THOROUGHBRED STYLE

STYLE

Racing dynasties – the horses, the owners, the studs

THOROUGHBRED STYLE

Racing dynasties – the horses, the owners, the studs

Anne Lambton • John Offen

Foreword by The Rt. Hon. The Earl of Derby

Salem House Publishers
Topsfield, Massachusetts

First published in the United States by
Salem House Publishers, 1987
462 Boston Street, Topsfield, MA 01983

Library of Congress Catalog Card Number:
86-60418

ISBN: 0 88162 196 X

**Designed and produced by
Robert Adkinson Limited, London**

Editorial Director	Clare Howell
Editor	Keith Spence
Art Director	Christine Simmonds
Picture Researcher	Mira Connolly

Phototypeset by Yale Press Ltd, London
Colour and black-and-white origination by
La Cromolito, Milan
Printed and bound by
Graficromo, Cordoba, Spain

Title page: Actaeon beating
Memnon in the Great
Subscription Purse at York,
August 1826, by John Frederick
Herring Snr (1795-1865).

CONTENTS

Christchurch with foal by Mill
Reef at Sandringham Stud.

FOREWORD

My grandfather was fortunate to have probably the greatest ever stud manager in Walter Alston. On one occasion my grandfather wrote to him saying a friend of his was going to start a stud and could Walter give him any rules. He replied 'there are no rules'. How true this is. How many great racehorses fail as stallions; great racing fillies when they go to his stud produce nothing of their own class. How totally unalike two brothers and sisters can be. It is equally true that the best looking and most expensive yearling can be useless.

The enormous costs of racing and breeding today have turned it into an industry rather than a sport, but, for all that, what enormous pleasure one can still derive from either owning or breeding a winner.

Thoroughbred Style gives a delightful picture of the thoroughbred industry in the four main breeding countries of the world. It will be invaluable as an introduction to anyone who has just started breeding horses or who is thinking of doing so, and will appeal to all racing enthusiasts.

The Rt. Hon. The Earl of Derby M.C.

INTRODUCTION

Left: The paddock at Royal Ascot.

This book was prompted by the public's growing interest in horse-racing. Attendance at all the world's most important race-courses is on the increase, and millions go racing in front of their television sets. We therefore felt there was a need for a book that would be both a guide to the history of the sport, and would take readers into the world of thoroughbred breeding that lies behind the brilliant spectacle.

We have not, however, made any attempt at compiling an all-embracing directory of stud farms. We have chosen instead a selection of farms that cover the spectrum of the thoroughbred scene. Some exemplify traditional racing families and personalities; others represent their region, are associated with some great champion, or are run commercially and are highly promoted; while others have a new architectural form to them. However different, they are all linked by success at the highest level, either past or present. These establishments differ from one another in terms of their size, the character of their owner and their aims and approach. All will have experienced good and bad years, as that is the nature and thrill of horse-breeding. Indeed, risk is the life-blood of the business, the challenge that has drawn so many different people together.

Racing today is a multi-million dollar industry. The escalation of bloodstock values, primarily brought about by the Arabs, has so inflated the cost of horse ownership that a new type of owner has emerged. This is the man who has joined a syndicate and owns, together with his fellow shareholders, a stud farm, nominations to stallions and a few horses in training. Whereas 50 years ago the same man might have owned the whole operation complete, he now has ten or more colleagues, with the result there may be as many as 50 people, all feeling involved in the running of a certain race, who will have joined the syndicate-owner for the pleasure of going racing. This can only bring good to the industry, since such a syndicate can only be run by a professional, who in turn employs other professionals. Thus there is enough money in reserve to withstand the inevitable lean year, and there are many more people to celebrate the victories.

We have concentrated on the élite regions of horse-breeding – England, France, Ireland and the United States – as these are the countries where horse-racing has developed over the centuries and where a large part of the population finds one of its most passionate interests on the racecourse. From being a minority concern, carried on by a few monarchs or aristocrats on remote heath or downland inaccessible to the man in the street, horse-racing has become one of the most democratic of all sports, uniting the millionaire and the factory worker in enthusiasm for an activity that links high finance with the perfection of animal strength and stamina.

As one would expect, most of the world's thoroughbred foals now come from North America, where some 40,000 are born each year. Though England and Ireland, with a total of about 9,000 foals, cannot compete with this flood of newcomers as far as sheer numbers are concerned, their long traditions of horse-breeding continue to ensure quality, shown by the fact that England exports about 2,000 thoroughbreds each year to more than 40 countries. The Old World can still challenge the New when it comes to centres of excellence.

With the speed of modern transportation by air, the actual provenance of a horse, as opposed to its bloodline, has lost a good deal of its importance. When a stallion can be flown in a few hours from France to cover a mare in the United States, or a colt can be sold at Newmarket and whisked out the next day to the Middle East, the old distinctions between French, British and American begin to break down. Colts and fillies are now as interchangeable as gold futures, and as much a part of the world of high finance. The wonder of horse-racing is that, for all the concentration of bloodstock into a few hundred pairs of extremely rich hands, the enjoyment of it remains accessible to everyone.

THE THOROUGHBRED
IN GREAT BRITAIN

The British people's love of outdoor sports, country life and animals unite in their passion for horse-racing. This universal appeal has formed the richness of horse-racing in this country, where the knowledge and involvement of spectators, and the traditions of races and racegoers, have been heightened by the thrill and fun of the sport. Development and evolution have been constant in the history of British horse-racing and breeding. In former centuries the horse was a status symbol in the same way as the car is today, and it is significant that in that supreme picture of medieval society, the *Prologue* to Chaucer's *Canterbury Tales*, almost every character's horse is described, each horse giving some indication of the personality of its rider. In such a society the trade in horses would be considerable; and what better way to demonstrate the quality of the horse for sale than by a race?

It is probable that the Romans raced in Britain on a considerable scale, and certainly horses were bred for two-horse chariot racing which went on throughout the Empire, so it is likely that there was a trade in better stock from mainland Europe. During the Dark Ages such trade naturally ceased, to revive in Norman times, when the Norman passion for hunting gave a great boost to the development of a new breed. The Crusades educated Western Europe in the superiority of horses from the East: it is known that King John imported horses for hunting and founded the Royal Stud at Eltham in Kent in the twelfth century. Richard II similarly was known to have had many foreign horses at the Royal Studs, but there is little reliable indication as to their breed. Henry VII kept horses for racing at Greenwich and was an important patron of equine sports, and under the Tudors racing began in earnest. The courses were generally set up by towns and cities, as the peace that followed the endless wars of the Middle Ages produced increasing wealth and leisure. Among the more famous courses were those at Chester, Salisbury, Croydon, Richmond in Yorkshire, Doncaster and Newmarket. The trophy was often a bell given by a city or by the monarch himself.

The royal patronage of Newmarket by King James I was a turning point in the history of racing. He was particularly attracted by the area for sport and had a house built at Newmarket on the site of the Griffin Inn. While hunting partridge, duck and hare were equally his pleasures, the royal stables were considerable and he kept 'two riders for the races'. He spent much time there, though the growing Puritan element in the House of Commons was already concerned at the amount of time the King spent on such pleasures. In 1621 the Commons even petitioned him not to put Newmarket before his public duties. This was hardly likely to have much effect on a monarch who enjoyed heavy gambling as a way of life. He was finally taken ill on return from hunting at Newmarket in March 1625, and died two weeks later.

James's successor, Charles I, similarly neglected state affairs for hunting and racing. His court had a worthy reputation for magnificence in the eyes of Europe, and Newmarket shared in this display, though its splendour was short-lived. The mood of the country was against Charles I, whose extravagance and display were strongly resented. The King last visited Newmarket in 1646 under military guard, a prisoner of Parliament. For the next ten years the bleak reign of the Puritans weighed heavily on the English, as almost all forms of public enjoyment were proscribed. Meetings were forbidden in 1655, Newmarket Heath was ploughed up to prevent hunting, and the King's house in the town stood empty.

From the days of the Stuarts Newmarket was pre-eminent in the development of the thoroughbred, and it is significant that this Suffolk town was so close to the great agricultural improvements that were going on in East Anglia at this time.

Before the Civil War in the 1640s, the Royal Studs were naturally the largest and best-stocked establishments in England. There were four principal ones: at Eltham Palace and Hampton Court Palace, on the east and west sides of London respectively, at Malmesbury in Wiltshire and at Tutbury in Staffordshire. When Charles I was beheaded in 1649, Cromwell closed them down,

Newmarket racecourse in the seventeenth century. The 'sport of kings' was patronized here by British monarchs before and after the Civil War.

Previous two pages: The Start for the Memorable Derby of 1844 by John Frederick Herring – memorable because it was regarded as the dirtiest Derby in history.

but the horses were not lost at their closure. Some went to Ireland, and after the Restoration others found their way to Hampton Court. Cromwell himself bred some for chargers rather than for racing. During the Commonwealth many members of the aristocracy retired to the country and began to take a serious interest in breeding, which had important effects by the end of the seventeenth century.

The horses in the Royal Studs, and other studs of importance, were of Spanish and Barb blood (that is, Arab blood imported during the Middle Ages into Spain when it was part of the great Arab empire, or directly from North Africa and the Middle East). The word 'Barb' is a corruption of 'Barbary', meaning the Maghreb (Morocco, Algeria, Tunisia and Libya). The Arab breeds, which originated from the Near East and the Mediterranean, are characterized by their lightness, quality and courage. By contrast, the native breeds of Western Europe are bigger overall, with large heads and a sluggish nature. During the medieval period the light Arab horses were dispersed throughout the Mediterranean. The Moorish domination of Spain, and its influence in southern Italy and Sicily, resulted in excellent breeds being established. When Spain regained her territory at the end of the fifteenth century she had acquired a reputation for horses of remarkable quality, which were traded throughout Europe. The historian Gervase Markham, writing in the early seventeenth century, believed that pure Arabians from the East were the best stallions. Evidence suggests that they had been imported since the Middle Ages, while the Barbs from North Africa were the next in demand. In the seventeenth century the Duke of Newcastle kept horses from the East in his extensive stables at Welbeck in Nottinghamshire, which were even heated. He also kept horses in both Paris and Antwerp, and his well-known book on horsemanship was translated into French about the middle of the century. Lord Fairfax, the commander of Cromwell's New Model Army who ultimately supported Charles II's Restoration, kept both Morocco Barb and Eastern stallions and was well-known for his writings on the subject, to which he devoted his retirement.

Horse-racing in the reign of Charles II. After the Restoration the British took up with glee pleasures denied them under Cromwell.

Typical of the horses prior to the Restoration were the fast ponies bred in the North and known as Galloways. Never more than 13 hands high, their Irish counterparts were known as Hobbys. There must have been a considerable trade in horses, and many native breeds would have been crossed with imports from Spain and Italy, who in turn would have had some Arabian and Barb blood.

When the Monarchy was restored in 1660, the country took to pleasure with an enthusiasm which made up for lost time. Charles II returned to Newmarket in 1663 having already been racing at Banstead Downs at Epsom in 1661. The King himself took an active part in the racing scene, even occasionally riding in a race, thus becoming the only English monarch to have personally won a race. His riding skill was legendary and in 1675 he won the Newmarket Town Plate, the first of numerous such Royal Plates. Charles generally made two annual visits to Newmarket, which subsequently became the traditional spring and autumn meetings of today. The diarist John Evelyn, who was in Newmarket in October 1671, found 'the jolly blades racing, dancing, feasting and revelling more resembling a luxurious and abandoned rout, than a Christian Court'.

In 1664 the King founded the Town Plate, which was to be run on the second Thursday in October for ever. Interested in training as well as riding, he is reputed to have sat for hours at the top of Warren Hill at the King's Chair, a summerhouse he had built. He also became the arbiter in disputes where courtiers had wagers of thousands of pounds relying on his judgement. The King himself had a favourite hack called Old Rowley, which became both the nickname of the King and the name of the Rowley Mile Course. The scene of the court at Newmarket was extravagant in an age of extravagance. Pepys tells of £15,000 won one night at a gambling house run by Lady Castlemaine and £25,000 lost the following night. Before long there were inevitable murmurings of discontent and Parliament refused to grant supplies to Charles. The spring meeting at Newmarket of 1681 was cancelled, and Burford in Oxfordshire was substituted. The royal horses were brought from Newmarket, and for a time it looked as though Burford would take Newmarket's place as the country's racing centre. The situation settled down and Newmarket recovered, only to be swept by fire, causing considerable damage. The King made plans to transfer all royal racing activities to Winchester, where a sumptuous new palace was to be built, but his death in 1685 saved Newmarket from decline.

Although Charles's successor James II was enthusiastic about racing while he was Duke of York, when he came to the throne he was so preoccupied with turning England Catholic that he had little influence. After William Prince of Orange was crowned in 1689 he paid several visits to Newmarket, and re-established the Royal Stud at Hampton Court. Queen Anne (1702-14) was an energetic supporter of the sport. Famous for her foundation of Ascot on a corner of the Great Park at Windsor, she presented the new race with a plate of 100 guineas, and was similarly generous in her patronage of York Races, where in 1709 she presented a gold cup. At Newmarket she had the royal residence redecorated, contributed to local charities and fully endorsed the town's position as the centre of English racing. She established a racing stable under the remarkable Tregonwell Frampton, who held the illustrious title of 'Keeper of the Running Horses', and was paid £100 a year for each of the Queen's horses he kept in his stable. For three reigns Frampton remained in office, and by all accounts never changed his manner of dressing or coarseness of speech and bearing.

In the century after 1660 it is difficult to be sure how many mares were imported, and it was more likely that the stallions rather than the mares were of foreign pedigree. The three most important of these imported stallions were the Byerley Turk, the Darley Arabian and the Godolphin Arabian, from whom all modern thoroughbreds descend in the male line.

When Budapest was captured from the Turks in 1686, the Byerley Turk was taken as a spoil of

The Byerley Turk, from the original by John Wootton, one of the three foundations sires to whom all English thoroughbreds can be traced.

war by a Captain Byerley. He was sent to stud at Goldsborough Manor in Yorkshire and sired Jigg, from whom can be traced the powerful lines of Tourbillon and The Tetrarch. The Darley Arabian, foaled in 1700, was a horse of exceptional beauty. He came from Aleppo in Syria, where the finest Arabians were believed to be bred, and was shipped to England by the Consul in Aleppo, Thomas Darley. Put to stud at Aldby in East Yorkshire, he founded a most important male line which includes such names as Phalaris and St Simon. He died at the age of 30. The

Godolphin Arabian, foaled in 1724, was also famous for longevity, for he died in 1753 at the age of 29. The subject of much folklore, he is said to have been discovered drawing a water-cart in Paris. He is supposed to have been employed as a 'teaser' to Hobgoblin at Lord Godolphin's Gogmagog Stables near Newmarket. Legend says that he fought Hobgoblin for the mare Roxana and, having won the battle, covered her. As a result she produced Lath, and then Cade by a later mating with the Godolphin Arabian. Cade's male line has continued down to the present with Precipitation and Hurry On.

The Godolphin Arabian, in an engraving by G.J. Stubbs after his father George Stubb's painting. This may be the only example of Stubbs not working from life – the horse died some 40 years before Stubbs was commissioned to paint him.

These horses did not race; they were imported because they had qualities which it was felt needed to be passed on to subsequent generations. The current stock in England at that time was highly mixed, and needed the Arab and Barb breeds that had been bred true to type. Two great racehorses of the eighteenth century became legends. The first was Flying Childers, a brown or bay colt, bred by Leonard Childers near Doncaster in Yorkshire in 1715, and owned by the Duke of Devonshire during both his racing and stud careers. On 26 April 1721, he beat the Duke of Bolton's Speedwell over 4 miles for a sum of £500, and in October 1722, he beat Lord Drogheda's Chaunter for £1,000 over 6 miles from Six Mile Bottom to Cambridge Hill at Newmarket. In the same year he beat the leading horse of the time, Fox, winner of three King's Plates, by more than 1½ furlongs. Flying Childers was described as 'the fleetest horse that ever ran at Newmarket or was ever bred in the world'. He was an excellent sire of broodmares and remained at the Duke of Devonshire's Chatsworth Stud until 1741, covering only mares that belonged to the Duke. In the male line, his son Snip was poor, but his son Snap was one of the best racehorses of the period. Snip was the maternal grandsire of the Derby winners Saltram (1783) and Sir Peter Teazle (1787).

George I (1714-27) was indifferent to horse-racing, and the royal residence was allowed to fall into disrepair; however, he continued the Hampton Court Stud and maintained Tregonwell Frampton in his post. George II (1727-60) increased the number of Royal Plates by a third, as part of the growing interest in the sport among all levels of society. Money prizes were being offered

The Darley Arabian, from a painting by J.N. Sartorius. The most influential horse in the history of the thoroughbred was bought in Aleppo in exchange for a rifle.

to the equivalent of the plates, and such was the enthusiasm for racing that by the mid eighteenth century laws were passed to discourage the small meetings, and to establish minimum weights, thereby encouraging quality breeding. It seems unlikely that this law, which forbade any race under the value of £50, would have curtailed popular village racing, but it is significant that racing had become so widespread that it should warrant control. Racing younger horses continued throughout this period. Four-year-olds were racing at Hambleton in Yorkshire by the late 1720s and three-year-old racing began in the next decade, but it did not spread south to Newmarket until the mid eighteenth century. It took another 30 years to make two-year-old racing an established feature.

Through Flying Childers's brother Bartlett's Childers, the permanent male line of the Darley Arabian was formed. Bartlett's Childers sired Squirt, who was a good winner and who in turn sired Marske. Marske belonged to William, Duke of Cumberland, who as Ranger of Windsor Forest established his stud there. Marske was mated with Spiletta, and the result was the chestnut colt Eclipse, named after the eclipse of the sun in 1764, the year of his birth. This horse became a brilliant racehorse, the legendary successor to Flying Childers. He was never beaten, and when he was removed from training in October 1770, he had won ten races, of which six had been walkovers. He was 15.3 hands high, with a fiery temper and a remarkable stride. The Duke of Cumberland died in 1765 and so did not see Eclipse's great racing career.

Cumberland also bred King Herod (1758-80) by Tartar (the Byerley Turk's great-grandson)

The Starting Post at Newmarket by John Wootton (1686-1765). In the early days of racing it was usual for spectators, also mounted, to accompany the runners on the course.

This is the third of George Stubbs's portraits of Gimcrack, painted for his owner, Lord Grosvenor, in 1770, the year Gimcrack won the coveted Whip at Newmarket at the end of a brilliant racing career.

out of Cypron. Herod was an enormous success, winning races at Newmarket and Ascot before becoming one of the most prolific stallions of his period. The Duke of Cumberland's stud thus produced one of the most successful lines ever. Among those that trace Eclipse in the tail male line are Northern Dancer, his son Nijinsky, Mill Reef, Roberto, Vaguely Noble, Grundy and Bustino.

The Eclipse-Herod cross was a milestone in the development of the thoroughbred. Eclipse's progeny were speedy and temperamental, whereas those of Herod were hard and resolute. Their

complementary qualities were to be shown many times in the next decades, and they particularly possessed those qualities necessary for the Classic races which were being established at this time. The St Leger, run at Doncaster, was founded in 1776, the Oaks at Epsom in 1779, and the Derby, also at Epsom, in 1780. These Classic races established the ultimate test for horses capable of running distances from 1 mile to 1¾ miles at three years of age. Speed and early development were the vital qualities for success.

Another famous horse of the day was Gimcrack, after whom the Gimcrack Stakes at York, run in August for two-year-olds, were named. An extraordinarily tough horse, he was the first English animal to have great success in France. In 1776, when six years old, he won a match over 22½ miles within an hour. Grandson of the Godolphin Arabian, his influence was spread in America by his son Medley.

Three-year-old races became the most in demand in the late eighteenth century, developing into the Classic races we know today. The St Leger, named after General Anthony St Leger, was first run at Doncaster in 1776, for three-year-olds over 2 miles. By the 1770s, Epsom became one of the most important courses in the country, and in 1779 the 12th Earl of Derby and his sporting friends instituted the Oaks, run for three-year-old fillies only, taking the name of the race from the converted inn that Lord Derby used as his house. The following year they planned a race for three-year-old colts and fillies; according to tradition Sir Charles Bunbury and Lord Derby tossed a coin to decide the name of the race. Derby won, thus naming what was to become the most important race in the world. Newmarket retained its position as the leading centre of racing

Eclipse, the most famous racehorse of the English Turf in an engraving after a painting by George Stubbs. He sired 335 winners, and the most important male line in English bloodstock descends from him.

throughout the eighteenth century, and by 1800 had seven meetings a year. Ascot went through several periods of decline after Queen Anne, but revived again under the Duke of Cumberland.

The rules governing horse-racing in Britain did not begin with the Jockey Club, founded around 1752, since in 1751 *Pond's Calendar* was published as a collection of such rules. The word 'jockey' at this time still meant an owner of horses, as well as rider, and the distinction was further blurred by the fact that many gentlemen still raced their own horses. The Jockey Club was typical of many clubs that were set up in the eighteenth century as informal groups of men with like interests. When its members were in London, they met at the Star and Garter in Pall Mall. The first property they bought in Newmarket was the Coffee Room, reputed to be on the site of the Jockey Club today. Sir Charles Bunbury, virtual President of the Club, transformed it into a body of considerable national importance. He was responsible for encouraging speed in the thoroughbred and for the introduction of races for younger horses, carrying lighter weights over shorter distances. Bunbury emerged as the most important arbiter and legislator at Newmarket. Since other courses followed Newmarket, his influence and that of the Jockey Club became nationwide.

Royal patronage returned to racing in style with the Prince of Wales, later George IV. His first success was in 1784 with his horse Hermit. The Prince loved Newmarket life, where he could race and gamble with his brothers, and he was the first member of the Royal Family to own a Derby winner – in 1788, with Sir Thomas. By 1791 he had as many as 40 horses in training, but his success was marred by scandal. The Prince's horse Escape, ridden by Sam Chifney, finished last against three mediocre horses, even though Escape was the favourite. The next day Chifney rode Escape in a race with five runners, including two from the day before. Escape won easily, and it

Flying Childers, 'ye fleetest horse that ever ran at Newmarket' or (as generally believed) was ever bred in the world, from a contemporary painting of about 1725.

21

was alleged that Chifney had backed Escape in the second race and had pulled him in the first. After a Jockey Club enquiry, the Stewards told the Prince that if Chifney rode his horses again, 'no gentleman would start against him'. The Prince accepted Chifney's version, sold his stud and left Newmarket. The Stewards of the Jockey Club had exercised their new-found authority, and shown that the rules they had laid down were to be observed by all, no matter what their rank.

The 4th Duke of Portland was instrumental in establishing the Jockey Club as a landowner in Newmarket. He lent the Club money to purchase the Coffee Room and added to his ownership of the Heath. He improved the land by clearing it and re-seeded and fertilized the turf, and he established the right of the Jockey Club to warn offenders off the Heath. The Jockey Club leased the Heath from him and, together with its own purchases, by 1819 was in control of almost all of it, ensuring security for the future. At this time, the Jockey Club, in a deliberate bid to raise the standing of Newmarket, had sponsored the Two Thousand Guineas (begun in 1809) and the One Thousand Guineas (1814). The Jockey Club was certain that the headquarters of racing was to be at Newmarket. There was no challenge to the Club from other course authorities, who frequently referred decisions to it, but by 1832 the Jockey Club announced that it would refuse to deal with disputes unless meetings were operating under Newmarket rules. In 1835 it published its first membership list, to make sure that provincial executives knew where its power lay. A number of scandals in the 1830s and '40s showed the need for firm control – for example, two of the runners in the 1844 Derby, the most important race for three-year-olds, turned out to be four-year-olds.

The most influential stud in England in the first two decades of the nineteenth century was that of the Dukes of Grafton at Euston Hall, near Newmarket. The 3rd Duke of Grafton had

A painting by George Stubbs of one of Lord Grosvenor's horses, Bandy, who in spite of his crooked near fore had a successful racing career.

been Prime Minister from 1767-70 and frequently upset Cabinet meetings by being absent at Newmarket. He founded his stud with the purchase of Julia, whose sire Blank was by the Darley Arabian. She was the dam of Promise (by Snap), whose daughter Prunella (by Highflyer) bred Pope, winner of the Derby in 1809. She also bred Pelisse, who won the Oaks in 1804, and Penelope, whose offspring Whalebone in 1810 became the Duke's third horse to win the Derby.

The Duke was a notorious eccentric, who ordered a grassed avenue of trees to be planted covering the 18 miles from Euston Hall to Newmarket, so that his carriage could drive to the races over grass. However, he forgot that he did not own the last 6 miles of land, so the avenue came to an abrupt halt. He took to writing religious pamphlets at the end of his life, leaving the stud to the management of his son, the future 4th Duke. Between 1819 and 1827 the 4th Duke had an unprecedented run of successes, winning the Two Thousand Guineas five times and the One Thousand Guineas eight times. In addition, he won the Derby with Prunella's son Whisker in 1815, and the Oaks six times. The key to the Duke's success was Waxy, who was a perfect example of a Herod-Eclipse cross and the principal stallion to perpetuate the male line of Eclipse.

The 3rd Duke of Grafton by Pompeo Batoni, 1762. Passionately interested in racing and Prime Minister from 1767 to 1770, he founded the stud at Euston Hall, one of the most influential studs in England in the early nineteenth century.

The Eclipse-Herod cross also founded the fortunes of the great stud of the 5th Earl of Jersey at Middleton Stoney in Oxfordshire. He started with Web, a sister of Whalebone, the origin of several strains of winners. Her daughter Filigree bred Cobweb, the winner of the One Thousand Guineas and the Oaks of 1824. Cobweb produced three Classic winners, Clementina, Achmet and Bay Middleton, the 1836 Derby winner.

By the mid nineteenth century, the breeding of the thoroughbred had been the subject of careful improvement for some 200 years. Admiral Rous of the Jockey Club wrote in his *On The Laws and Practice of Horse-Racing*: 'The clearest proof of the improvement that has taken place in the English Racehorse is the fact that no first or second cross from the imported Arab, with the exception of one mare by the Willesley Arabian (Fair Ellen), is good enough to win a £50 Plate in the present day; whereas in 1740 our best horses were the second or third crosses from the original stock'.

Admiral Rous and contemporary opinion laid great store by the claim that these advances had been made because thoroughbreds were 'true sons and daughters of the desert'. Since that time, many authorities have suggested that while Arab stock introduced greater genetic purity and bred to type, it was not solely responsible for the quality of speed inherent in the English racehorse. It is now generally thought that there was a native English element in the stock that was already working when the development of the thoroughbred began.

When Queen Victoria came to the throne in 1837, royal patronage sank to a level unknown since the Hanoverians. Although she had visited Ascot and York as heir-apparent, she expressed no interest in the sport. Indeed, she set herself against the scandalous behaviour of the Regency, in which her uncles had played so large a part. In 1840 she attended the Derby; but although the Epsom Committee went to great efforts to improve the facilities, her visit was a disaster. The start was late, the crowd was unenthusiastic, and the Queen never returned. Newmarket was also disapproved of; only Ascot remained on the Queen's list, and then only while the Prince Consort was alive. She did all she could to prevent the Prince of Wales (later Edward VII) from becoming interested in racing. Significantly, the royal residence at Newmarket was sold and a Nonconformist chapel was built on its site.

One of the dominant members of the Jockey Club in the first half of the nineteenth century was Lord George Bentinck. A ruthless man, he was determined to eradicate lawlessness and corruption on the Turf. In 1844 he changed the method of starting a race, which was often open to abuse and false starts. The dropping of a flag was to mark the start, and any jockey who held back was liable to be heavily fined. Each horse was allocated a number that had to match the race-card, and the board and saddling had to take place in one area away from spectators. Races had to start on time, and failure meant a fine. Jockeys' uniforms had to be of silk or velvet to be easily identified. Improvements were made at both Goodwood and Epsom. Many of these formalities, taken for granted today, imposed a discipline and order that made for efficient and honest racing.

Horse-racing could not have become a successful popular entertainment if it had not been for the Jockey Club's deliberate efforts to impose its regulations on all courses. By the 1870s its control was almost absolute. Under Admiral Rous the Club drew up the *Rules Concerning Horse-Racing in General*. It refused to recognize those courses that did not run under Club rules, refused to publish the programmes and results of unrecognized meetings, and penalized any trainer, jockey or official who took part in such meetings. By the end of the nineteenth century the system of licensing was in operation, whereby trainers, jockeys, officials and racecourse authorities all had to apply for a licence.

Admiral Rous set out the calendar for the flat-racing season, made 5 furlongs the minimum distance for a race and restricted the racing of two-year-olds. Jockeys could be given on-the-spot warnings for misconduct, and the Club even issued a warning to Parliament when it was to

Two of the great nineteenth-century reformers of British racing, (*above*) Admiral Henry Rous (1795-1877) and (*below*) Lord George Bentinck (1802-48).

consider a bill concerning the weight horses should carry. After the Club had made it clear that these matters were its concern only, the bill was withdrawn. In 1876 the Club published *The Rules of Racing as made by the Jockey Club at Newmarket*, which became a point of reference throughout the world. The Club continued to buy up parts of Newmarket Heath, so that it came to control the largest training area in the country. The unrecognized courses with their criminal elements were squeezed out and inevitably collapsed.

One of the most important influences on the growth of horse-racing in Britain during the nineteenth century was the railway. The gradual extension of railways became a rapid expansion after the 1840s, so that by the 1870s the country was covered by a complete network, and the 130-odd meetings were all well served by cheap public transport and the famous 'racing specials'. Although formerly racing enthusiasts had managed well enough without trains, in some cases walking overnight to be in time for a meeting the next day, the convenience and speed attracted a

A dramatic finish for the Two Thousand Guineas at Newmarket between 'Mr Day's The Ugly Buck and Lord George Bentinck's The Devil to Pay'.

MR. DAY'S "THE UGLY BUCK," AND LORD GEORGE BENTINCK'S "THE DEVIL TO PAY."—RACE FOR 2000 GUINEAS, AT NEWMARKET.

much wider audience. The transport revolution did not simply affect passengers. The trains could carry horses, which in turn assisted the growth of two-year-old racing, since these horses could not have stood up to the strain of walking long distances to the racecourse. Meetings began to be national in nature rather than local, since they could now attract horses as well as racegoers from the country as a whole.

The system of vanning had been popularized by Lord George Bentinck, when he sent his horse Elis to the 1836 St Leger at the last possible moment in order to lengthen the odds; but the practice was not new. Graziers had sent prize livestock to market for years in padded vans or horsedrawn carts. This had great advantages, but it was expensive. What it did was to make the advantages of railway transport immediately apparent. Clearly railways were much faster, enabling horses to travel on the days of the race, while security was much stronger. By the 1850s there was no suitable alternative. This resulted in a change in traditional patterns, and certain major races evolved with a hierarchy of races below them. Greater specialization began to occur, as leading jockeys and the best officials could all travel to more meetings, and this in turn led to greater professionalism. The traditional training-ground of the North was severely affected. It was no longer necessary to have trainers close to a racecourse, and London's social attractions became easily accessible from Newmarket, which grew at the expense of more distant areas.

The railway companies were quick to exploit this expanding interest in horse-racing. Not only did they carry the spectators and the horses, but they actually sponsored races. Prize money increased, though it was not as good as it might have been, as revenue did not come from entrance fees but from the owners themselves and from the subscriptions of local business people, who stood to profit from the races. Nearly all authorities had relied for some years on letting space at the course for gambling and refreshments. The result of this insecure income meant many failures, and it was not until the enclosed gate-money meetings that a new secure era evolved.

Of the several trends that were emerging from the extraordinary growth in racing in the first half of the nineteenth century, one which was to give trouble later was the growing concentration on precocious speed. Within the Jockey Club, Sir Joseph Hawley was leader of a group convinced that the racing of immature animals had gone too far. He took on Admiral Rous, and in 1869 proposed firstly, that no two-year-olds should be allowed to run earlier in the season than 1 July, and secondly, that the Jockey Club should contribute none of its money to any race involving the entry of two-year-olds. Hawley's support within the Jockey Club was limited, and two-year-old racing was banned only from 1 May. Even this was dropped after some years because of pressure from course operators.

The promoters of the new enclosed park courses were well aware of the type of racing that made money. Their audiences were interested not in long-distance races, but in races for two-year-olds, where uncertainty and speed meant excitement. The emergence of these new courses and spectators had resulted in considerable competition which in turn had increased prize money. On the other hand, tests for stamina were excellent for the bloodstock industry but were not so good for gate-money. Nevertheless, the concentration on two-year-old races could not be a good thing. Rous deplored the change but felt that it was impossible to do much about it. 'It is much to be regretted,' he wrote, 'that the old system of not training horses until their powers are fully developed has been abolished.' Regrets, however, were not enough, and by the turn of the century the Jockey Club's hand had been forced. In 1899 it was obliged to place substantial curbs on two-year-old racing. Up to the Epsom summer meeting they were restricted to 5 furlongs, and before 1 September to no more than 6 furlongs. June was to be the starting-point of two-year-olds competing with three-year-olds, and there were to be no handicap races for older horses. By the end of the nineteenth century British vulnerability as a result of the emphasis on youthful speed was clearly exposed by American competition.

Right: The Race for the St Leger, 1830. The Start by James Pollard. First run in 1776, the St Leger is the last of the Classics to be run, taking place in September.

The encouragement of handicaps also hindered British competitiveness. The Classic races are the best test of the thoroughbred, because the contestants are largely equal in terms of weights and weight-for-age, whereas the handicaps are important because they allow a greater amount of racing, which in turn promotes more ownership and gambling. Even mediocre horses have a chance to win, thus maintaining owners' interests; but the negative aspect of handicaps is that they can permit an excessive amount of mediocrity, and that can be, as Admiral Rous put it, 'a boon to bad horses with no other prospects of success'. By the 1860s the French were showing that their emphasis on excellence in Classic middle distances was paying off. The victory of their horse Gladiateur in the Two Thousand Guineas, the Derby and the St Leger in 1865 showed that English success was no longer to be taken for granted.

The problem of handicapping had reached a peak by the mid nineteenth century, and the Jockey Club was forced to act. In order to be good at handicapping, one has to recognize form in hundreds of horses, which means full-time observation. This was not always possible in the early nineteenth century when communications were difficult, particularly in remote areas, so the Jockey Club decided to appoint a public handicapper. The first to hold the post was Admiral Rous, appointed in 1855 at the ripe age of 60. One of the great characters of the period, Rous had written that a public handicapper should be man of independent circumstances in every sense of the word, a spectator of every race in the country and beyond suspicion of accepting bribes. He had already allotted weights for the historic match between Voltigeur and The Flying Dutchman at York in May 1851. The Flying Dutchman won and went on to found one of the most important

Gladiateur, the French horse who was the English Triple Crown winner in 1865.

lines in France. After Rous's death, public handicappers were appointed to succeed him, the first being the Weatherby family. The founder of the family, James Weatherby, first published his *Racing Calendar* in 1773, and the family began a close association with the Jockey Club which lasts to this day. They acted as secretaries to the Club, receiving entries to races, and dealing with the registration of colours and acceptance of horses for the *General Stud Book*.

The development of reliable and accurate records concerning the racing and breeding of racehorses is of immense importance to the thoroughbred industry. The earliest record known was John Nelson's Register at Newmarket in the late seventeenth century, followed by the Calendars of race results kept by Pond, Heber and Cheyney in the eighteenth. The *Racing Calendar*, first

Voltigeur and Flying Dutchman, two horses of great merit who both won the Derby and the St Leger – Flying Dutchman in 1849 and Voltigeur in 1850.

published by James Weatherby in 1773 and continued by the family ever since, was bought by the Jockey Club at the end of the nineteenth century. Records of the pedigrees of bloodstock were begun by Weatherbys in an introductory volume of 1791, under the title of *General Stud Book*, which continues to the present day. For elegibility of entry in the original editions, Weatherby took direct descent from about 100 mares, which he considered to be the foundation stock of the thoroughbred and which existed in the second half of the seventeenth century. Any earlier records were piecemeal and inadequate. The eighteenth century records listed Eastern stallions and their progeny deliberately imported to improve the lines of blood. The work was vital to the British breeding industry, which expanded enormously and without any competition in the first half of the nineteenth century.

Newmarket itself, although pre-eminent in the racing world, remained outside nineteenth century changes to some extent. It was a place of privilege, it did not need extra spectators, and it even went to considerable lengths to discourage them. When the Great Eastern Railway began cheap excursions to Newmarket, the Jockey Club fixed the finish of one race and the start of another on a different course, so that only those on horseback could see both. The railway line to Newmarket was allowed because of its convenience for transporting horses, not spectators. The upper classes watched on horseback, and facilities for spectators remained primitive. Newmarket

Right: John Singleton on Bay Malton by George Stubbs. Singleton was a Yorkshire jockey who rode for the Marquess of Rockingham; Bay Malton the successful horse who even defeated Gimcrack.

The Ascot Gold Cup, 1834 by James Pollard. First run in 1807, the Gold Cup is today the principal race of the Royal meeting. It is run over 2½ miles.

could not, however, remain outside current developments, and by the mid nineteenth century it had ceased to be the leading training area for Derby winners.

With incomes rising and improved transport, many dubious new meetings were established as speculative ventures. Courses on the fringes of London encouraged the worst elements, and those at Enfield and Bromley were notorious. Often organized by publicans, these meetings encouraged fraud and robbery to such an extent that the Metropolitan Racecourse Act was passed in 1879 banning all race meetings within a certain distance of London.

As a result of this the 'park' or 'enclosed' courses were set up along lines laid down by the Jockey Club. Such courses charged entrance fees at varying prices, aimed at the respectable members of the public, and marked the beginning of racing as an organized leisure business. When General Owen Williams, a member of the Jockey Club, opened Sandown Park in 1875, he required an entrance fee from all racegoers, and the speculation proved an enormous success. Starting with two annual meetings, Sandown had reached five by 1880. In 1878 S.H. Hyde opened Kempton Park, and by the 1890s Hurst Park, Lingfield and the popular Gatwick had followed. Outside the London area, Newbury was established in 1906 and further afield Derby in 1880 and Leicester in 1884.

The centre of British racing: the Jockey Club headquarters at Newmarket drawn by F.G. Kitton.

An irreverent look at the deliberations of the Jockey Club in 1875.

The success of these enclosed courses was largely due to the willingness of the public to pay for a day's racing in comfort, which in turn led to better-quality sport. Lady spectators, who were now able to attend, provided an important source of income. Before the park courses, only those that were part of the social season such as Ascot, Goodwood and Epsom made any provision for women. Nevertheless, racing remained a bastion of male society: women were not allowed to be trainers or officials, and certainly not jockeys. Where they were owners, they raced under pseudonyms throughout the century – Lily Langtry raced as 'Mr Jersey' and the Duchess of Montrose as 'Mr Manton'.

The improved organization and layout of the courses meant that, even for those only partially interested, racing provided a pleasurable day's outing. Saturday afternoon racing was established to capture the market for commercialized entertainment, and no park course was far from a station. The new spectators preferred two-year-old racing and handicaps, which made for uncertainty and excitement. The quality of the new courses and the increase in revenues enabled prize money to increase. In 1886 Sandown began the Eclipse stakes, the first ever to carry a stake of £10,000. The success of the move was instantly shown by the quality of the horses it attracted, which in turn drew in ever more spectators.

The racecourse and grandstand at Ascot in 1846, the stands packed as full of spectators as they are at meetings today.

The success of the enclosed courses was largely confined to those within reach of London's growing population. Increasing commercialism made the Jockey Club nervous and, in order to maintain quality, they imposed a dividend limitation of 10 per cent on any race company. Regulations regarding the amount of prize money required were also laid down. Open meetings were forced to increase their earnings from admission to grandstands and private boxes. Those that were part of the social calendar, such as Ascot, Epsom and Goodwood, thrived; but other open courses felt competition from enclosed courses strongly. Even Newmarket was obliged to make changes. Stands were built and enclosures made, and only those on foot were allowed free entry. The character of racing had ceased to be rural and local in context, and for many people in country areas the traditional social event became the point-to-point.

The second half of the nineteenth century had seen several spectacular pedigree influences. Voltigeur's son Vedette mated with Flying Duchess, daughter of the Flying Dutchman, to produce Galopin. The latter was renowned for speed, won the 1875 Derby, and sired St Simon out of St Angela. Bred by the Hungarian Prince Batthyany, St Simon was bought by the Duke of Portland for 1,600 guineas. Highly temperamental, he was notorious for great bursts of speed. He was entered for nine races and won them all, taking the Ascot Gold Cup by 20 lengths. A spectacular sire of winners, St Simon was champion stallion from 1890 to 1896 and again in 1900 and 1901. Ten of his progeny, including Persimmon and Diamond Jubilee, won 17 Classic races between them. Among them, Memoir won the Oaks and the St Leger, and Semolina won the One

Right: St Simon by Lynwood Palmer (1906). Foaled in 1881 by Galopin out of St Angela, he was even more successful at stud than on the racecourse. He sired the winners of 571 races; ten of his progeny between them won 17 Classic races.

The Owners' Enclosure at Newmarket towards the end of the nineteenth century, painted by Isaac Cullen.

Thousand Guineas. In 1897, the year of Queen Victoria's Diamond Jubilee, St Simon created another record by siring the winners of all the Classics. His sons sired 12 further Classic winners, including Ard Patrick and Sceptre. Galopin, St Simon and St Simon's sons dominated the list of winning sires for over 25 years. Three of the finest horses of the twentieth century, Hyperion, Nearco and Ribot, are St Simon's direct descendants. Other countries have also benefited from his influence, notably France, where Rabelais, Prince Palatine and St Bris were from his line.

Queen Victoria's disapproval of racing did not stop the Prince of Wales's interest in the sport. In 1863 he attended the Derby and received a hearty welcome from the crowd, and in the following year he became a member of the Jockey Club, which the Royal family approved of. In 1874 he registered his colours and began his stud at Sandringham, He had a series of successes – Persimmon by St Simon out of Perdita II won the Derby and the St Leger of 1896, and in 1900 Persimmon's brother Diamond Jubilee won the Triple Crown. The Prince was not frightened of showing his enjoyment of the sport, and as King he became immensely popular, all of which gave great encouragement to the racing world. Six lean years followed at the Royal Stud when the King almost left Egerton House, but his luck returned in 1909, when he won his third Derby with Minoru, trained by Richard Marsh.

The days of King Edward's patronage as Prince of Wales were remembered by many as the golden years of English racing. Indeed, these were the last years in which racing was entirely English and largely dominated by a small body of aristocrats. Several of those who were members

Persimmon, by St Simon out of Perdita II, was owned by the Prince of Wales (on the left).

of the Jockey Club were also members of the Government during this period, among them Lord Rosebery, who as Prime Minister in 1894 won the Derby with Ladas. The pleasure of the ruling élite was increased by the fact that the Jockey Club had managed to curb corruption, and the period produced legendary performances from horses and jockeys. Racing had become a profitable industry, which in turn financed better quality. This state of affairs, added to the enormous wealth accruing to Britain at this time, and the conspicuous spending that went on lavish house parties for race weeks, makes it easy to see how this reputation as a golden era came about.

Racing appealed particularly to the Edwardians. Money and leisure existed in plenty, and excitement and glamour were something they were looking for after the rather dull middle years of the nineteenth century. Fortunes were spent not simply on buying and breeding horses but on stables, country houses for race meetings, lavish hospitality and betting. Heirs to vast fortunes like George Baird spent the equivalent of £70 million in ten years; but equally there were members of the great aristocratic families, backed by enormous resources, who were interested in breeding and owning the finest quality. The Dukes of Portland and Westminster were two such men, and others, like Alfred de Rothschild, claimed that the finest publicity a man could buy was a racehorse. By the end of the nineteenth century racing was a well integrated part of the social calendar, and gone were the days when there were only 100 ladies in the Royal Enclosure at Ascot. When the Prince of Wales became King in 1901, he was surrounded by an unusually wide circle of friends. He enjoyed the company of the rich; and wealthy men with new fortunes, such as Maple the furniture businessman and Baron de Hirsch the Hungarian-born financier, found

Iroquois, the winner of the 1881 Derby, and his jockey Fred Archer. The American-bred Iroquois won the St Leger in the same year.

that spending on racing opened many doors.

There were few barriers in the nineteenth century to international racing, and the English played a large part in continental horse-racing throughout the century. Americans had come to Britain as early as 1856, when Richard Ten Broeck brought some of the best American horses to Newmarket. His Pryoress won the Cesarewitch of 1857, and in 1861 he followed this up by winning the Goodwood Cup with Starke and the Ascot Stakes with Optimist. After a gap of 20 years, similar American successes were repeated, when James Keene won the Cambridgeshire with Foxhall, and Pierre Lorillard took the 1881 season by storm. His colt Iroquois won the Derby and the St Leger as well. By the 1890s the Americans were making a serious impact, not simply by winning but by introducing new training methods. Horses were given much more fresh air than was usual in Britain, where boxes often resembled hothouses. The Americans used better fitting shoes, much lighter running plates, estimated to give a horse an advantage of four lengths in a mile. Their approach to racing was quite different, in that they were not interested in a tight finish, aiming instead to win long before the winning post. The English preferred the jockey to win the race, but to do no more than win it. They loved a tremendous rush on the post and encouraged a waiting race, which in itself was considered a great art. The Americans did not ride flat out, as no horse could manage that, but they were determined to get out in front. Their courses tended to be extremely flat, and this enabled them to be very good judges of pace.

The most visible change the Americans brought was the modern style of riding – 'the monkey up a stick', as it was called. Folklore suggests that this style was taken from the Red Indians, but more likely it was from the southern Negroes, who were simply thrown up without saddles, and naturally gripped the mane and balanced on the neck with their knees. The first jockey to ride in

Left: Lord Rosebery's Ladas, Winner of the Derby in 1894, painted by Emil Adam.

TOMMY and TODDY.

Tod Sloan, the American jockey who popularized the modern style of riding, with short leathers and crouched forward position, with Tommy Loates at Newmarket. Painted by G.D. Giles in 1898.

this fashion was a coloured jockey called Sim, who appeared at Newmarket in 1895, but it was Tod Sloan who made it popular. Sloan was a remarkable jockey who was an extraordinary judge of pace, but his judgement of people was his downfall. He arrived in 1897 with a group of rogues whose shady dealings and betting frauds cost the betting ring an estimated £2 million. The Americans' short stirrup leathers and crouching seat proved to be superior, reducing wind resistance and giving better distribution of weight on the horse. Gradually English jockeys adapted to the style, but the end result was to some extent a compromise. The knees of most jockeys did not overlap the withers, nor were reins so tightly held as in the pure American style.

Ten years after this revolution the American invasion was over. Many of the Americans had been warned off by the Jockey Club. Certain trainers had imported sophisticated doping techniques and had few qualms about it. Doping was not made illegal until 1904, when the Jockey Club outlawed the practice after George Lambton had demonstrated the remarkable effect of cocaine on a horse. Sloan was finally disciplined after the 1900 Cambridgeshire, when it transpired that he had tried to bribe the favourite's jockey and stood to win £66,000 if his own horse had won. His licence was never renewed, and he died in poverty in Los Angeles in 1933.

By 1908 a second invasion was about to occur. Anti-betting legislation, sponsored by Governor Hughes of New York, had brought racing in America almost to a standstill. This legislation had encouraged Americans to try their luck in Britain, where the breeding industry was fearful that it would be swamped by large numbers of horses of doubtful pedigree. American pedigrees could not always go back far enough to show that they came originally from bloodstock exported from Britain. In 1901 the Jockey Club decided that, if eight to nine crosses of pure blood could be proved 100 years or more back, and the Turf performances of the horse's immediate family was such to warrant purity of the blood, then the horse could be registered in the *General*

An elegant and fashionably dressed visitor to Ascot in 1910.

The great railway age in Britain for the first time made race meetings accessible to large numbers of ordinary people: this scene is of Waterloo during Ascot week.

Stud Book. However, eight years later it looked as if there was little chance of a revival of racing in the United States. In September 1909, the previous amendment was removed, and from then on no horse was eligible for the *Stud Book* unless it could be traced to an acceptable strain in early volumes. In 1913 Lord Jersey went further and passed the rule which prohibited the acceptance in the *Stud Book* of any horse, unless it could be traced without flaw on both sire's and dam's sides of its pedigree to horses already accepted. This became known as the Jersey Act and caused fury across the Atlantic, as it branded many American horses as half-breeds. American exports of bloodstock abroad slumped, and the Americans were convinced this was simply an attempt to make the international thoroughbred trade a British monopoly. The Jersey Act remained in force until 1949.

War was declared in August 1914, and military requirements immediately took precedence over all others. No meetings could be counted on as reliable, and anyway they were subject to cancellation as railway facilities became impossible. Attendances were well down, and there was a strong body of opinion against race-going. Other major sporting events were abandoned, and some breeders such as the Duke of Portland pulled out of Epsom and Ascot in consideration of the mood of the times. Finally, the Jockey Club was asked to abandon racing to enable the railways to be uncongested. Representations were made for exemptions for Newmarket, where it

Derby Day has traditionally been regarded as a favourite day out for Londoners from all levels of society.

was feared that insufficient racing would harm the industry. By 1916 the Jockey Club was allowed to hold more meetings at Newmarket to prevent ruin, but by then there was an acute petrol shortage. In 1917, the most critical year of the war, the Jockey Club voluntarily abandoned all meetings, largely because it felt that, if it did not do so, the government would legislate accordingly. The move was a serious blow to the industry, and led to the founding of the Thoroughbred Breeders' Association under Lord D'Abernon to safeguard breeders' interests. By now the yearling price had dropped by half, and the complete abolition of racing was proving disastrous. The government gave way, realizing how important the racecourse test was for the thoroughbred, which in turn was vital to light-horse breeding as a whole. Eighty days of racing were approved for the 1918 season, half of which were to be at Newmarket.

When war ended and restrictions lifted, the public took to racing as never before. Racing reflected the immediate postwar economic boom, but, like the boom, it collapsed in the spring of 1920. Throughout the interwar years course administrations were anxious about the ability to pay entrance fees, on which they were completely reliant. Unemployment was high, but it was concentrated in certain areas. Even at its peak some 80 per cent were still in work, while in the South-East, where many courses were situated, there were periods of considerable prosperity. One of the greatest problems was to increase competition in the face of other popular entertainment industries, as the cinema had reached a peak of popularity and greyhound racing was introduced commercially. The former offered warmth and comfort in some luxury, and both entertainments were on the doorsteps of the customer. As regards betting, the greyhound tracks used the totalizator and therefore were able to make admission charges extremely low. Football pools were taking up a considerable amount of the money available for betting and appealed to many who would not have normally gambled publicly. By the mid 1920s there had been a noticeable fall in course attendances.

The facilities at the racecourses now came under severe attack. Lord Dalzell's report of 1919 complained about the state of many course facilities, but little was done. By the end of the 1920s he suggested that courses should amalgamate. The Jockey Club was against this, and only in the few years before World War II were funds made available from the totalizator surplus. Since these were distributed according to turnover, no course received enough to have much effect. As the Jockey Club pointed out in a report made in 1943, England had fallen behind other countries in many respects. Some courses introspectively looked after existing customers, rather than seeking expansion of their share of the leisure market.

The 17th Earl of Derby dominated breeding in Britain between the wars (for the story of his Stanley House Stud, see page 90). He bred Hyperion, son of Gainsborough out of Selene, one of the greatest horses of this century. Notorious for his good temper, Hyperion won the Derby in 1933 – the smallest horse ever to do so. His win was in record time. He became the leading sire of winners in England six times, the best total since St Simon. In the next generation his son Aureole, bred by King George VI, became the most successful English Classic sire, and in the United States his sons Khaled, Alibhai and Heliopolis had an enormous influence.

Two other stallions of the period were to have immense influence on international racing and breeding – Nearco and Ribot. Nearco, the second famous descendant of St Simon, was bred by Federico Tesio, founder of the famous Dormello Stud on Lake Maggiore in Italy. Foaled in 1935, he was undoubtedly the finest horse ever bred in Italy and won all the 14 races he ran. He was purchased by Martin Benson for the Beech House Stud at Newmarket, where he spent 19 years. During World War II an air-raid shelter was specially built for him. An astounding horse at stud, he was leading sire in 1947 and 1948, and for more than a decade was never out of the top ten. His sons included Dante, Nearctic (sire of Northern Dancer), Amerigo (sire of Fort Marcy), Sayajirao, Nimbus and Nasrullah. By the time Nearco died in 1957 some 80 of his offspring were standing at stud throughout the world.

Ribot, foaled in 1952 and the third great descendant inbred to St Simon, was also bred by Tesio. He was the winner of the Prix de l'Arc de Triomphe twice and won 16 further races. At stud at Dormello in the late 1950s he later went to America, where he died in 1972. Among his progeny were the American Classic winners Tom Rolfe and Arts and Letters, the Prix de l'Arc de Triomphe winners Molvedo and Prince Royal II, and Ragusa, Ribocco, Ribero, Boucher, Regal Exception and Long Look.

Racing continued during the World War II on a very limited scale, with the Derby transferred to Newmarket in 1940-5. Many Members of Parliament complained about the waste of petrol in bringing large crowds to Newmarket, and stud-farm lands were ploughed up by law for food production. The Thoroughbred Breeders' Association was particularly worried about vital rations for breeding stock. The Ilchester Report of February 1943, called to consider the future of racing, recommended strongly that good-class horses should be kept longer in training, assisted by the provision of races with substantial prizes for horses of four years and upwards. The recommendation was reiterated many times afterwards, as the increasingly commercial nature of the industry led to early retirement to stud.

Postwar racing was dominated by France, as Marcel Boussac's studs reached their peak of success. In many ways this had been helped by the fact that throughout the war racing had continued in France. From 1947 to 1960 there was only one year in which the French were not successful in the English Classic races. At this time the Aga Khan transferred his operations to France. There were many reasons for the phenomenal French success rate. Some said that the English concentrated too much on two-year-old racing, and that breeders needed to produce

The jostle and excitement just before a race, caught by Sir Alfred Munnings in his *Study for the Start of the Cambridgeshire*, which is held at Newmarket over the Rowley Mile Course.

those horses that would beat the French as three-year-olds. Others emphasized that French racing management was superior to British, since in France modern starting stalls, watering systems and photo-finishes were all being used. Moreover, all legal betting there was by means of the state-owned totalizator, the proceeds of which meant higher prize money and more modern facilities.

Once again the profits of war and the coming of peace brought new money to racing. Foreigners, attracted as ever by the historical and social background of British racing, began to breed and race in greater numbers. They tended to look at the sport in increasingly financial terms, and this was to grow considerably over the next 30 years. Nevertheless, in the early 1950s the chief prizewinners still mostly relied on horses that they had bred themselves.

Racing was extremely fortunate to have the enthusiastic and knowledgeable support of Queen Elizabeth II from the beginning of her reign. With Captain Boyd Rochfort as her trainer, her horse Aureole came second in the 1953 Derby, and in the following year won the King George VI and Queen Elizabeth Stakes, making the Queen the leading owner of the season and Captain Boyd-Rochfort winning trainer for the third time. He had achieved 13 Classic winners by the time he retired in 1968, when he was knighted for his services to the Royal Family.

Foreign progress in breeding did not appear to worry British breeders until after World War II. Most were perfectly happy with the 1913 Jersey Act, though the Americans viewed it as a blatant piece of protectionism and felt that it was deliberately designed to make the international bloodstock trade a British monopoly, since it effectively labelled many of their horses as half-breeds. Its disastrous effects were shown in 1948 when the Two Thousand Guineas and the St Leger were respectively won by the half-bred horses My Babu and Black Tarquin. In 1949 the Jersey Act was repealed, returning to the 1901 entry conditions for the *General Stud Book*. Fifteen years later the Derby had been won by Galcador, Never Say Die, Larkspur and Relko, all of whom would have been excluded under the Jersey Act conditions.

After the war British thoroughbreds were continually defeated. Prize money in Britain was rising much more slowly than in France and the United States, which as a result greatly increased their importation of top-class bloodstock. In 1965 the Duke of Norfolk's Committee on the Pattern of Racing was set up to examine the improvement of the thoroughbred and the programme of races. It endorsed two principles: firstly, that the racecourse test was the only test for the value of the thoroughbred; and secondly, that speed was the principal criterion of excellence. The Norfolk Committee found that there were not enough races for good three-year-olds over 1 mile, and that there were not enough valuable races to keep the best four-year-olds in training. In 1967 the Porchester Committee set up the first 'Pattern of Racing', to produce the correct distribution of races between speed and stamina, and to give incentives to breeders to help them compete internationally.

The greatest problem was the range and lack of specialization in the breeding industry in Britain, which spread from sprinters to steeplechasers. None of Britain's major competitors bred with such a wide range. The Horserace Betting Levy Board was formed in 1961 to raise funds to increase prize money, and thus make British races more internationally competitive. French races were offering better prizes, and many English horses raced in France. However, success had encouraged the French to buy from Britain and Ireland, so that the British-bred horses were still doing well in middle-distance races.

By the late 1950s it was clear that something would have to be done about raising money within the industry if it was to remain internationally in the front rank. Prize money was way below France, and the standards and amenities at racecourses were poor in comparison with those abroad. As early as 1943 the Ilchester Report had recommended action, but little had been done. The Betting and Gaming Act of 1960 legalized betting outside the racecourse, imposed a betting tax and set up the Horserace Betting Levy Board to collect revenue from the Tote and from bookmakers alike. The revenue from bookmakers was intended to improve horse-racing, breeding and veterinary science.

Until the opening of the park courses in the 1870s racing was not widely seen as a popular entertainment, and that aspect was rather frowned upon; but from the time of enclosed courses and entrance fees, racing became a serious commercial business. By the mid nineteenth century gate money was not enough to support the industry, and there was general agreement that the best way to raise funds was to maximize betting turnover, which nowadays is annually in the region of £2,500 million. The British Bloodstock Agency was founded as far back as 1911 to cater for commercial breeders, and the rise in the price of first-quality bloodstock reflects the demand. No longer could the breeding of the best horses be confined to a few aristocratic families. With the dislocations of war, costs of maintenance were rising sharply, and owners began to sell nominations to their stallions. The only way to pay for the rising costs was to take a profit on the increase in the capital value of a winner, and even in the immediate postwar period owners were finding it difficult to keep a good three-year-old. Today many horses that have won only one significant race are taken out of training and put to stud.

David Robinson, who made a fortune from pioneering radio and television rentals, was one of the first men in England to set out to make a commercial business out of racing. The good horses that he sold annually as stallions were expected to pay for the expenses of his others. In 1969 he was leading owner, and in 1973 he had more winners in one season than any other owner ever. He is estimated to have made a return on his capital of 20 per cent and at the peak of his operation he had over 150 horses in training.

By the mid 1960s there was much talk abroad of the decline of the British breeding industry, though there were still owners, such as Jim Joel, who had bred every winner themselves, and there were foreigners who enjoyed racing in Britain because of its sporting attitude. While

A string of racehorses exercising on Newmarket Heath in 1947. The large numbers of Newmarket-based horses are still exercised on the famous gallops and heathlands surrounding the town.

American-bred horses dominated the best races in Europe at this time and few British owners could afford the fees of American studs, the fascinating element of knowledge and chance could still produce surprises. Arthur Budgett's two Derby winners, Blakeney in 1969 and Morston in 1973, were both out of Windmill Girl by the celebrated Brigadier Gerard, who won all but one of his 17 races.

Right: Jockeys at the Start from an oil painting by Sir Alfred Munnings.

As if American domination of world-class racing were not enough, the economic recession of the 1970s had a serious effect on British breeders, and the future looked bleak. However, in the mid '70s a complete turnaround took place, the effect of which remains to this day. Robert Sangster set out in 1968 to make the breeding of racehorses a commercial business. He aimed to gain control of the world's greatest stallions by buying the best yearlings rather than proven winners. The racing careers of his best colts are fully advertised in order to win as much prize money and publicity as possible, to create a profitable demand for shares in the stallion. Once the colt has won this reputation he is sent to stud. Sangster took a great gamble, and in partnership with Ireland's Vincent O'Brien is now one of the world's biggest owners, with 34 stud farms stretching from the United States to Australia.

In the 1970s Sheikh Mohammed Bin Rashid Al Maktoum and his two brothers, the sons of the ruler of Dubai, ventured into the thoroughbred world, in a strong financial position to buy the best American bloodstock. That they chose to base their operations in England was very much to that country's advantage. Their intention was not to make money; it was simply to buy and race the best. In so doing they followed the best of British traditions. Where they departed from tradition was in the scale of their operations. In 1983 they spent £50 million, and a year later they bought one-third of the top 18 lots at Tattersalls' Newmarket Highflyer sales. Today, Sheikh Mohammed is Britain's largest single racing owner. King Khaled Abdullah, of the Saudi Arabian Royal Family, runs his thoroughbred interests on firm commercial lines. He does not always buy at the same level as the Maktoum brothers, but he has been highly successful, most recently with Dancing Brave. He keeps most of his horses in England and owns the Juddmonte Farms in Berkshire.

Foreign competition was becoming acute by the late 1970s, particularly from Ireland. In England, many large traditional studs had been dispersed due to taxation, and many horses had been exported. There were now many small breeders who could not hope to afford the current inflated prices. As in so many sectors during the 1970s, high rates of inflation prevented the necessary level of reinvestment of capital. However, in recent years the situation has stabilized. Horse-racing and breeding in Britain today rely almost exclusively on overseas investors. In 1984 only a quarter of the most successful owners lived in Britain. Britain has enormous appeal to foreign owners and breeders. Its racing programmes are very varied; it has a skilled and devoted labour force, and a wealth of research, veterinary and managerial skill; and its bloodstock resources of the top class are considerable. Such quality, which stands on its own two feet with almost no Government support either directly or in the form of taxation advantages, assures Britain's lasting position in the bloodstock world.

The transformation of the British thoroughbred industry has been phenomenal during the last ten years. Prices have risen some 500 per cent, and Britain's standing has risen internationally. Once again the best racehorses are also trained in Britain, and so the entertainment value of racing has improved. The widespread enthusiasm and knowledge of British racegoers, which contributes so much to the unique atmosphere of British racing, has attracted foreigners for decades, and makes it as fascinatingly international as it has ever been in the past.

BRITISH STUDS

Horses training on the famous heath at Newmarket, the headquarters of British flat racing.

NEWMARKET

Newmarket is unique in England and probably the world as a town that is devoted almost exclusively to horses. It is to Charles II that Newmarket owes its proud position as the principal centre of British racing. Situated in the heathlands of Suffolk, 61 miles north-east of London, its accessibility, combined with its unmatched facilities, expertise and institutions, attracts many trainers and breeders the world over to set up their establishments here.

The approach from London is particularly impressive. A long straight road leads past the Egerton Stud and training establishment, with a mile or more of split fencing. Formerly owned by Richard Marsh, who trained King Edward VII's horses and those of King George V, the stud was recently purchased by M. Parrish and is being restored to its former glory. Beyond this property lies the National Stud, surrounded by beech trees and bordering the July Course where the summer race meetings take place. On the principal and more exposed racecourse, the Rowley Mile Course, the first two Classic races are run — the One Thousand Guineas and the Two Thousand Guineas — as well as the two most important autumn handicap races, the Cesarewitch and the Cambridgeshire.

The start of the High Street gives no indication of Newmarket being anything but a typical English country town, although the observant eye will notice the late seventeenth- and eighteenth-century buildings concealed by Victorian and Edwardian shopfronts.

A sign directs international buyers to the Tattersalls sales paddocks, on the west side of the town. Nearby are the offices of the British Bloodstock Agency, The Curragh Bloodstock Agency, and the Thoroughbred Breeders' Association. The Jockey Club, racing's ultimate authority, was formed in 1752 to protect and safeguard the interests of racehorse owners. The Club acquired ownership of Newmarket Heath, and in 1858 directed that the *Rules Concerning Horse-Racing in General* should be enforced at all race meetings. Thus, the pattern for horse racing the world over became established. The Jockey Club has as its headquarters an impressive Georgian-style house in the High Street. A few doors away is the recently-established National Horse Racing Museum and Library.

At the Clock Tower, the road divides. To the south-east lies Cheveley, and some of Newmarket's 45 stud farms that stretch out into the surrounding countryside. Along the Snailwell Road is the bronze statue of the famous Derby winner, Hyperion. On the east side is the Bury Road, where the houses south of the road back on to training grounds and those on the north, such as Stanley House, adjoin paddocks and stud-farm land. High walls dominate the roadside with the occasional famous name on a gate-post. The training stables of the Wraggs and Henry Cecil lie almost opposite each other.

With each year that passes the town strengthens its position as the headquarters of the British Turf. The Animal Health Trust, founded in 1942, has created the impressive Equine Research Station at Balaton Lodge. Under Lord McAlpine of Moffatt another trust was set up in 1982 to form an apprentice school, which now turns out over 100 qualified stable employees annually. While ever conscious of its role as guardian of the standards of British racing and breeding, the Jockey Club has acquired a further 80 acres of what was once Lord Derby's private gallops. With land suitable for stud farms being snapped up almost before it is placed on the market, Newmarket continues to hold and to expand its unrivalled position as the pre-eminent centre of the thoroughbred world.

ANGMERING PARK STUD, WEST SUSSEX

When an Englishman hears of the Dukes of Norfolk, he immediately recalls Arundel Castle. The family seat for over five hundred years, the massive grey fortress was built even before the Norman Conquest and occupies a commanding position overlooking the River Arun and the famous Sussex Downs. The castle is often described as a smaller version of Windsor Castle, and, much restored and rebuilt, now approaches its medieval splendour. The Dukes of Norfolk are the premier peers of England and the hereditary Earls Marshal. To the Earl Marshal falls the onerous task of arranging state occasions, principally the coronation of the monarch. Richard III created John Howard the first Duke of Norfolk in 1483. Since the Reformation the family has remained the leading Catholic family in England.

It was into this background that Bernard, 16th Duke of Norfolk, was born in 1908, inheriting the title at the age of eight. He adored cricket and later became both President and Manager of the MCC. The Duke's interest was kindled by Sir Henry Abel Smith, who also persuaded him to join the Royal Horse Guards. Here his interest in racing deepened so that by the time he was twenty-six he was elected a member of the Jockey Club. His influence there was unparalleled this century. He was Steward for three periods – 1946 to 1948, 1953 to 1955, and 1965 to 1967.

In 1937 the Duke married Lavinia Strutt, whom he had met while hunting with the Quorn in Leicestershire. The Duchess was extremely knowledgeable about racing: her stepfather, the 6th Lord Rosebery, had been one of England's most important owner-breeders. An exceptional judge of horses, she has devoted herself to the Duke's horses, successfully developing the stud as well as supervising those in training. One of the foundation mares of the Angmering Park Stud was given as a wedding present by Lord Rosebery and named Lavinia. She bred the winners Minster Lovell and Blue Angel and in turn Blue Angel produced Caerlaverock by Hyperion who won the Free Handicap at Newmarket in 1952.

The other notable mare in the early days was Honest Penny who bred Baccarat, Garrick and Silver Penny, who won their owners fourteen races in all. Honest Penny bred seven winners in all and did much to establish the Norfolks' reputation as breeders. The small private stud grew considerably after the war. The training grounds were improved inside the Park and all-weather gallops and canters were set up, making it unnecessary to take the horses up onto the Downs. The first trainer was Fred Bancroft, followed by Willy and Gordon Smyth; John Dunlop then developed the stable into a public training operation for some fifty owners and some hundred horses.

In the thirty years after the war the Duke of Norfolk's prestige in the racing world was unrivalled. His management of Ascot was exemplary. He extended the Royal Ascot meeting of four days in June to give quality racing throughout the year. He began the King George VI stakes in October 1946 and the Queen Elizabeth Stakes in 1948, both reaching international standing very quickly. The two races were amalgamated in 1951 as part of the Festival of Britain celebrations. Such was the quality of runners in the first race that it became a permanent international test for middle distance. In 1955 the Queen Elizabeth II Stakes took over from the Knights Royal Stakes to become the last important race in the calendar for three-year-olds to compete with their seniors.

Arundel Castle, the home of the Dukes of Norfolk for more than 500 years, is open to the public at certain advertised times during the summer.

As part of his policy to develop racing at Ascot, the Duke took pains to ensure that it remained the most important meeting of the year. The Gold Cup was to be the ultimate test for stayers, as the King's Stand Stakes was for sprinters. The pageantry and dress regulations for the Royal Enclosure, during Ascot week, remained as traditional as ever in a period when standards of dress were becoming more and more lax. It was a policy that paid off. The traditional event is now more popular than ever and has proved to be a great success commercially. The only other meeting that approaches it as a social event is Goodwood, which marks the end of the London season.

Perhaps the greatest achievement of the Duke of Norfolk was his work in examining the Pattern of Racing in Britain. Together with Geoffrey Freer, a former senior handicapper, and Peter Willett, the leading throughbred expert, they formed a Jockey Club committee in 1965. They were charged with making recommendations about the programme of all races and stakes, with special attention being paid to the top class horses of all ages, the prestige races, and the improvement of the thoroughbred. The Norfolk Report made it clear that there should be appropriate races of the right distance at the right time of year, in order to test the best horses of all ages. They also stressed the importance of training and racing horses long and often enough to test them for constitution and soundness. The Race Planning Committee was set up under the chairmanship of Lord Porchester to establish the necessary series of races to carry out the requirements of the Norfolk Report. The Porchester Report of 1967 brought about the 'Pattern Races' which were to be a series of tests of the best horses for all ages and types. These races were both innovative and extremely influential and the idea was taken up in Ireland, France, Germany and Italy. America followed by instituting their stakes in three grades paralleling the European groups.

The Angmering Stud had considerable post-war success. Burpham won the mile Britannia Stakes at Royal Ascot in 1949 and Eternal City won nine races for his owners. By the late 1950s the Duchess had purchased a number of fast two-year-olds. The soundness of this decision was shown in 1959 when Sound Track won the July Stakes. This was followed in 1960 by Skymaster winning the Middle Park Stakes, and in 1961 Sovereign Lord won the Richmond Stakes and the Gimcrack Stakes. Further winners of the period were Ballymacad, Ragtime, Conspirator, and Golden Plume. The best mare bought at this time was La Fresnes who brought much-needed speed to the bloodstock, although not with her immediate offspring. Her daughter Fotheringay by Right Royal V, while of little distinction herself, had Hyperion blood, and when mated with Ragusa (by Ribot) she bred Ragstone. Ragstone won the 1974 Ascot Gold Cup, an important win for the Duke in view of his personal association with the course.

When the Duke died in 1975 the Duchess of Norfolk continued the operations at Angmering. She currently keeps ten mares and is assisted by her Stud Manager, John Dunlop, with whom some of her horses are also in training. The original stud farm has been divided into two independent operations: one where her mares and foals are housed, the other a racing stable for her daughter, now a professional trainer. With its independent yard and all-weather gallop at Arundel Park, this relatively mild part of England has proved a successful place to train horses, as John Dunlop bears witness, having trained many Classic winners including the 1978 Derby winner, Shirley Heights.

The best winner bred at Angmering was Castle Keep by Kalamoun out of Fotheringay who has won an impressive ten races, including the Grand Prix de Prince Rose, and finished second in the 1981 Princess of Wales Stakes at Newmarket and the Geoffrey Freer Stakes at Newbury. Retired to stud in 1983, he currently stands at the Lavington Stud near Petworth, founded by the late Lord Woolavington in 1904, and is now owned by Lord Woolavington's daughter, the Hon. Lady Macdonald-Buchanan.

Castle Keep, by Kalamoun out of Fotheringay, is the best winner bred at Angmering with ten major races to his credit.

BANSTEAD MANOR STUD, NEWMARKET

Banstead Manor Stud was bought by H. E. Morriss in 1926. Morriss was a well-known Shanghai businessman as well as the editor and proprietor of the prestigous *China Daily News*. He spent the greater part of his life in China and remained there after the Communist revolution. He bought Banstead Manor in 1925, the year that he won the Derby with Manna.

Set on the edge of Cheveley village, Banstead is south-east of Newmarket, reached by an impressive driveway with lawns separating the house from an ornamental lake on which pelicans once lived. There are other curiously oriental features about the stud and the stud farm itself is separated from the house by a high wall in which oriental statues are set into niches. The manor house is a three-storey Georgian-style house typical of the 1920s, with large reception rooms opening onto a broad terrace at the rear, clearly designed with lavish Newmarket race week parties in mind.

In the stud farm the loose boxes are built around a square yard behind which are the stallion box and 370 acres of prime agricultural land. After the Communist revolution H. E. Morriss no longer returned to England for the flat racing season and his son, Nicky, became Manager of the stud farm. Nicky lived amongst his father's collection of oriental carpets, jades and ivories running the stud in a gentlemanly fashion until his death in 1963, being succeeded by his son Hugo.

Ile de Bourbon, by Nijinsky out of Roselière by Misty IV, now stands at Banstead Manor Stud. He is the sire of winners of 19 races and over £88,500, including Glowing With Pride and Kishi Lagoon.

Today, the focus of Banstead Manor has shifted to the stud farm and its adjoining office. The foaling unit has been enlarged, fourteen boxes have been added and there is an isolation unit for visiting mares. Questions of hygiene and security are now the order of the day. The stud is a very successful company with twelve mares permanently at stud and two syndicated American-bred stallions, Beldale Flutter and Ile de Bourbon. Hugo Morriss grows most of his own fodder and he typifies the modern approach to bloodstock, while at the same time he has all the urbane charm of a Newmarket man who knows his subject backwards. Such a combination typifies the kind of racing family that has formed the backbone of Newmarket for generations.

Beldale Flutter, the American-bred horse by Accipiter out of Flitter Flutter, currently stands at Banstead Stud.

BLOOMSBURY STUD, WOBURN, BEDFORDSHIRE

The Dukes of Bedford have owned Woburn since the time of Henry VIII. Anxious to secure the Tudor dynasty, Henry ennobled and enriched many powerful families who had done him service in return for their loyalty, among them the Russell family. They received the ruined Cistercian Abbey from which Woburn takes its name and the surrounding estates. Although today these amount to some 3,000 acres, they are only a fraction of the size they were in the last century.

The family were in the forefront of agricultural improvement in the seventeenth century. They drained 6,000 acres of swamp in the Fens, turning it into some of the most fertile agricultural land in the country. As their landholdings increased, so did their power; and in the late seventeenth century the title of Duke was granted in recognition of the services and support the family had given in establishing a Protestant monarchy. Meanwhile, Lord William Russell married one of the daughters of the Earl of Southampton whose dowry was an area known as Bloomsbury Farm. Over the next 300 years that area of London was continually developed, so that the famous names of Russell Square, Woburn Place and Tavistock Square all echo the associations of this illustrious family.

Woburn Abbey, the magnificent eighteenth-century stately home of the Marquess and Marchioness of Tavistock, designed by Hollard and Flitcroft.

The Canaletto Room, Woburn Abbey.

Much of the area today has been sold to pay death duties and it has been Woburn itself that has commanded attention in the last few decades. The present Duke was one of the first to recognize that great houses could be opened to the public commercially, in order to safeguard their fabric for the future. The scale of Woburn is considerable, with the immense house itself, the Safari Park, restaurants, and some 40 antique shops.

The treasures within are all that one expects of one of the greatest houses in England, containing one of the world's most important private collections of paintings, and an important collection of both English and French eighteenth-century furniture. Such is the attraction of Woburn to visitors and tourists that the family have even advised the Polish government about the care of their historic palaces.

The Marquess and Marchioness of Tavistock were obliged to take on this vast operation and responsibility in 1974 when the present Duke and Duchess retired abroad. They had been living near Newmarket, where the Marchioness was an enthusiastic but not yet successful breeder. Woburn itself had been famous for its stud in the eighteenth and nineteenth centuries. The 5th Duke of Bedford was the founder of the Bedford racing interests. He bred three Derby winners at Woburn — Skyscraper (1789), Eager (1791) and a colt known as the son of Fidget (1797), the only unnamed horse ever to have won the Derby. The 7th Duke of Bedford was also successful on the Turf. He employed the famous Admiral Rous to run his racing stable at Newmarket from 1840, where for 20 years he brought the Duke an annual income of over £1,500 from racing success.

The Marchioness of Tavistock with Mrs Moss, the Bloomsbury Stud's outstanding foundation mare.

BLOOMSBURY STUD

After resting for well over a century, the 150 acres of paddock of the Bloomsbury Stud are being put to good use once more, and a stud farm that in the past bred renowned racehorses is doing so again. The Tavistocks bought their first filly foal in 1965; but the real revival began in 1975, when they bought a broodmare, Mrs Moss, at the Newmarket October Sales. Bred by Sir William Piggott Brown, Mrs Moss was by Reform out of a mare by Whistler. She had won only one race (the Alice Hawthorn Stakes at Chester) and had a club foot; but there was something about her head that made Lady Tavistock bid for her. It turned out to be an inspired purchase for Mrs Moss is one of the most outstanding mares currently at stud as she has proved herself to be a leading foundation mare. Her first nine foals have all won races, she has two sons at stud and she was voted Broodmare of the Year in 1984. Her offspring have won over £450,000 in some 40 races. Mrs Moss's most illustrious progeny, Precocious by Mummy's Pet, now stands at New England Stud, Newmarket. He won five races including the Gimcrack Stakes and the Norfolk Stakes, and was retired to stud unbeaten. Since then, out of 46 mares covered, he has got 43 that have foaled. Lady Tavistock owns 31 shares in him and has also eight shares in Good Times, a winner of nine races including the Italian Two Thousand Guineas. He, too, stands at Newmarket at the Ashley Heath Stud.

Lady Tavistock manages Bloomsbury with Walter Wik, her Stud Groom. She currently has 14 mares, with eight boarders, and her policy is to breed yearlings for sale and also to have horses in training. She is present at the foaling of her mares whenever possible and believes in handling the animals at as early an age as possible. All the yearlings she retains herself are trained by Henry Cecil, Clive Brittain, William Jarvis or Charlie Nelson. She has also sent mares over to Mill Ridge Farm, Kentucky, where Pushy (out of Mrs Moss by Sharpen Up) has spent the whole of her stud life. Here she has produced Eye Drop (by Irish River), Pushoff (by Sauce Boat), and Blue Book (by Secretariat). The Bloomsbury Stud has produced winners of eight group races, 14 group placings and four listed races. The Tavistocks' son, Lord Howland, just back from Harvard and as enthusiastic about bloodstock as his mother, now works for Tattersalls. The Bloomsbury Stud looks set for a lasting revival of its fortunes.

The Marchioness of Tavistock with Mrs Moss and three of her famous offspring. *From left to right:* Jupiter Island by St Paddy, winner of 11 races and retiring to stud for the 1987 season; Pandemonium by Mummy's Pet, born in 1985; and Precocious, full brother to Pandemonium, undefeated as a two-year-old and winner of the 1983 Gimcrack Stakes was retired to stud in 1985.

BROOK STUD, NEWMARKET

The Brook Stud at Cheveley, named after the picturesque stream that runs through its 200 acres, was founded in 1926 by a professional gambler, Archie Falcon. He was a Newmarket-based racing correspondent whose principal task was to tip winners for the readers of sporting newspapers. In order to do this he had to be out on the Heath six mornings a week, his field glasses carefully trained on the various strings of thoroughbreds as their trainers worked them. Trainers do not take kindly to the likes of Archie Falcon and will go to great pains to hide the weights which their horses are carrying, whenever they set up a trial gallop. Falcon was therefore obliged to worm this information from the jockeys and the stable lads and edge his way close enough to eavesdrop.

Falcon, however, was no ordinary tout. In 1922 he backed Captain Cuttle in the Derby and won £80,000. It was a time when Newmarket was enjoying singular success and when admittance to the Members enclosure was severely restricted. There were then thirty-two days of important mid-week racing, including the One Thousand and Two Thousand Guineas Stakes for three-year-olds and the two important autumn handicaps, the Cambridgeshire and the Cesarewitch. All these races were very popular with gamblers, who regularly took advantage of the opportunity afforded by those bookmakers who offered anti-post betting on both races. Anyone with inside knowledge could back an animal well in advance, when the odds would be far longer than on the actual day of the race. But Archie Falcon, having had such a spectacular win, turned his skill and

View of Brook Stud and its stables.

knowledge to a far more respectable game of chance: that of becoming an owner-breeder.

At first he bought Woodditton Stud and his horses were owned and raced in partnership with Mrs Edgar Wallace. After three years he sold the stud as a going concern, including the mares and foals, to Sir Victor Sassoon. It was with the proceeds of this sale that he was able to buy the 200 acres at Cheveley and build Brook Stud. He designed and built himself two large stallion boxes with thirty-two timber and tile-roofed boxes for the mares and thirteen smaller yearling boxes. Sadly Falcon died five years later, before he had made his mark. His widow leased the property until 1934, when it was bought by Sir Alfred Butt.

Sir Alfred Butt was fifty-six and a gambler, at home in the casinos at Monte Carlo and Deauville as well as at Newmarket. He was also a successful and astute entrepreneur and with typical dash he had his trainer Frank Butters buy him a colt by Sansovino out of Irish Melody for 1,500 guineas. The price paid for this colt, bred at Sledmere, was then a record for a yearling and three times the current price of the average yearling sold by Tattersalls. Bloodstock was suffering at this time from the world depression which may account for the reason why Sir Alfred Butt, who spent so lavishly, was regarded by some as unlucky; for although his horses won a number of races, the top prizes seemed to elude him. He had no theoretical knowledge of breeding and was just as happy gambling on a selling race as he was on a Classic.

During 1948 Sir Alfred added many new loose boxes to Archie Falcon's original main yard. He turned the stud into a company and made his son Kenneth a member of the board. Kenneth Butt was a serious student of bloodstock, and was particularly impressed by the success the Aga Khan was having by breeding from dams with speed. He had great difficulty persuading his father that the fundamental aim of Brook Stud was to breed top quality animals, either to go for training or for sale at Tattersalls. Gradually Kenneth Butt took over the administration of Brook Stud and by the mid 1950s it had been divided into twenty-one paddocks, all double-fenced, double-gated, drained and carefully treated with basic slag every three years. The remaining 80 acres, which up to that point were arable, were turned over to grass and fenced to give an additional nine paddocks. The modernization was completed by building two sets of isolation boxes and a covering yard. At the end of each covering season, when the visiting mares left Brook Stud, Kenneth Butt brought Hereford and Friesian cattle from his own farm to graze the paddocks.

The enlargement of Brook Stud has meant that all forage since the mid 1950s has had to be bought. Philip Mitchell, the stud's present manager, considers this to be an advantage since it widens choice and allows only the best to be fed to the animals. It has taken over twenty years from the time Archie Falcon began building for Brook Stud and its progeny to become a force to be reckoned with in the thoroughbred world.

The list of horses bred by the Butts is long, but Petition by Fair Trial out of Art Paper deserves special mention for Sir Alfred bred him, raced him, and stood him at stud. As a two-year-old he won the New Stakes at Royal Ascot, the Richmond Stakes at Goodwood, the Gimcrack Stakes, and the Champagne Stakes at Doncaster. As a three-year-old he beat Sayajirao at Hurst Park, though he was beaten in both the Two Thousand Guineas and at Goodwood. As a four-year-old he regained confidence, winning the Victoria Cup and the Eclipse Stakes in record time. He was retired to Brook Stud and syndicated with each of the forty shares being valued at £1,500 and his nomination fee fixed at 250 guineas. As a sire of winners he was exemplary and was the leading sire of 1959. Sir Alfred Butt died in December 1962 at the age of eighty-four. The year before his death the stud bought Tina II from the Aga Khan to send to Petition; she never raced but amply repaid her purchase price by becoming the dam of six notable winners.

David Harris bought Brook Stud from Sir Kenneth Butt in 1981. His trainer was Gavin Hunter and among the horses he owned was Greenwood Star. With a background of accountancy and an introduction to horseracing as a result of acting for Joe Coral, David Harris has accurately gauged the needs of enthusiastic business people who cannot devote themselves to racing and breeding full-time. Investment in Brook Bloodstock PLC fulfils such a need. The group owns fifteen broodmares, nine yearlings, two stallions (Kalaglow and Never So Bold) and five horses in training, one in a half share and one in a quarter share. The stud is managed by Philip Mitchell who began as a student at Sir Victor Sassoon's Beech House Stud, then spent a year with Sir Noel Murless before becoming a stud manager in 1972 at Herringswell Stud. From the beginning David Harris has had his eye on the international market. He bought Brook Stud complete and proceeded to assemble a group of broodmares of the highest quality by both buying and selling, his overall policy being to race such fillies as he wished to retain for breeding and to sell all the colts born at the stud.

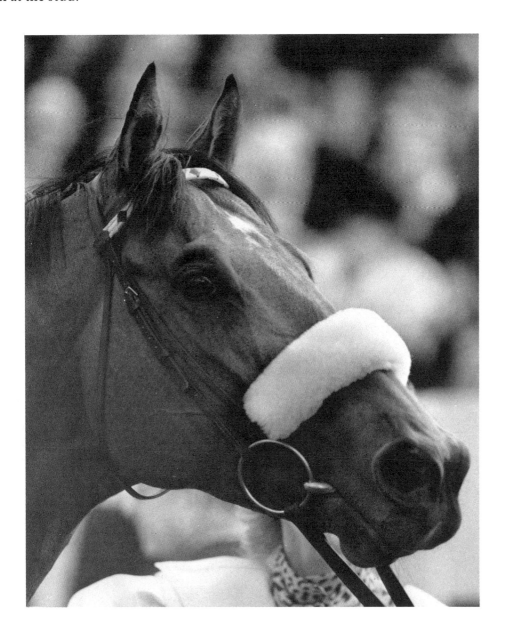

Never So Bold, by Bold Lad out of Never Never Land by Habitat. European Champion Sprinter in 1985, Never So Bold won ten races, including the King's Stand Stakes, the Norcros July Cup and the William Hill Sprint Championship. He currently stands at Brook Stud.

DALHAM HALL STUD, NEWMARKET

Sheikh Mohammed Bin Rashid Al Maktoum is the largest single owner in British racing today. The second son of the ruler of Dubai, and his country's Minister of Defence, he divides his time between the political role he plays in the Arab world and his passionate interest in animals, in particular the breeding and racing of thoroughbreds.

The last ten years have seen the gradual and significant build-up of Sheikh Mohammed's bloodstock interests, which now include three studs in England and one in Ireland. In 1981 he acquired Dalham Hall Stud from the Hon. J.P. (Jim) Philipps, who sold the stud as a going concern to include all the bloodstock. The 160 acres of wind-protected paddocks, on a favoured location between Duchess Drive and Woodditton Road, had been in the Philipps family for two generations and its yearlings were among the most prominent to be sold by Tattersalls. Founded in 1928 by Lord Milford, on a different site to the present day stud, it had a fine and established record. Many of Dalham Hall's current bloodstock trace back to the stud's foundation mare, Lady Peregrine, including Great Nephew (out of Honeyway) who sired many Classic winners, notably Shergar.

Oh So Sharp, ridden by Steve Cauthen, is led in by Sheikh Mohammed after her spectacular win in the 1985 Gold Seal Oaks at Epsom.

Among the former Dalham broodmares was the outstanding Oh So Fair, now in America. Bought by Jim Philipps at the Newmarket December Sales in 1970, she was the dam of Oh So Sharp, Sheikh Mohammed's first home-bred Classic winner of the St Leger, the One Thousand Guineas and the Gold Seal Oaks, all in 1985. His elder brother, Sheikh Maktoum Al Maktoum, already owned three Classic winners — Shareef Dancer (currently standing at Dalham), Touching Wood, and Ma Biche.

Sheikh Mohammed's prime concern has centred on the modernization of the stud itself. Leaving the old yard as it was, he has constructed what is said to be the largest timber-structured building in Europe as a foaling barn. Measuring some 200 by 130 feet and 42 feet high, this vast and sophisticated structure houses 23 boxes and two foaling units, one with four foaling boxes, the other with two. Each unit has its own integral exercise area and closed circuit television cameras as well as the traditional sitting-up room. Dalham Hall is a stallion station for the highest-class sires, and with this unique foaling barn its impact on racing and breeding worldwide will no doubt be significant. To date Sheikh Mohammed owns a string of some 225 horses and over 100 broodmares.

Shortly after Sheikh Mohammed acquired Dalham Hall, the Rutland Stud came on to the market. This 340-acre property, which belonged to the late Edgar Cooper Bland, is to become the annex of Dalham Hall. It has a fine residence in which the General Manager, the Hon. Robert Acton, will live, with responsibilities for the management of Sheikh Mohammed's stud interests. Robert Acton came to Dalham from the National Stud, where he was assistant to Michael Bramwell. Sheikh Mohammed is also advised by his Stud Manager, Alec Notman, who before working for Jim Philipps was Lord Derby's second man at Woodland Stud. With the expertise of

Shareef Dancer, by Northern Dancer out of Sweet Alliance was bought as a colt by Maktoum Al Maktoum for $3 million. Winner of three Classic races, including the 1983 Irish Sweeps Derby in the second fastest time ever recorded, he retired to Dalham Hall Stud in 1984 and was syndicated for $40,000.

The new foaling unit at Dalham Hall Stud also has its own scanner. The barn, now completed, is said to be the largest such timber construction in Europe.

Charles Spiller in charge of matings and Anthony Stroud, the Racing Manager, the Dalham Hall operation is likely to be a potent international force in the coming years. Two hundred acres of cereals have been turned over to paddocks and a lake has been dug for irrigation purposes. A further 150 boxes have been built to house the yearlings, and more trees have been planted on a property that has always been known to be one of Newmarket's most sheltered and protected stretches of land. Rutland Stud is to be used as an interim home for yearlings bought at the Keeneland, Saratoga and Fasig-Tipton sales.

Sheikh Mohammed's first winner, in 1977, was a filly named Hatta, bred by Alan Lillingston at Mount Coote. Bought for the Sheikh by Colonel Dick Warden of The Curragh Bloodstock Agency, she won four races as a two-year-old, and the Molecomb Stakes at Goodwood. She is the dam of Al Amead, a home-bred colt by Brigadier Gerard. Until he bought Dalham Hall, it could be said that his enjoyment came from winning races.

While Dalham Hall is the centre of the Sheikh's racing empire, he also owns Aston Upthorpe at Didcot, in Oxfordshire, where 20 mares are permanently at stud on 130 acres purchased from Sir William Piggot-Brown, and Woodpark Stud on 500 prime acres in Co Meath where most of his broodmares are based. Weanlings from both Dalham and Aston Upthorpe are sent to Woodpark. He has bought nominations to some of the leading Kentucky stallions: Affirmed,

The stables at Dalham Hall. The newly modernized stud is to be Sheikh Mohammed's stallion station.

Blushing Groom, Damascus, El Gran Señor, Nureyev, Seattle Slew, Slew O'Gold, The Minstrel, and Topsider. To take advantage of these nominations he flies selected mares from his other stud farms and boards them in Kentucky.

At the beginning of 1986 Sheikh Mohammed bought a half-share in the two most expensive Northern Dancer colts bought by the Sangster syndicate at Keeneland in July 1985, the condition being that these two horses would run in the Sheikh's colours. The colts, Imperial Falcon (out of Ballade) and Obligato (out of Truly Bound), cost the Sangster syndicate $54 million. They are to be trained by Vincent O'Brien. Both names were chosen by the Sheikh who, in common with many other racehorse owners, believes that a horse with an ugly name never won a good race.

The Maktoum family's enormous financial stake in bloodstock does not end with owning and breeding. They are directly helping racing through sponsorship of individual races. The Dubai Champion Stakes run at Newmarket is for three-year-olds; Sheikh Mohammed sponsors the Dalham Chester Vase and the Woodpark Stakes at Phoenix Park in Ireland; Sheikh Maktoum sponsors the Gainsborough Stud Fred Darling Stakes; and their brother Sheikh Hamdam sponsors the Derrinstown Stud Derby Trial Stakes.

Inevitably, the arrival on the racecourse of a new group of owners leads to much speculation. The world of racing has always been so and Newmarket is no exception. The Maktoums have brought vast wealth into racing and theirs is a different scale of values, one which makes them the world leaders in the buying market. Nevertheless, the generous pricing of their stallions has shown that they are happy to let other breeders have access to their bloodlines. The reasons they give for owning racehorses are sportsman-like, as summed up by Sheikh Mohammed: 'People tend to get the wrong idea about our attitude to racing. We don't want to throw our weight about, and we don't try to alter your conventions. We enjoy our horses. We don't bet. We run them all honestly and fairly, and we thoroughly enjoy British racing.'

Top Ville, Dalham's new resident stallion, by High Top out of Sega Ville, broke the time records for both the Prix du Jockey-Club and the Prix Lupin in 1979.

The impressive entrance to Dalham Hall Stud.

HIGHCLERE STUD, HAMPSHIRE

Lord Porchester's stud farm at Highclere, in Hampshire, fulfils the layman's romantic conception of such a place. Set within the grounds of Highclere Castle, the 250 acres turned over to horse-breeding lie on chalk downs five miles south of Newbury. The many giant Lebanon cedars are reminders of the family's association with the Middle East, as is the mausoleum, erected on Beacon Hill within the estate, where Lord Porchester's grandfather, the 5th Earl of Carnarvon (1866-1923), lies buried. A distinguished Egyptologist, Lord Carnarvon assembled the group of archaeologists that discovered the tomb of Tutankhamun. He also sailed round Cape Horn and was an enthusiastic motorist and photographer. Ahead of his time in many respects, he once turned up at the Goodwood races wearing a pair of co-respondent shoes — a touch of eccentricity which earned him a sharp rebuke from Edward VII.

Highclere Castle was built in 1838 by Sir Charles Barry, and the stud farm was founded at the beginning of this century by the 5th Earl. It originally consisted of about thirty boxes, including a stallion and foaling box. In its early days, it did not breed a Classic winner, but it afforded Lord Carnarvon such pleasure that in his will he requested to be buried on a site from which it was possible to see both the stud farm and into his bedroom window. He was not elected to the Jockey Club until near the end of his life — no doubt his avant-garde photography and style of

View over Highclere Stud set in the grounds of Highclere Castle.

Highclere Castle, built in 1838 by Sir Charles Barry, is the seat of the Earls of Carnarvon.

dressing were responsible. At any rate, on being awarded this honour, he gloomily observed: 'I suppose I must regard this as my death warrant.' He died a year later, in 1923. The most famous of Lord Carnarvon's home-bred horses was Blenheim who won the 1930 Derby. An outstanding success at stud, Blenheim got Mumtaz Begum, dam of Nasrullah, Donatello II, and Whirlaway.

In the early 1960s many of the present Earl of Carnarvon's horses were trained by a former Grenadier Guards officer, the Hon. Arthur (Atty) Corbett, at Compton, a few miles from Highclere. One colt in particular, Queen's Hussar, showed real ability from his first gallop, and as a two-year-old won the Cannon Yard Plate at Windsor, the Cuddington Stakes at Epsom, the Rous Memorial Stakes at Newmarket and the Washington Singer Stakes at Newbury. He won the last-named race by 10 lengths while wearing blinkers, which he always raced in from then on. In 1963, as a three-year-old, Queen's Hussar won two important mile races, the Lockinge Stakes at Newbury and the Sussex Stakes at Goodwood, and as a four-year-old he won the Cavendish Stakes at Sandown — in all seven races from five furlongs to a mile, worth £21,105. He retired to stand at Highclere, with a good reputation for being a genuine miler, at the modest fee of £250. No one could foresee that he would sire one of the outstanding British horses of the century, Brigadier Gerard.

Brigadier Gerard, owned and bred by John and Jean Hislop, won 17 out of his 18 races, over distances varying from five furlongs to a mile and a half. He earned over £200,000 in prize money, and in the 1971 Two Thousand Guineas he beat his great contemporary Mill Reef decisively. After this Queen's Hussar's stud fee escalated rapidly, as did his reputation, for he also sired both the Queen's filly Highclere, who won the 1974 One Thousand Guineas and the Prix de Diane, and another seven-times winner, Shiny Tenth.

Lord Porchester (the Earl's son) had always been enthusiastic about Queen's Hussar. By producing £2,000 at the right moment, he managed to buy Jojo, Queen's Hussar's 12-year-old dam. She rewarded him by producing Hiding Place who was the dam of Little Wolf, the 1983

Teenoso, by Youth out of Furioso, won six races including the 1983 Epsom Derby by three lengths. Lester Piggott also rode him to victory in the King George VI and Queen Elizabeth Diamond Stakes in the same year. He retired to stud at Highclere in 1985.

Ascot Gold Cup winner. In 1979 Lord Porchester took over the ownership and management of the Highclere Stud from his father. Queen's Hussar died in 1981 and in his place stood Troy (now deceased) and Homing, both trained by Dick Hern. Troy won the 1979 Derby, the Irish Sweeps Derby, the King George VI and Queen Elizabeth Diamond Stakes, and the Benson and Hedges Gold Cup, while Homing was the best miler in Europe. Teenoso, winner of the 1983 Derby, has been sent to Highclere to stand — proof, if any were needed, that Lord Porchester runs a highly competent operation.

The stud has been enlarged since his grandfather's day, and now comprises 100 boxes, two veterinary examination rooms, a laboratory, new foaling units, foaling boxes with closed-circuit television and a security officer — a precaution that many stud farms have been obliged to take. The need to take the maximum precautions against disease, especially virus abortion, is also common to all stud farms, as is the need to isolate groups of animals: the mares waiting to foal cannot be allowed in contact with the yearlings, while the visiting mares are kept apart from the home-bred mares. The influence of Arab breeders has increased this demand for better technology, which now plays an important part when a stud owner is trying to promote a stallion for syndication. Once the horse is proven, the facilities become less significant.

Lord Porchester is steeped in the traditional background of racehorse breeding, yet is flexible enough to accept the promotional drive of the Americans: John Gaines, for instance, has initiated deferred payment arrangements for syndicated stallions over a five-year period as a way of attracting breeders. Lord Porchester, currently the President of the Thoroughbred Breeders' Association, is sympathetic to the smaller breeder and at the same time brings international standing to his presidency. For the past twenty-five years he has played a leading role in local politics. He is Chairman of the Newbury Racecourse Company, which now has a comprehensive scheme for rebuilding and refurbishment, and as Her Majesty the Queen's Racing Manager, although he is modest with regard to what this entails, he advises her on the matings of her many thoroughbred mares.

He has three mares in the United States, (two at Lane's End Farm, Kentucky, with William S. Farish III), and in return he keeps one of William Farish's mares at Highclere. The purpose of this is to outcross in the States, bring back the progeny, and then inbreed here. Thus he keeps class speed within his stud, with the ultimate aim of gradually upgrading his band of broodmares. He has already obtained a record price of £400,000 for a yearling at the Highflyer Sales at Newmarket.

Troy, by Petingo out of La Milo, winning the 1979 King George VI and Queen Elizabeth Diamond Stakes with Willie Carson. Bred in Ireland at the Ballymacoll Stud, he raced 11 times with eight wins. He dominated the finish of the 1979 Epsom Derby by seven lengths – his most important win. He retired to stud at Highclere in 1980 where his syndication for stud was a European record valuation of £7.2 million. He died in 1983.

The stables at Highclere Stud which now comprises 100 boxes. There are 15 mares permanently at stud and two resident stallions standing: Homing and Teenoso.

KIRTLINGTON STUD FARM LTD, OXFORDSHIRE

Kirtlington Park was bought by Hugh Maitland Budgett in 1922. Situated in the heart of Bicester hunting country, it lies on the Oxford-Bicester road and consists of 800 acres of prime agricultural land. Its current owner is Arthur Budgett, the only Englishman ever to have owned, bred and trained two Derby winners. He was brought up with horses, his father being a keen hunter and author of the authoritative work on the subject, *Hunting by Scent*.

At Oxford he had captained the University Polo team and on coming down in 1939 he took out a trainer's licence. During the war he served in Burma and the Middle East and it was not until 1946 that he was able to train again. In 1947 he saddled his first winner — Fair Mile, owned by his brother, who won the Novices Chase at Newton Abbot.

Arthur Budgett began to be recognized as a trainer of top-class horses with Commissar. This colt foal by Sir Cosmo out of Salar was bought by the Budgett brothers at the Newmarket Sales in December 1940 for 270 guineas. That same day they were offered a handsome profit by Sam Armstrong, the Newmarket trainer, which fortunately they turned down. Commissar was sent to Stedhall for training, and his brother left for India.

Commissar failed to win as a two-year-old, sprung a tendon as a three-year-old and was turned out to grass at Kirtlington to await the return of the brothers. Finally, as a six-year-old, he justified the trainer's belief in him by winning the Stewards' Cup at Goodwood. Shortly afterwards Arthur Budgett moved to East Ilsley, near Wantage, to be near Stedhall's training gallops. His string comprised Commissar, now very unsound, the novice chaser Fair Mile and four other horses.

The Lincoln Handicap of 1948 proved Budgett's faith in Commissar. At the opening of the flat racing season a trial gallop between the favourite for the race, Flexton, and Commissar showed the latter in good form. Billy Rickaby, who was riding that winter in Bombay, was cabled to return to ride Commissar in the Lincoln. That year the race had a record number of starters and 2 furlongs from home Commissar drew clear to win by two lengths. A month later he won over 6 furlongs at Bath ridden by Gordon Richards. In his last race he broke down irretrievably and was pensioned off to run with the yearlings. He died at the age of 28, having established Arthur Budgett's name with the racing public.

Arthur Budgett's next significant move was to rent Whatcombe, one of the leading stables in the country, and of great historical significance, for it was here that Dick Dawson had trained his Derby winners. Nearby was Woolley Down with its wonderful turf, perfect for summer gallops. Whatcombe House itself, a small Queen Anne house, recalled the days when racing was popular at nearby Enborne Heath, Newbury, in the eighteenth century. A mile west of Whatcombe on higher ground lay Summer Down, which drained well and was ideal for spring and autumn training. Just as the move was made, Arthur's father died and left him Park Farm. He was now able to increase the number of broodmares, sell the yearlings, and buy the occasional foal for re-sale as a yearling. He took in boarders belonging to his brother, Horace Renshaw, and Sir Gervais Tennyson d'Eyncourt, and put the whole operation on a sound commercial footing.

KIRTLINGTON STUD LIMITED

Few men are Arthur Budgett's equal as a judge of yearlings. He bought only six yearlings costing more than £6,000 throughout his career as a trainer. His winners or their dams were bought by him for modest sums or they were home-bred by their owners. Windmill Girl was one such purchase. By Hornbeam out of Chorus Beauty, she came up for sale as a foal at the Newmarket December Sales of 1961 and failed to reach her reserve of 1,000 guineas. Arthur Budgett bought her in partnership with his brother-in-law, Peter Towers-Clark, for the reserve price with the idea of re-selling her as a yearling. Two weeks before she was due to be sold the following October, she developed a swelling on her inside off fore, and it was decided to keep her. She ran only twice as a two-year-old and according to her jockey, Lester Piggott, the second time out she showed great promise. Budgett never hurried his two-year-olds. He rarely bought sprinters, preferring middle distance horses most likely to be at their best as three-year-olds. He believes his horses will let him know when they are ready to race, which may indeed account for the many winners he has produced as four- and five-year-olds. He also believes that horses need plenty of time to digest their morning feed before work. His horses are fed English and Scotch oats crushed on the spot, linseed mash twice a week, vitamins in moderation, and dandelions to whet the appetite.

The Groom's Cottage at Park Farm, Kirtlington, with the stables behind.

Windmill Girl's first race as a three-year-old was very disappointing, but she was allowed one more chance in the Oaks Trial at Newmarket, which she won easily. The Oaks of 1964 was one of the wettest on record and the going extremely soft. Windmill Girl was thought in the weighing room to have next to no chance. Ridden by Joe Mercer, she suddenly sharpened with a furlong to go and finished second. A fortnight later she won the Ribblesdale Stakes at Ascot.

Windmill Girl made her name and that of Arthur Budgett, as the dam of Blakeney and Morston, his two Derby winners of 1969 and 1973. Blakeney, by Hethersett, was a typical small first foal, and like his dam failed to reach his reserve at the Newmarket yearling sales, so Budgett kept him, selling a half share to Horace Renshaw. Windmill Girl foaled for the fourth time at Baron Guy de Rothschild's Haras de Meautry in April 1970. A chestnut colt by the St Leger winner Ragusa, he was named Morston. When mare and foal returned to Kirtlington, Budgett decided that this colt was not for sale. Morston was not hurried, indeed the 1973 Derby was only his second appearance on a racecourse. He won comfortably by a length and a half.

Although most breeders of thoroughbred horses run cattle on their paddocks, Arthur Budgett prefers sheep, claiming that they tread the paddocks more evenly and leave the grass sweeter. He believes that the later the foal is weaned the better for the animal, providing the mare shows no signs of tiring. The Budgetts have an open mind on breeding theory and prefer common sense and instinct and, when necessary, an unorthodox approach to an individual animal.

A yearling out of Creake by Mummy's Pet in front of Park Farm.

Three mares in foal in front of Kirtlington House, currently undergoing restoration.

THE NATIONAL STUD, NEWMARKET

The National Stud has a record of achievement that few other stud farms can challenge. Between 1972 and 1980 its stallions sired eight Classic winners. Both Mill Reef and Grundy would have left England, had they not been acquired by the Stud. However, in recent years the world-wide escalation of stallion values has made it extremely difficult for The National Stud to acquire top-class stallions with the money it has available.

The history of the National Stud began with the generous offer of his stud at Tully, Co Kildare, made in 1915 by Colonel Hall Walker, MP for Widnes in Lancashire, to the British Government. He offered them bloodstock comprizing six stallions, 43 broodmares, ten two-year-olds, 19 yearlings, and more than 300 head of Shorthorn cattle, at a time when our army on the Western Front was facing the second bleak winter of World War I. It took the House of Commons four months to vote the necessary £50,000 towards the cost of establishing this stud, which was for the benefit of the British Army. The National Stud was formed under the control of the Ministry of Agriculture, who appointed as Director Sir Henry Greer, who was both a Steward of the Jockey Club and a member of the Irish Turf Club.

The National Stud. Its policy today is to concentrate on the standing of stallions and the holdings of shares in top-class syndicated stallions.

View across the paddocks to the stud.

From 1916 until 1933, with Sir Henry Greer as Director, the National Stud flourished. It bred Blandford, who sired four Derby winners, Trigo (1929), Blenheim (1930), Windsor Lad (1934) and Bahram (1935).

Sir Henry Greer was succeeded by Mr Noble Johnson. In 1937 Peter Burrell was appointed Director, and horses like Stardust, Big Game and Sun Chariot further enhanced the Stud's already excellent reputation. With the outbreak of World War II the history of the National Stud radically altered. The Government sold Tully to the Irish Government, and Peter Burrell was faced with finding somewhere suitable to accommodate the Stud's valuable horses. From the executors of Lord Furness he purchased the 400-acre Sandley Stud at Gillingham, in Dorset, leasing a further 600 acres of land at West Grinstead, in Sussex, as an annex. On this combined acreage he could grow all the required foodstuffs, and also graze cattle.

Sir Percy Loraine, as Chairman of a Committee set up in 1955, recommended that the future policy of the National Stud should be to stand one or more stallions of the highest class, and to maintain 15 broodmares, who would represent the best blood-lines and thus ensure continuity. The other members of the Committee were the Duke of Norfolk, Marcus Wickham-Boynton and the late Jack Jarvis, whose task was to make proposals for the acquisition and disposal of bloodstock. These recommendations, which have come to be known as the Loraine Report, had far-reaching effects. In 1963 Christopher Soames, as Minister of Agriculture, transferred the Government responsibility for the National Stud to the Chairman of the Horse Race Betting Levy Board, Field-Marshal Lord Harding; thus it no longer had Government support.

The stables at the National Stud. The stud was purpose-built to accommodate the stallions and their visiting mares.

Under the auspices of the Levy Board, the National Stud was obliged to become self-supporting and to create its own identity. Once again the policy was changed. The stud at Gillingham was sold, the proceeds going towards the building and creation of the National Stud at Newmarket. The Stud would concentrate on standing high-class stallions. Broodmares were thought to be in competition with the commercial breeder, and were no longer retained.

The National Stud's buildings were purpose-built to accommodate six stallions and their visiting mares. As much space as possible was allowed between the covering yard and the loose boxes, with a wider dispersal of all stud buildings than had hitherto been usual, so as to minimize the spread of disease. The paddocks of this 500-acre property were ploughed and re-sown with good grass seed, and many hundreds of trees, principally Canadian maple, were planted; thus all paddocks have some shade in summer. The buildings cost £290,000 out of a total of £400,000. By the autumn of 1966 the stud farm was sufficiently advanced for the first two stallions, Never Say Die and Tudor Melody, to take up residence.

On 17 April 1967 the National Stud was officially opened by Her Majesty the Queen. The policy was to prevent proven high-class stallions from being exported, by purchasing them. In 1985 the Sparrow Committee, under the chairmanship of Sir John Sparrow, submitted its proposals for the direction and financing of the National Stud. In 1986 a new Board of Directors was set up, with Chris Collins as Chairman, aided by Bruce Hobbs, David Gibson and Peter Willett; and Miles Littlewort was appointed Manager. Their brief is to maintain the stud's standard of excellence, and to guarantee its viable future as a producer of bloodstock and a model for other studs to follow.

Visiting mares and their foals at the National Stud. In 1964, the National Stud sold all its broodmares and yearling fillies in accordance with its new policy not to breed in competition with commercial studs in England.

PLANTATION STUD, NEWMARKET

Slip Anchor with owner Lord Howard de Walden and trainer Henry Cecil.

Lord Howard de Walden owns three stud farms: Plantation Stud at Newmarket, Thornton Stud near Thirsk in Yorkshire, and Templeton Stud, part of his Berkshire home. Although he cannot be said to be competing with the Arabs, in 1986 he had 100 mares, foals, yearlings and horses in training. His involvement as an owner-breeder is strictly sporting.

In winning the 1985 Derby with Slip Anchor, he fulfilled an ambition that had taken him 37 years to accomplish. This is not to say that his all-apricot silks had failed to pass the winning-post first on any number of occasions; but breeding a Derby winner is the ultimate achievement, and in Slip Anchor Lord Howard had also proved one of his cherished breeding theories. This was that the outcross of the right German mare with an élite stallion of the Nasrullah male line would prove worthwhile. So his Racing Manager, Leslie Harrison, paid a visit to the famous Gestüt Schlenderhan, near Cologne, and persuaded Baroness von Oppenheim to sell him one of her mares, Sayonara, for the equivalent of £25,000. Sayonara already had two stakes-winning sons to

Slip Anchor winning the 1985 Epsom Derby, ridden by Steve Cauthen. By Shirley Heights out of Sayonara, Slip Anchor was Lord Howard de Walden's first home-bred Derby winner.

her credit when she was sent to Shirley Heights and produced Slip Anchor. In 1980 Lord Howard secured a nomination to Mill Reef, the result being Slip Anchor's three-parts sister Sandy Island, winner of the Lancashire Oaks. Sandy Island is now retired to the Plantation Stud, an interesting new recruit to Lord Howard's broodmare band.

Lord Howard de Walden bought his first yearling — Sanlinea, a Precipitation filly — for 8,000 guineas; that same year he also acquired Jailbird, a colt by Devonian, bred in Ireland at the Kildangan Stud. Jailbird was his first winner, winning at Chepstow, while Sanlinea became one of his two foundation mares. The other, Silvery Moon, was bought from the executors of Lord Fitzwilliam. All three horses had a link with Lord Derby's Hyperion, the 1933 Derby winner, so it would seem that from the outset Lord Howard had an eye on his ultimate goal. Hyperion was the grandsire of Jailbird, and the maternal grandsire of Sanlinea. It was not until 1958 that Lord Howard acquired a stud; up to that time his mares had been boarders at the Cheveley Park Stud, near Newmarket.

Plantation Stud is a neighbour of Lord Derby's Woodland Stud, with Snailwell Road dividing them both from Stanley House, in an area of Newmarket always thought to have the best paddocks. In 1967 Lord Howard bought Thornton Stud in North Yorkshire from Lady Sassoon. The deal included the ageing resident stallion, Hard Sauce, who was rising 20 and died two years later during the covering season, to be replaced by another top-class sprinter, So Blessed.

The third of Lord Howard's studs, Templeton, is a part of Avington Manor, his country house, near Hungerford, in Berkshire. It was created in 1961 within the parkland running down to the River Kennet. Both Plantation and Thornton Studs are public studs, inasmuch as Lord

Kris, by Sharpen Up out of Doubly Sure, was a champion miler and winner of 14 races. Retired to stud in 1981, he currently stands at Thornton and is the sire of winners of over 20 races, including the Classic winner, Oh So Sharp.

Howard sells nominations to his stallions Pharly (by Lyphard out of Comely by Boran) and champion-miler, Kris (by Sharpen Up out of Doubly Sure), who are visited by broodmares from other studs. At Templeton, on the other hand, the 70 acres of the 3,000-acre estate which have been turned into paddocks are retained exclusively for his foals. As soon as they are weaned they go to Thornton, where they remain until they return to Plantation Stud as yearlings en route to their various trainers.

Lord Howard has three principal trainers, all within the vicinity of one or other of his stud farms. Henry Cecil trains for him at Newmarket, Peter Walwyn at Lambourn in Berkshire, and Ernest Weymes at Middleham in Yorkshire, with Leslie Harrison acting as the overall Racing Manager. Lord Howard has been the Senior Steward of the Jockey Club on three separate occasions. He considers buying shares in stallions to be a good investment. The most remunerative of those he currently owns is in Shirley Heights who won two Derbys and is sire of two Derby winners (Darshaan and Slip Anchor) — a transaction which took place while he was staying with Lord Halifax at the same time as the Queen. Like Her Majesty, Lord Howard is one of the few owner-breeders left who never sells any of his yearlings.

Some of the mares and foals at Plantation Stud.

THE ROYAL STUDS

Founded at Hampton Court in the sixteenth century, the Royal Studs have a history as long as that of the thoroughbred itself and have been closely involved with its evolution. Although thoroughbred breeding was discontinued at Hampton Court in 1976, the Royal Studs at Sandringham, Wolferton and Polhampton today constitute one of the leading establishments in Great Britain. Horses bred at the Royal Studs over the last 200 years have won virtually every major race in Britain and have exerted an important influence on thoroughbred racing and breeding throughout the world.

The Royal Paddocks at Hampton Court were originally established in the sixteenth century by Henry VIII, principally to breed horses to hunt with the Royal Buckhounds but also to race, although they were not thoroughbreds. King James I bought the Markham Arabian in December 1616, and Charles II sponsored the importation of stallions and mares from the East, which resulted in the development of the modern thoroughbred.

Mares being led past the Royal Stud office at Sandringham.

Neither King George I nor King George II showed much interest in the Turf, although the latter's son, the Duke of Cumberland, bred the great sire King Herod in 1758 and the even more illustrious Eclipse in 1764. The Prince of Wales, later Prince Regent and in 1820 to become George IV, played a prominent part in racing as an owner and breeder, breeding the Derby winners Gustavus and Moses.

Queen Victoria did not race the produce of the Royal Stud, the yearlings being sold at an auction arranged each year by Tattersalls. Prospective buyers would drive down by coach to Hampton Court some twelve miles from Hyde Park Corner, when the carriages would be drawn up in a circle and the senior partner of Tattersalls would conduct the sale. Among the many winners bred at Hampton Court were two foals born in 1887 who were, between them, to win the Derby, Oaks and St Leger. Sainforn won the Derby, while the filly Memoir won the Oaks and St Leger.

In 1894 there was a dispersal sale of all the thoroughbreds at Hampton Court. The Prince of Wales had established the stud farms at Sandringham and nearby Wolferton in Norfolk in the 1880s, and these were to carry on the history of the Royal Studs. However, one of the last drafts of yearlings to be sold at Hampton Court included the great racemare La Flèche, who won sixteen races, including the One Thousand Guineas, the Oaks, St Leger, the Ascot Gold Cup and was second in the Derby.

The first of the Sandringham mares to achieve fame was Perdita II. This wonderful mare produced three full brothers to St Simon, Florizel II, Persimmon and Diamond Jubilee. Foaled in 1891, Florizel II won many high-class races including the St James's Palace Stakes, and was a

Mares and foals in front of a blossoming cherry tree at Sandringham.

Christchurch, and filly foal by Shirley Heights, standing beside the statue of Persimmon, bred by the Prince of Wales, later King Edward VII, and winner of the 1896 Derby and St Leger.

successful sire. Persimmon, foaled in 1893, won the Derby, St Leger, Eclipse Stakes, Ascot Gold Cup and Jockey Club Stakes and was an immediate success at stud, among his first crop of runners being Sceptre, the great filly who won every Classic race apart from the Derby. Diamond Jubilee, foaled in 1897, won the Triple Crown as well as the Eclipse and Newmarket Stakes. A very difficult horse to handle both in training and at stud, he was sold in 1906 to South America, where he did extremely well. The next really high-class horse to emerge from the Royal Stud was Friar Marcus, foaled in 1912. This most effective sprinter retired to the Wolferton Stud in 1917, where he became a consistently successful stallion.

During the 1920s several good horses were bred, including Scuttle, winner of the One Thousand Guineas of 1926. In 1934 King George V bought Feola, a filly by Friar Marcus out of Aloe, who was second in the One Thousand Guineas and third in the Oaks and was to found one of the most influential thoroughbred families in the world. Her daughters included the Classic winner Hypericum, the dams of Round Table, Aureole, Doutelle, Above Suspicion and the Argentinian champions Sideral, Sederea and Sagittaria, and the grand-dams of Highclere and Ben Marshall.

The greatest success in the reign of George VI was the victory of Hypericum in the 1946 One Thousand Guineas. Avila, later to become a highly successful broodmare, won the Coronation Stakes of 1949, and Above Board, a daughter of Feola, won the Yorkshire Oaks that year and the Cesarewitch the following year. The foundations were being laid for one of the most successful periods in the history of the Royal Stud. At this time the horses were trained at Freemason Lodge, Newmarket, by Captain, later Sir Cecil, Boyd Rochfort and managed by Captain Charles Moore.

The first year of the present Queen's reign saw the victory of Stream of Light in the Lancashire Oaks, the first of over 80 Pattern and Listed races won by horses bred by Her Majesty. The following year, 1953, saw the colt Aureole run second in the Derby; and as a four-year-old in 1954 he established himself as the best horse in Europe by winning the Coronation Cup, the Hardwicke Stakes and the King George VI and Queen Elizabeth Stakes. He retired to the Wolferton Stud, where he stood for over 20 years, being twice Champion Sire.

Aureole's success was followed during the next six years by a stream of high-class winners which twice put The Queen at the head of winning breeders. These included Doutelle, the Two Thousand Guineas winner Pall Mall and the fine staying filly Almeria. Doutelle was an instant success at stud but tragically died from an accident after only four seasons. Pall Mall retired to Ireland where he proved a highly effective stallion.

By comparison with the 1950s, the 1960s were a somewhat lean period, although in 1965 Canisbay won the Eclipse Stakes. After a period at the Sandringham Stud he was exported to Italy where he proved a great success, becoming leading sire in that country.

The 1970s proved a very successful period for the Royal Studs with the achievements of Albany, Example, Highclere, Escorial, Joking Apart, Dunfermline and Tartan Pimpernel. In 1974 Highclere won the One Thousand Guineas and then the Prix de Diane at Chantilly, watched by Her Majesty The Queen, who received a tremendous reception from the French crowd. Highclere then ran second to Dahlia in the King George VI and Queen Elizabeth Stakes, with the winners of both the French and English Derbys behind them. Highclere became the first filly trained in England or Ireland to win over £100,000 in a single year.

Jimmy Scallan, the Sandringham Stud Groom, with a foal by Shirley Heights.

Dunfermline, winner of the 1977 Oaks and St Leger in the Queen's colours, with a colt foal by Dance in Time.

Dunfermline, a bay filly by Royal Palace out of Canisbay's half-sister Strathcona, is probably the best racehorse to have carried the Queen's colours. She won the Oaks and the St Leger in the Queen's Silver Jubilee year of 1977. In the St Leger she had a titanic struggle with Alleged, winning by three-quarters of a length with the rest of the field far behind. She ended her three-year-old career as the best three-year-old in Europe and the only horse ever to have beaten Alleged.

The run of success has continued in the 1980s with high class winners like Milford and Height of Fashion, the leading two-year-old in Europe. Every crop of foals since 1971 has produced at least one 'black-type' winner, and the total number of races won by horses bred by Her Majesty exceeds 400. Today some 25 mares are kept, nearly all of them Pattern race winners, daughters or half-sisters to Pattern race winners or themselves dams of Pattern race winners.

In addition to the Queen's mares, five mares belonging to Queen Elizabeth the Queen Mother are kept to breed steeplechasers and hurdlers. The Queen Mother keeps a small but highly successful string of jumpers with Fulke Walwyn at Lambourn, and since 1952 has won over 360 races. Notable home-bred steeplechasers include the half-brothers Inch Arran, Colonius and Isle of Man who won some 40 races between them, while Tammuz, bred by the Queen and a half-brother to Highclere, won the Schweppes Gold Trophy Hurdle. Insular, also bred by the Queen, won the 1986 Imperial Cup Hurdle at Sandown.

All the mares, on returning from the stallions they have been visiting, are kept at Sandringham and Wolferton. These stud farms, on the Royal Estate in Norfolk, have large well-sheltered paddocks. Most of the buildings are of Carr stone, an attractive local ironstone, and the boxes, erected in the 1870s, are solidly built with excellent insulation.

Sandringham and Wolferton each house a stallion and in the season have visiting mares. Bustino (by Busted out of Shipyard) stands at Wolferton, where Barrie Lister is the Stud Groom, and Shirley Heights (by Mill Reef out of Hardiemma) at Sandringham, where Jimmy Scallan is Stud Groom. Both these stallions are owned by syndicates in which the Royal Studs have a significant interest.

Above and right: Bustino, the Wolferton resident stallion, won five races, including the St Leger and Coronation Cup.

Bustino won the St Leger and as a three-year-old proved himself the best of his generation. He ran twice as a four-year-old, breaking the 1½-mile course record at Epsom in the Coronation Cup and then, with Grundy, ran the 'Race of the Century' in the King George VI and Queen Elizabeth Stakes at Ascot. Giving Grundy more than weight-for-age, Bustino was beaten by half a length in the fastest 1½-mile race ever run in Europe, with the great racemare Dahlia third. The first three horses broke the European distance record and the first five broke the course record.

Bustino's sire, grandsire and great-grandsire have all been Champion sires, and he comes from the illustrious family of Rosetta, which has produced so many Classic winners and successful stallions. He himself has sired a steady stream of Pattern and Listed race winners, including Height of Fashion.

Shirley Heights won the Derby and the Irish Derby and has proved an instant success at stud, siring the French Derby winner Darshaan and the Epsom Derby winner Slip Anchor from his first three crops, in addition to such high-class winners as Acclimatise, High Hawk, Head for Heights and Elegant Air.

Yearlings are kept at the Polhampton Lodge Stud, near Kingsclere, where Michael Norris is the Stud Groom. This is next door to one of the Queen's trainers, Ian Balding, and only a few miles from her other trainer, Major Dick Hern at West Ilsley.

Lord Porchester is the Racing Manager, and Michael Oswald is the Stud Manager. The Queen takes a very close interest in the Stud and is consulted on all important decisions. Very few British breeders have bred more high-class winners and few, if any, know more of what is involved. The Royal Studs have a long and illustrious history and, with their very impressive collection of young mares, their future looks bright.

Mares and foals at Sandringham Stud.

Shirley Heights, winner of two Derbys and sire of two Derby winners in his first three crops, currently stands at Sandringham.

ROBERT SANGSTER'S RACING WORLD

Left: The Minstrel, by Northern Dancer by Fleur, was bought in 1975 on behalf of Robert Sangster for $200,000.

When in 1975 Robert Sangster decided to give his full attention to the breeding and racing of thoroughbreds, he took his plans to Vincent O'Brien. He had been an owner for over ten years, but without any notable success. He liked the gambling and the Saturday-afternoon aspect of the sport appealed to him; but the amateurish attitude that surrounded bloodstock made him, in his own words, 'want to shake the industry by the neck'. He proceeded to do just that.

Sangster is first and foremost a businessman, and in Vincent O'Brien he found one of the world's great experts on thoroughbreds. O'Brien had achieved almost every goal possible, and from a comparatively humble start had built up a wide international following. Like Sangster he is compelled to move forward. Thus their great racing partnership began — a partnership that has led some racing experts to compare their success and influence to the late Aga Khan and the late George Lambton. But there is also a significant difference. The old Aga Khan sought success on the racecourse as a distraction that would occupy his mind and at the same time bring return on his money; Robert Sangster entered the thoroughbred industry having studied the commercial possibilities of racing and breeding for over ten years. He had horses in training with Eric Cousins, near his home at Swettenham in Cheshire, where he was born. He had first-hand insight of how easily money could be lost, and of where businessmen like himself went wrong; and from these first early experiences he developed a formula whereby someone with his energy and drive could make big returns on capital investment.

He calculated that the surest way to make money through thoroughbred horses was to buy the best colts, especially those bred in America, race them in England and Ireland, and then syndicate them back in Kentucky. The fact that Northern Dancer became the leading sire in Britain on four separate occasions without ever leaving the United States is largely due to the Sangster-O'Brien alliance. Together they bought and established no less than 15 of Northern Dancer's sons, including Sadler's Wells, winner of six races, who now stands at Coolmore Stud, and Nijinsky, whom Vincent O'Brien bought for one of his American clients, Charles Engelhard.

Sadlers' Wells, sired by Northern Dancer, winning the 1984 Phoenix Champion Stakes.

Like all serious professional gamblers, Sangster hedges his bets. This is the key to his whole Turf attitude, and the reason why so many of his horses are owned in half-share and why he favours partnerships. His income is derived from four sources: first, the prize money earned by his horses; second, the sale of some of the yearlings he breeds; third, the syndication of his winning racehorses while still in training (here Sangster is very astute, since it requires up to six years to establish a stallion); and fourth, fees from breeders who send their mares to his stallions.

Since he entered racing seriously in 1977, Robert Sangster has continued to expand and diversify. He is now one of the world's largest breeders, with shares in 34 European stud farms, his major interest being his third share of the Coolmore Stud in Co Tipperary. He has stallions standing in Kentucky and interests in stud farms in Australia, South Africa, and Venezuela. He has also acquired two racing magazines, *Pacemaker* and *Stud and Stable*, amalgamating them to form *Pacemaker International* and turning this into a thriving medium for American breeders to advertise their horses.

Phoenix Park racecourse, just outside Dublin, owes much of its recent refurbishing to Robert Sangster. He has also become involved in race sponsorship with the Swettenham Stud Sussex Stakes, the most valuable race run over a mile in Europe, and with Stavros Niarchos has sponsored the Phoenix Champion Stakes.

Always moving forward, always expanding and using his imagination, Robert Sangster could justly be termed one of the world's greatest salesmen. Now he no longer bids against Stavros Niarchos when an expensive yearling comes up for sale but has reached an arrangement whereby they share some of these expensive animals. In 1986 he visited Sheikh Mohammed Al Maktoum in Dubai and sold his two half-shares in recent American purchases — two colts that will be trained by Vincent O'Brien and run in the Sheikh's colours. By such astute manoeuvring he has his two greatest non-American rivals not exactly as partners, but co-operating in a venture from which they all stand to gain.

It is impossible for an outsider to estimate Sangster's expenditure on bloodstock. He openly admits that he needs major successes every year to pay the running expenses, and the 400 or more horses he has in training are with the best and most expensive trainers. Taking into account veterinary fees and the amount spent on entries, it can be estimated that each horse in training costs £12,000 a year to keep. Although he owns enough shares in stallions to avoid paying a fee for his own mares, rearing each foal costs around £10,000. Other annual expenses are security, advertising, and insurance, which has soared in cost since the abduction of Shergar. Sheikh Mohammed, for instance, has had to pay out $8 million to insure Shareef Dancer for five years.

The main yard at Swettenham Stud, the former headquarters of Robert Sangster's racing operation in Britain.

Thanks to an inspired yearling purchase, in 1977 Sangster won the English and Irish Derby with The Minstrel, proving that his theory of buying the best available American bloodstock was sound from the outset. Since then he has kept constantly on the move, using his private jet as others might a car.

The family fortune stems from Robert's grandfather, Arthur Sangster, who in 1926 had the brilliant idea of setting up football pools, an idea carried out by his son Vernon. The family business of Vernons Pools now has an annual turnover of around £500 million. Even so, it must have taken some courage for Robert Sangster to confront his father in the boardroom of Vernons and ask for a float of £6-7 million to launch himself into the bloodstock business, for Vernon Sangster had already courteously declined previous invitations to invest in bloodstock. Nevertheless, the request was put, and the loan was advanced.

When Sangster first went to the yearling sales in 1975 to put into practice his theory of how big money could be made, he was well aware of the enormous risk he was taking. He has never lost sight of the risks of racing, but by going about it professionally and on a larger scale than anyone else before him he has succeeded in minimizing the risks. By so doing he has pointed the way for others who prefer the excitement of the great outdoors to the confines of City boardrooms. His success is paramount and since 1977 he has been leading owner in Britain five times.

Robert Sangster presenting the Swettenham Stud Sussex Stakes Cup to Khaled Abdullah, whose horse, Rousillon, was the 1985 winner.

STANLEY HOUSE AND WOODLANDS STUDS, NEWMARKET

The Derby family has had a long and influential record as owner-breeders of many of the world's classically-bred racehorses. The 12th Earl of Derby gave his name to the race which has remained the premier prize in the racing calendar, while the Oaks, which he won in 1779 with a filly called Bridget, was named after his house at Epsom. However, it was not until 1893, when the 16th Earl of Derby inherited the title from his childless brother, that the great racing dynasty was founded.

Stanley House, an agreeable residence complete with a stud farm and training stables, was only part of Lord Derby's investment in Newmarket, where he also bought the Woodlands and Plantation Studs at the instigation of his son. At the Duchess of Montrose's dispersal sales at Newmarket, his son, Lord Stanley, bought for his father the yearling filly, Canterbury Pilgrim, and the five-year-old mare Broad Corrie. These two were to be the foundation mares which resuscitated the Derby breeding operations, divided to this day between Knowsley Stud in Lancashire and Woodlands Stud in Newmarket.

It was in the summer of 1893 that young Lord Stanley asked the Hon. George Lambton, the fifth son of the Earl of Durham, to become his private trainer — a somewhat unconventional step since trainers in those days were seldom the social equals of their patrons. The third member of the team was the experienced Stud Groom John Griffiths, formerly in the employ of the Duchess of Montrose. It was on Griffiths's advice that Canterbury Pilgrim was purchased, even though she had a short neck and very low withers; she also had a mean and spiteful nature and as a two-year-old had failed to win a race. To calm her down, George Lambton placed an old gelding in her stable; he became her companion, devotedly accompanying her at exercise. The trick worked, and as a three-year-old in 1896 she won the Oaks, the Liverpool Cup, the Park Hill Stakes, and the Jockey Club Cup. Retired to stud, she was the dam of Chaucer and Swynford, two stallions that were to play a very influential part in the Derby-Lambton racing association.

Lord Stanley succeeded to the title in 1908, having an active part in the breeding and racing of his father's horses. Walter Alston became the Stud Manager; and the combined efforts of the 17th Earl of Derby, George Lambton and Walter Alston remains as remarkable today as it was then, for it resulted in 16 winners of 20 Classic races in the span of 29 years, including no fewer than three Derby winners — Sansovino (1924), Hyperion (1933), and Watling Street (1942). Lord Derby was first in the list of leading owners in Britain eight times, and first in the list of leading breeders nine times. Hyperion was leading sire six times, Fairway four times, Phalaris twice, and Swynford and Pharos once each.

Nor were the Derby bloodlines confined to England. Hyperion has been one of the most potent and enduring factors in thoroughbred breeding all over the world. Swynford founded a dynasty through his son, Blandford, and Pharos's son, Nearco, is a pervasive and universal influence in Classic pedigrees as the male-line ancestor of great stallions like Northern Dancer, Royal Charger and Nasrullah. The Fairway male line lived on in the Derby winners Grundy, Troy, and Shergar. Phalaris's son Sickle stands at the root of the flourishing American male line that leads through Native Dancer to Raise A Native, Exclusive Native, and Mr Prospect. It is no exaggeration to say that the cornerstones of top-class thoroughbred racehorses in the second half of the twentieth century come from Woodlands Stud and Knowsley.

The 17th Earl of Derby with his racing manager, the Hon George Lambton.

The object of every owner-breeder aspiring to breed Grade 1 thoroughbreds is to win the Derby. The 17th Earl of Derby (grandfather of the present Earl) succeeded in doing so three times, and with a band of far fewer mares than any other breeder who has since succeeded in dominating the Classic scene. In 1914 his broodmares numbered 26, in 1930 they had risen to 31; but by 1947 they were down to 26 again. He gave top priority to speed on the dams' side, and believed that a well-prepared mating should be put into practice at least three times to give it a chance to succeed. The repeated matings of Gondolette with Swynford and of Scapa Flow with Phalaris are examples of this mating policy.

Following in the footsteps of the 12th Earl's experiment at inbreeding his 1787 Derby winner Sir Peter Teazle with his three-quarter sister Wren (a winner of 15 races, who produced four valuable offspring with her near-brother), Lord Derby inbred using only proven individuals of the highest class, like Galopin and his son St Simon, and Pilgrimage and her daughter Canterbury Pilgrim. Of his 16 individual Classic winners, only three (Herringbone, Swynford and Toboggan) did not have a duplication of one of those four ancestors at least as close as third and fourth removes. All his Derby winners were inbred: Sansovino was inbred to Pilgrimage in the third remove, and Hyperion and Watling Street both had duplications of St Simon in the third and fourth removes.

Classic-winner High Top, by Derring-Do out of Camenae, won the 1972 Two Thousand Guineas at Newmarket. The sire of Top Ville, Cut Above and My Top, he currently stands at Woodlands Stud.

It was Sansovino's Derby win in 1924 that placed Lord Derby at the head of leading owner-breeders. Not since 1787 had an Earl of Derby won the race that carried his name. In 1923 he wrote to George Lambton: 'To be head of the winning owners and breeders: to have the racehorse of the year which has won more money than any other (Tranquil): to have the winning stallion: and to have four stallions in the first 25 (Swynford 1st, Stedfast 8th, Phalaris 12th and Chaucer 24th) is a record which I should think has never been equalled, and certainly never beaten, and it is to you that all this is due.'

Yet it is Hyperion, not Sansovino, who has been immortalized, life-size and in bronze, set against a ring of cropped cypresses on the road leading from the back entrance of Stanley House to the town of Newmarket. Hyperion, born in 1930, was a late May foal. Small but tough, he developed so rapidly that by Royal Ascot in 1932 he had won the five-furlong New Stakes in record time (his time of 61 seconds was 0.4 seconds faster than the best three-year-old sprinter, Gold Bridge, who won the Granville Stakes run over the same distance on the same afternoon). The fact that Hyperion was bred to win over 1½ miles and had produced such a turn of speed made George Lambton concentrate all his energies on getting him to the peak of fitness by the next Derby Day. Hyperion's preliminary race was the Chester Vase, which he won effortlessly; he then won the Derby by four lengths, in the record time of 2 minutes 34 seconds. He went on to win the St Leger — a triumph, however, that was followed by the break-up of the Derby-Lambton racing partnership when George Lambton was dismissed on health grounds.

Life-size bronze statue of Hyperion, bred and owned by the 17th Earl of Derby and winner of the 1933 Epsom Derby and St Leger.

Above: Champion sprinter Sharpo, by Sharpen Up out of Moiety Bird.

Lord Derby died in 1948, ten years after his son. John Derby succeeded as 18th Earl at the relatively young age of 30, inheriting more than Hyperion on his grandfather's death. His responsibilities are mainly centred around Liverpool and Merseyside and he was Lord-Lieutenant of Lancashire from 1964 to 1968. These activities have tended to keep him away from Newmarket for the greater part of the year, though his enthusiasm for racing is as great as that of his grandfather.

The Woodlands Stud is now a company (Stanley Estate and Stud Company) with a combined acreage of 200 acres and is owned by the present Earl of Derby. There are 12 resident broodmares, and two syndicated stallions, High Top and Sharpo, and the stud is managed by John Waugh. Sharpo, by Sharpen Up out of Moiety Bird by Falcon, is a sprinter who has won seven races, including the Prix de l'Abbaye at Longchamp, the July Cup, the William Hill Sprint Championship (three times), the Prix de Saint-Georges, and the Temple Stake. He has yet to prove himself as a sire. High Top, by Derring-Do out of Camenae by Vimy, won five races including the Newmarket Classic, the Two Thousand Guineas. Syndicated by the British Bloodstock Agency, he was retired to stud in 1973 and has sired winners of 266 races, the most notable being Cut Above, who won the St Leger, and Top Ville, winner of the Prix du Jockey Club, and My Top, who won the Italian Derby.

Thus the tradition of Stanley House lives on. The yearling colts are sent up to Knowsley to benefit from a change of air in the summer months and the famous paddocks are maintained along traditional lines, with bullocks grazing on them in winter.

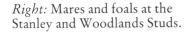

Right: Mares and foals at the Stanley and Woodlands Studs.

Below: A young foal at the Woodlands Stud.

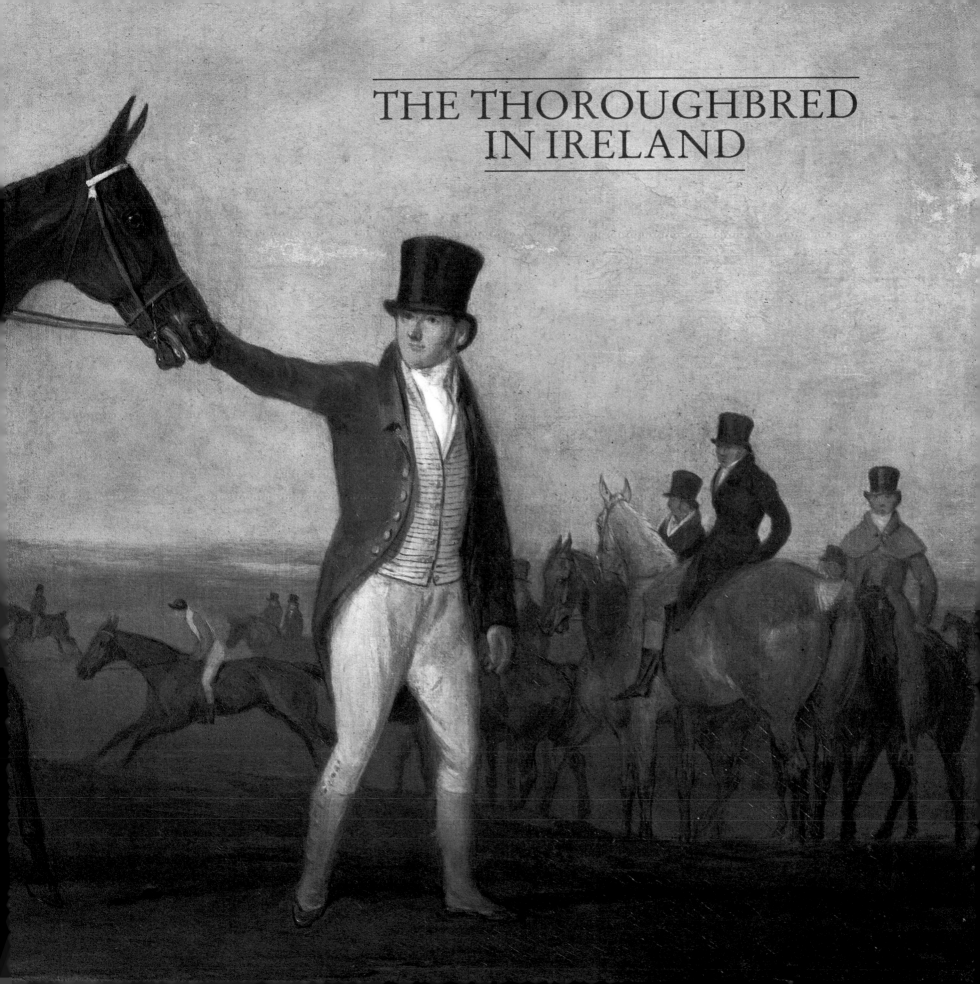
THE THOROUGHBRED
IN IRELAND

The Irish people have a unique reputation for their love of horses, which is ingrained in their culture. Even in the Dark Ages, there was more racing in Ireland than in the whole of the rest of Europe. The seventh-century illuminated manuscript known as the Book of Kells shows many horsemen riding bareback without saddles but with bridles; unusually for the period, they were clearly not warriors. Ireland's principal racecourse, The Curragh, in County Kildare, is said to have begun in the third century AD with the 'Tenach Life' ('Fair of the River Liffey'), and Ireland's ninth-century legal code, the Brehon Laws, made many references to horse-racing. One of the charms of the pre-Christian Irish heaven was that there was to be unlimited racing there.

There is no certainty as to whether horses were imported from abroad, but it is traditionally supposed that there was a considerable trade. Racing was so popular that people came from as far as Scotland to the fairs at which the races were run. Horses were imported from Spain and elsewhere in Europe throughout the medieval period, and much contact that would have encouraged the trade was made with the Middle East during the Crusades. The Hobby, similar to the Scottish Galloway, was the earliest breed of Irish horse. Small and tough, it was rarely bigger than 13 hands high. By Tudor times these were the horses Ireland was particularly known for. Gervase Markham in the early seventeenth century remarked on their importation to England, where they were to be found at the Royal Stud at Tutbury in Staffordshire. Racing took place predominantly at the fairs, where violence was notorious, and beaches were often used as racecourses at low tide, but The Curragh remained the national centre. A celebrated match took place there in 1634 between Lord Digby's and the Earl of Cork's horses.

As in England, Charles II's Restoration in 1660 marked an increase in racing enthusiasm. At Dublin in 1665 the Lord Deputy gave a plate for races at which there were over 5,000 spectators. Sir William Temple made the greatest contribution during this period. He wanted to establish at The Curragh an Irish equivalent of Newmarket, where he had been greatly impressed by the horses he saw grazing, and set up the King's Plate, run every September, for which the King gave £100. Improving the breed was the principal motive for the race. The next Lord-Lieutenant, the 2nd Earl of Clarendon, reported favourably on his visit to The Curragh, where he found the turf finer than at Newmarket; but any possible development was cut short by the Revolution of 1688 and the defeat of James II two years later at the Battle of the Boyne.

By the 1730s, however, a revival had taken place, leading to the remark in *Dickson's Dublin Intelligencer* that 'horse-racing is become a great diversion in the country'. In 1741 John Cheyney's *Racing Calendar* recorded an Irish race for the first time. This was for a £60 prize at The Curragh and was won by Lord Bessborough's Amazer. Other entries in the *Calendar* suggest that races had been held at Mullingar in Co Westmeath, Limerick, and Mallow in Co Cork, but races did not always succeed because of lack of entries. The most famous race of the period was between Irish Lass (known as the Paddereen Mare) and the English Black and All Black. When the former won, with the assistance of a rosary (in Irish *paidrin*, hence Paddereen) tied to her neck, she became a national heroine. All the gentry had backed the English horse, while the common people betted on the Paddereen. The writer Oliver Goldsmith remarked on the astonishing amounts of money that had been bet on the match. National enthusiasm for racing was rife when Black and All Black won against Lord March's Bajazet at The Curragh in September 1751, and bonfires were lit in the streets of Dublin to celebrate.

The Irish Turf Club was founded in 1750. By 1757 disputes were being submitted to the Jockey Club at Newmarket for a decision, and Cheyney's *Racing Calendar* was listing meetings in Ulster, Limerick, Meath and Galway. Twenty years later 18 courses were mentioned by Pat Sharkey, whose *Irish Racing Calendar* was first published in 1789. The success of these courses seemed to be fragile, as the lists vary from year to year; nevertheless, The Curragh was well established as the headquarters of racing. The Irish Turf Club was increasingly active by the late

Previous two pages: A gentleman holding a bay racehorse with a jockey up on The Curragh, Co Kildare. Painted by John Doyle (1797-1868).

Right: Flyer, bred by the Earl of Drogheda, out of Bannister Mare by Hero in 1762, won a sweepstake of 900 guineas beating the Hon. Thomas Connelly's Fortune. Painted by D. Quigley.

1780s and properly organized by 1790. In Ulster, apart from the Maze Course at Down Royal, where both Charles II and William III had given plates, there was little interest in racing.

In the early nineteenth century Irish racing received a great boost when in 1821 George IV attended a special meeting at The Curragh. New stands were provided, and the King gave the Turf Club a whip to be run for, as had been done at Newmarket. There were setbacks, however. In 1817 there had been an attempt to set up the Irish Oaks Stakes at The Curragh, but this had been a failure. All the same, the general quality of racing was improving. Ireland's problems of poverty and famine hardly touched the sport, as the lower classes did not follow racing. By the 1820s some 16 King's Plates were being run, with over 40 stallions standing at stud throughout the country.

A Bay racehorse with jockey, one of a set of five paintings by D. Quigley thought to have been commissioned by Windham Quin of Adare (1717-1789). The painting shows a scene of The Curragh with the cathedral of Kildare in the background. The jockey is in the racing colours of Windham Quin.

Above: Portrait of Pat Connolly, one of the first well-known Irish jockeys in the 1830s.

Several horses began to make their names in Ireland during this period. Bran, bred by the Marquess of Sligo, won the spring St Leger at York in 1832, ridden by Pat Connolly, one of the first well-known Irish jockeys. In 1835 he was second in the Ascot Gold Cup. Another well-known horse was Bob Booty, bred by Denis Bowes Daly, friend of the Prince Regent. He did not run until he was four when he immediately won a King's Plate at The Curragh. In 1808 he was second at the Brighton Races before returning to Ireland, where he won the King's Plate and the Kildare Stakes at The Curragh. At stud he was a notable success, siring Guiccioli who was known to begin with as a 'cat of a thing' but went on to be a highly successful broodmare. She produced Birdcatcher and Faugh-a-Ballagh, both by Sir Hercules, who was owned at that time by Lord Langford at Summerhill, Co Meath, and was later sold to George Knox of the Brownstown Stud, Ireland's oldest stud, at The Curragh. Sir Hercules lived to the age of 29, siring Coronation, the 1841 Derby winner, and Leamington, the sire of Iroquois (the first American-bred horse to win the Derby, in 1881).

Birdcatcher, born in 1833, was slow to mature due to illness. After being sold to William Disney, of Lark Lodge Stud at The Curragh, he quickly recovered, demonstrating great speed in the Madrid Stakes at The Curragh and again with another win in the Milltown Stakes. In the Peel Cup, established in 1819 and run over 1¾ miles of the severest course at The Curragh, he was so

Right: Faugh-a-Ballagh, with H. Bell up, winner of the 1844 St Leger Stakes at Doncaster in which only nine of the 109 subscribers started. By Sir Hercules out of Guiccoli, Faugh-a-Ballagh was the brother of the famous Irish Birdcatcher.

far out in front that he won by over 500 yards and could not be brought to a stop for a further two miles down the road. He lived to the age of 27, and was twice the leading sire of British winners, including Daniel O'Rourke, who won the 1852 Derby, Songstress, who won the Oaks, and the St Leger winners Knight of St George and The Baron.

His two most successful sons were The Baron and Oxford. The Baron was bred almost by chance. George Watts, of Jockey Hall, Co Dublin, offered to sell his dam Echidna to a priest for £20, but the priest turned her down, so she was put to Birdcatcher. The Baron sired Stockwell, the 'Emperor of Stallions', who was the sire of Doncaster and grandsire of Bend Or, both Derby winners. Bend Or sired Ormonde, one of the greatest racehorses ever. Stockwell's male line passed to Phalaris, one of the most important stallions since World War II.

Though Oxford was not in the same class as The Baron, he was the male-line ancestor of Blandford, who was to be the major stallion in Britain and Ireland in the interwar years. The Ulsterman Tom Ferguson had bought Fanny Dawson from the Earl of Derby and had her covered by Economist. Harkaway was foaled in 1834. His start was not very encouraging, so for two years he was turned out with the cattle. As a three-year-old he beat Birdcatcher in the Northumberland Plate, and between 1836 and 1838 he won 18 of his 23 races. As a four- and five-year-old he won six races in England, with two successes in the Goodwood Cup. He was not an outstanding stallion. Ferguson originally set Harkaway's fee at 100 guineas (three times the usual price), a sum reduced to 31 guineas when he returned to Rossmore Lodge at The Curragh. However, Harkaway did get King Tom, who sired St Angela, the dam of St Simon.

Two men dominated Irish racing in the mid nineteenth century. Lord Waterford, who had been a leading member of the English Turf, returned home to Curraghmore in 1840. He became Master of the Waterford Foxhounds and did much to improve racing interests in the southern part of the country. As an administrator in the 'dictator of the Turf' style he combated abuses and laid foundations for the future. The horrors of the famine period in the 1840s, during which almost

Right: The opening of the new grandstand at The Curragh in 1853.

The Corinthian Cup, Punchestown, 1854, one of the major racing events in which jumpers, already proven on the hunting field, competed. Today, Punchestown remains the venue for the big Kildare and National Hunt Steeplechases, although the banks have been modified and turned into a park-course and there is also a flat-race track.

Two of a group of paintings commissioned by the 2nd Marquess of Sligo (1788-1845). A noted sportsman, his horses ran in the Derby and other major races during the first half of the nineteenth century.

Left: Steel, a bay racehorse, with Haslam up, painted by John Doyle on Lord Sligo's estate at Westport in 1819. By Sligo Waxy out of Miss Staveley, Steel won the Waxy Cup at The Curragh in 1817.

half the population of Ireland emigrated, did little to impede the progress of racing. Only in the extreme west, where the rich were heavily dependent on rents, was there really any setback, as public betting played little part in racing at that time.

The second leading figure was Lord Drogheda, who dominated the Irish Turf Club in the same way as Admiral Rous dominated the English Jockey Club. Lord Drogheda was a resident landlord at Moore Abbey, Co Kildare, and gained much respect for his care of his tenants during those difficult years. Like Lord Waterford, he trained and bred his own horses at home, although most Irish horses were trained at The Curragh by private training grooms. The first Irish Derby, run at The Curragh in 1866, was largely due to Lord Drogheda's encouragement. The race had an uncertain start. From 1866 to 1871 the distance was 1 mile 6 furlongs, reduced in 1872 to the Epsom distance of 1½ miles. All the same, it did not prove attractive to owners. James Cockin was one of several owners from England who began to raid Irish races. He won the first Derby with Selim in a field of only three, and again in 1867 with Golden Plover. The stewards of the Irish Turf Club passed regulations to prevent these invasions, so that by 1868 no horse was allowed to run in the Royal Plates, Royal Whip or the Lord Lieutenant's Plates unless it had been trained for six months in Ireland.

Right: Starch, a black racehorse with jockey up, the racecourse and grandstand beyond, by Henry Barnard Chalon, 1824. Starch was one of Lord Sligo's most successful racehorses of the period.

The Curragh's attractiveness improved greatly during the 1870s, when railways encouraged attendance, and the Derby was fixed in the summer, making it an event in the social calendar. Though the success of Irish racecourses had fluctuated enormously, in 1860 Baldoyle, Co Dublin, was opened and became financially sound almost from the start. Up to this time there had been little capital available, and there had also been considerable public apathy towards enclosed park courses, as Ireland's steeplechasing enthusiasts were always a strong interest group. As Baldoyle was the first to be established, it naturally was able to capture the best dates. In 1874 it changed its name to Dublin Metropolitan Races, and the same year it started its own Derby in May to rival that of The Curragh. Run over the same distance of 1½ miles, its great appeal was in its continuation of the practice of fixed weights and ages.

George Low, a Scotsman living near Athy in Co Kildare, bred Barcaldine by Solon out of Ballyroe. As a two-year-old Barcaldine was unbeaten in Ireland, and he won the Ascot Gold Cup of 1883. At stud he produced Mist (winner of the 1891 One Thousand Guineas and the Oaks) and Sir Visto (winner in 1895 of the Derby and St Leger). In 1895 he was second in the list of leading stallions. Barcaldine's most important son was Marco out of Novitiate by Hermit. Marco got Marcovil, who sired the enormously influential Hurry On. Bendigo was another important Irish horse of this period. By Ben Battle (Irish Derby winner 1874) out of Hasty Girl, he was bred by Moses Taylor of Newbridge, who sold him to 'Buck' Barclay. Bendigo won the first Eclipse Stakes at Sandown Park in 1886 and was third in the Hardwick stakes of 1887 against Minting and Ormonde. He retired to the Russian Imperial Stud.

Russia also bought the horse Galtee Moore. He and Ard Patrick were bred by John Gubbins, who inherited stud farms at Knockany and Bruree, Co Limerick, and won his first Irish Derby with Blairfinde in 1894. Gubbins was typical of the Irish breeders emerging at this period. Galtee Moore, named after the Galtee Mountains in Co Tipperary, was by Kendal, purchased from the Duke of Westminster in 1885, out of Morganette. Trained by Sam Darling at Beckhampton, he was the first Irish-bred and Irish-owned colt to win the English Triple Crown (1897). Added to these victories were the Prince of Wales Stakes at Ascot, the Sandringham Cup and the Sandown Foal Stakes. Gubbins was the first Irishman to become the winning owner in England. Ard Patrick, half-brother to Galtee Moore by St Florian out of Morganette, won his first race at Kempton and went on to win the 1902 Derby easily, beating the favourite Sceptre. Like Galtee Moore, he was sold abroad, to Count Lehndorff at Graditz in Germany.

Leopardstown racecourse on the outskirts of Dublin, opened in 1888, was to provide an excellent stimulus to racing and breeding in the years round 1900. It was the brainchild of an Englishman, Captain Quinn, who was attracted by the similarity of the site to Sandown Park and set about building a copy. With only £20,000 capital gathered from a group of friends, the land was bought up and the Sandown Park stands were copied. Teething troubles at the opening were enormous. Such was the publicity given that it proved impossible to deal with the crowds, and scenes were witnessed that echoed those of the first special trains to the Epsom Derby. The Leopardstown Grand Prize was offered in 1890 to the value of £1,000 – the first prize of such a sum ever offered in Ireland and one which guaranteed English runners. As ever, more investment in breeding followed better prize money, so that Ireland was able to boast several top-rank studs in the next 20 years.

Leopardstown racecourse had a stroke of bad luck. Being slightly cramped for space, the track had been laid out on a round 5-furlong course. The distance was exact, but many owners and riders disliked it because of the bends. When the number of entrants declined, Captain Quinn was forced to build a straight 5 furlongs. The new course began to throw up very odd discrepancies, and the trainer F. F. McCabe challenged the distance, which was found to be less than 4½ furlongs. Quinn was fined, and a new course was laid out. It was some years before the

Right: Galtee Moore, bred in Ireland by John Gubbins, was the 1897 English Triple Crown winner. He was sold to the Russian Government for £21,000 as a three-year-old.

The Member's Lawn between races at the inaugural meeting in 1902 at the New Phoenix Park Club.

authorities were able to buy the adjoining land that finally enabled both start and finish to be seen from the stands.

Phoenix Park, opened in 1902, was the next park course to be inaugurated. Proximity to Dublin and the success of Leopardstown had caused this demand, and this time it was Hurst Park that was the model. Phoenix Park was a great success. Its Phoenix Plate, worth 1,500 sovereigns, became the most important event for two-year-olds in Ireland. Moreover, apart from The Curragh it was the only course in Ireland which was for flat racing only. Although the old steeplechasing enthusiasts who had dominated country meetings were disparaging, smart Dublin society embraced it as part of their season. When the King and Queen arrived for the State visits of 1903 and 1904, Phoenix Park was inevitably part of the programme.

At the end of the nineteenth century Sir Henry Greer, subsequently Director of the National Stud, was an important figure in the thoroughbred world of Ireland. He bought Brownstown House at The Curragh in 1888, and the following year purchased Gallinule from George Baird. Gallinule, by Isonomy out of Moorhen, was mated with Tragedy (the first horse to race in Greer's colours), and sired Wallflower, who won the St Leger in 1898, and Slieve Gallion, who won the Two Thousand Guineas in 1907. From 1895 to 1901 he sired all the Irish Derby winners except one and was the leading sire of winners from 1903 to 1905. His most important offspring was Pretty Polly, who won the One Thousand Guineas, the Oaks and the St Leger in 1904.

In 1900 Colonel Hall Walker purchased the Tully Stud at The Curragh (see Irish National Stud, page 132). Solidly backed by the Irish Government, it was to be the spearhead of Irish thoroughbred policy. Several Irish trainers built up legendary reputations during this period. J. J. Parkinson, who had trained to be a veterinary surgeon, became successful as a jockey at Roscommon in the 1890s. He rode like Tod Sloan in the new American fashion, and spent some time in America learning their training and riding methods. On his return he bought Maddenstown Lodge, where he bred and raced, winning immense popularity in the next 20 years. Parkinson and Michael Dawson, at Rathbride Manor at The Curragh, became the leading trainers of their day.

One of the most colourful Irish owners of the period was Richard 'Boss' Croker. Born in Cork in 1841, he had emigrated to New York in 1848, after the famine. He led a varied and dubious career as a professional fighter and racketeer, ending up as leader of Tammany Hall, which controlled the Democratic Party in New York. When Theodore Roosevelt set up a commission of enquiry into its alleged corruption, Croker abruptly set sail for England, where with his considerable wealth he bought a training establishment in Berkshire. He was forbidden by the Jockey Club to have his horses trained at Newmarket, but no reason was given. Croker sold up and returned to his native Ireland, where he bought the Glencairn estate, near Leopardstown, on the outskirts of Dublin. Here he imported the American-bred broodmare Rhoda B. He first appointed Parkinson as his trainer and by 1905 was the leading Irish owner. After a dispute with Parkinson, Croker appointed F.F. McCabe as his trainer for Orby. By Orme out of Rhoda B, Orby won first time out at three years at the Liverpool sprint meeting. Ridden by the American jockey Johnny Reiff, Orby won the Derby of 1907 by two lengths. The Irish gave 'the Catholic horse' an enormous welcome, which was not shared by all spectators. After the race, King Edward VII refused to receive Croker. Orby was the first Irish-trained horse to win the Derby – a distinction not to be repeated for another 51 years. Croker became the leading owner again in 1911, but never became a member of the Irish Turf Club.

By 1900, Ireland's increased success in thoroughbred breeding was shown in quantity as well as quality, since she was producing almost a quarter of the mares bred in the British Isles. The outbreak of World War I saw the beginning of a period of stagnation in Ireland's position in the racing world. Meetings were held in 1915 and 1916 on a limited scale but, after the Easter Rising in 1916, racing was forbidden, and only permitted again after some time had elapsed. The Civil War of 1918 saw the end of steeplechasing, and The Curragh was requisitioned for the army. Despite the continuing troubles, some meetings continued until the peace of 1923, and during this period the meetings continued to make progress. The National Stud at Tully was well established, and new studs were set up in Co Dublin and Co Limerick. The most important influence was that of the Aga Khan, who had appointed Sir Henry Greer as his first Stud Manager in Ireland.

The Aga Khan's interest in horse-racing had been stimulated by Lord Wavertree as early as 1904, when the Aga Khan was a guest at Tully, at that time still Lord Wavertree's private stud. Between 1904 and the start of his interest in breeding the Aga Khan had been busy in politics, and in any case he did not have the necessary capital. Advised by George Lambton, he built up one of the most important studs of the twentieth century at five farms in Ireland. When his grandson, the present Aga Khan, took over these were reduced to two, at Ballymany and Sheshoon, but they have produced exceptional results, including Bahram the Triple Crown winner, Palestine the Two Thousand Guineas winner, Tulyar who in 1952 won the Derby and the St Leger, and Udaipur and Masaka who won the Oaks.

Pretty Polly, bred in Ireland in 1901 by Major Eustace Loder, was a chestnut filly by Gallinule and one of the greatest Irish racehorses. She won 22 of her 24 races, including the St Leger.

During this period both The Tetrarch and Blandford stood in Ireland. The Tetrarch, born in 1911, was bred by Edward Kennedy of the Straffan Station Stud in Co Kildare. Known as the 'Spotted Wonder', he was probably the fastest two-year-old ever. Major Dermot McCalmont bought him, and he was ridden by Steve Donoghue in seven races for two-year-olds, in which he was never beaten. Doubts about his fitness prevented him from running in the Derby of 1914, and he did not run again. He retired to stud at McCalmont's Mount Juliet Stud in Co Kilkenny, where he got Tetratema, who won the Newmarket Two Thousand Guineas and in turn sired Mr Jinks. The Tetrarch was known for exceptional speed, and his influence on the development of the modern thoroughbred was far-reaching. When he was mated with Lady Josephine, a mare also known for speed, the product was the 'Flying Filly' Mumtaz Mahal. She was the most important broodmare in the Aga Khan's empire, and from her descended some of the most prestigious horses of the twentieth century, including Mahmoud, Nasrullah, Abernant, Royal Charger, Kalamoun and Petite Etoile.

At the autumn Newmarket sales of 1920 the Tully Stud sold Blandford, a colt by Swynford out of Blanche by White Eagle. R.C. Dawson bought him, and at three years he won the Prince of Wales Stakes at Newmarket. Retired to Cloghran Stud in Co Dublin because of tendon trouble, he became one of the best sires of the period. His progeny included four Derby winners – Trigo, Blenheim, Windsor Lad, and Bahram. Bahram also won the Triple Crown in 1935. Blandford was leading sire of both France and England in 1935, and of England on two other occasions.

By the end of the war several important reforms had taken place, setting the scene for the extraordinary postwar development which was to put Irish bloodstock into the first rank. The British removed all their stock from Tully to Dorset in 1943, and the Irish Government took over as the Irish National Stud. The Racing Board and Racecourses Act was passed, giving the Board widespread powers of control, from the totalizator functions and the finance of racing to the improvement of amenities. Attendances rose sharply in the immediate postwar period, stake money reached record heights, and the Racing Board distributed grants for improvement, including a new stand at The Curragh. Breeders like McGrath remained pre-eminent, assisted by his purchase of Nasrullah, who became leading sire in 1951 and among many others got Never Say Die, Belle of All, Nearula and Musidora.

Considerable progress took place in the 1950s, but it was the 1960s which ushered in the brilliant period in Irish breeding and racing that has maintained momentum to this day. The establishment in 1962 of the Irish Sweeps Derby made the £30,000 race the most valuable race in Europe and placed Ireland firmly in the top level of the international racing scene, where it has remained. That same year Vincent O'Brien trained the Epsom Derby winner Larkspur, a colt of Never Say Die. O'Brien placed his trust in American horses for breeding, and in the next 20 years he won the Derby five times with Sir Ivor, Nijinsky, Roberto, The Minstrel and Golden Fleece. In 1970 Nijinsky was the first horse to win the Triple Crown since Bahram in 1935.

Ireland's thoroughbred industry attracted great tax incentives. In the Finance Act of 1939 earnings from stallions standing on a farm were exempt from income tax. The Finance Act of 1969 went further and made sales of stallion shares and nominations exempt from tax, thus making investment in top-class stallions highly profitable. Stud-farming is now Ireland's fourth largest industry, but success in this particular world does not come simply from fiscal manipulation. The Irish have an exceptional knowledge and love of horses, and this, combined with their training grounds, breeding expertise, climate and geographical location, will keep them firmly at the front in the thoroughbred world.

The Tetrarch, ridden by Steve Donaghue, was possibly the fastest horse to be seen this century. Bred in Ireland by Edward Kennedy in 1911, he was bought by Major Dermot McCalmont. He won all his races with ease and was the sire of numerous Classic winners, notably Caligula, Tetratema and Mumtaz Mahal.

IRISH STUDS

SOUTHERN IRELAND

Bloodstock breeding in Ireland encompasses a way of life and an approach to the business quite unlike any other country. In many ways it recalls the civilized owner-breeder of the eighteenth and nineteenth centuries, but beneath this romantic exterior it is fiercely commercial and its stud farms rank among the finest in the world. Many of the studs are still part of agricultural estates, often attached to beautiful Georgian houses and their parks for which Ireland is famous. Moreover, many of the houses are still lived in by families who for generations have earned their living from breeding thoroughbreds. The Irish are horse-lovers and few families do not boast some connection with horses. Thoroughbred breeding is the country's fourth largest industry. Racing in Ireland is not only an important source of entertainment, but also plays a significant part in the Irish economy. Horses are a major export, but more importantly the lush pasturage, famed all over the world, has attracted breeders from other European countries as well as from the United States to establish stud farms in Ireland, and particularly in Co Limerick, where many of the most famous stud farms are situated in the Golden Vale.

Both breeding and racing in Ireland are summed up by two words, 'The Curragh', which to the Irish are like Newmarket and Epsom rolled into one. Situated on the plain of Co Kildare, some 20 miles south-west of Dublin, The Curragh has grass that is perfect both for racing and producing strong young horses capable of winning races at an early age. In former centuries there were other Curraghs – the name means simply 'race-course' in Gaelic – but it was the one in Co Kildare that finally displaced all the others and won an immortal place in the history of the Turf.

Left: Triptych, by Riverman and trained by Vincent O'Brien, wins the 1985 Irish Two Thousand Guineas at The Curragh.

AIRLIE GROUP OF STUDS

Between the two World Wars, the migration of Irishmen seeking their fortunes on the Turf was predominantly one-way, with one notable exception: the Rogers family. Johnnie Rogers, from Cheltenham, was a distinguished amateur jockey and subsequently became one of Ireland's leading trainers. In 1935 he trained the Irish Triple Crown (the Two Thousand Guineas, the Irish Derby, and Irish St Leger) winner Museum, and collected the One Thousand Guineas and the Oaks with Smokeless — five Irish Classics in one year. In passing he also won the Ebor Handicap at York on Museum.

His son, Derby Rogers, trained in England for a period at Chitterne on Salisbury Plain, but without notable success, so he returned to Ireland, and bought Crotanstown Lodge at The Curragh.

At the outbreak of World War II, Derby's son Tim joined a British anti-aircraft unit in Northern Ireland where he became a great friend of Charlie Smirke, already a famous jockey who had won the Derby twice, on Windsor Lad (1934) and Mahmoud (1936). The pair of them would get weekend leave and travel south to Crotanstown, to enjoy the benefits of Ireland's neutrality and more especially the racing. Eventually Tim was commissioned into the 4th Hussars and sent to Cairo, where he was chosen by Winston Churchill to act as his ADC during the Prime Minister's morale-boosting visits to the troops in the combat zones.

His time as Churchill's ADC transformed the raw young subaltern, whose knowledge was confined to the Turf, into the self-assured individual Tim Rogers was to become. When he rejoined his regiment in Germany he saw to it that he always rode the best thoroughbred, Colonel Warden (code name for Churchill), and with Colonel Warden Tim brought off his first coup — at the Ascot military meeting at Freudenau, where he ran Colonel Warden and backed him, winning £2,000. He changed his winnings into liras, and with the money bought a small villa on the edge of the Italian Lakes.

After demobilization he returned to Ireland, where his father and younger brother Micky were training. There was clearly no room for a third family member to take out a licence, so instead Tim took over the management of his father's stud at Airlie. His wages were £5 a week and he was in charge of two moderate stallions. Life in those days in Southern Ireland was inexpensive and easy-going. Then in 1958 his younger brother won the Epsom Derby with Hard Ridden: Tim's old friend Charlie Smirke, at his nonchalant best, coasted home an easy winner by five lengths. Spurred on by this success Tim borrowed £7,000 from a family friend, and with his own winnings and savings bought Airlie from his father for £28,000, and set to work. Known to his staff as 'the Captain', Tim Rogers soon won a reputation for being equally astute at choosing horses and people to work with. At Airlie he is remembered for his willingness to get down to the most elementary jobs, such as mucking-out, and in the process he built up a great team spirit. His boast was 'I started with one mare and no money' — a small beginning for what has grown into a major thoroughbred empire. To encourage local breeders who could not afford escalating stud fees, Tim deliberately charged below-market rates for some of his finest stallions such as Tumblewind.

Habitat, by Sir Gaylord out of Little Hat, whose outstanding racing career is now matched by his tremendous success at stud. Four times Champion Sire, he stands at Grangewilliam Stud and has sired over 900 winners to date.

Tim Rogers syndicated his first stallion at the end of 1958. The horse Ommeyad, bred by Prince Aly Khan, was by Hyperion out of Minaret, and had won the Irish St Leger. Ten years on, Rogers was able to pay the Greek shipowner Marcos Lemos £200,000 for Petingo. The condition of the sale was that the money was to be paid before the running of the Sussex Stakes at Goodwood, which Petingo duly won, making him the most important miler in the country. Tim had gambled again and won, for he was able to syndicate Petingo for £5,000 a share. Unfortunately, the horse died prematurely of a heart attack while he was covering a mare. He was leading sire in England in 1979, siring Fair Salinia, winner of both the English and Irish Oaks, and Troy, winner of both the Epsom and Irish Sweeps Derby.

For some time Tim had had his eye on another top-class miler, Habitat, trained by Fulke Johnson Houghton. On the eve of the Prix du Moulin, Tim offered David McCall, the racing manager of Habitat's owner Charles Engelhard, $1 million provided Habitat won the race. There were no formal details, merely a note scribbled on the inside of a cigarette packet. Engelhard, an immensely rich American businessman, was amazed, but admitted afterwards that it was the easiest and simplest piece of business he had ever transacted.

The horse was syndicated at £10,000 for each share — a staggeringly high amount at the time, — but none of the original shareholders regretted their investment. Habitat topped the lists for first-season sires and for all sires of two-year-olds; the value of his shares and nominations escalated accordingly. Twelve years on Tim was asking a fee of £30,000 as a down-payment and a further £30,000 if the mare got in foal. Habitat is a powerfully-built horse, though he is thin-skinned and hates cold weather. Habitat is undoubtedly the most successful stallion to stand

Henbit, by Hawaii out of Chateaucreek, won the 1980 Epsom Derby during which he cracked his off-fore cannon bone. Since retiring to stud at Airlie, he has sired several winners in his first crop in 1985.

in Ireland since Nasrullah, and is sire of some of the fastest horses in Europe with 78 individual Stakes winners to date. Tim Rogers refused many tempting offers to buy Habitat. He was not only a brilliant judge of stallions: he also knew how to promote them, and had an uncannily accurate instinct when it came to assessing what the current market could stand. His horses in training have included Ela-Mana-Mou, Northern Baby, Le Marmot, and Najar. Ela-Mana-Mou, the grandson of Petingo, and winner of the 1980 King George VI and Queen Elizabeth Diamond Stakes, now stands at Airlie alongside Derby winner Henbit. Ballad Rock was the second leading UK-based sire of 1984, the top position being held by his stable companion Habitat.

Ela-Mana-Mou, by Pitcairn out of Rose Bertin, whose consistent racing performance won him much acclaim, stands at Simmonstown Stud.

AIRLIE STUDS

The stud farms of Airlie, Grangewilliam, Simmonstown, Loughtown, and Kilmacredock are all within a few miles of each other, near the borders of Co Dublin and Co Kildare. Grangewilliam and Simmonstown form the heart of the stallion operation, while the 100 broodmares, either owned outright or in partnership, are kept at Airlie. The studs are on some of the best grassland in Ireland, lying on limestone which builds up plenty of bone in young horses, making them ready to race at an early age.

Tim Rogers was a man who always looked ahead. In the late 1970s he was one of the few foreigners permitted to buy land in New Zealand (permission that was granted at prime ministerial level) in return for assurances that he intended to invest in the breeding industry. He bought a 300-acre property in the North Island, which he renamed Grangewilliam, and assembled a dozen high-class broodmares and installed the stallion Standaan, winner of the Goodwood Stewards Cup. Nearer to home, he took a close interest in the Irish National Stud and the Irish Equine Centre. He was already a shareholder of Goffs.

In 1977 Tim was diagnosed as having leukaemia and given two years at most to live. In fact, with the support of his wife Sonia (who came from a prominent English owner-breeder family), he survived until New Year's Day 1984, alert and at work to the end. His brother Micky, who had retired from training in 1970 to live a tranquil life at his Rathbride Stud, became Sonia's assistant manager; he died in 1985. Sonia herself is the owner and manager of nine stallions and more than 100 broodmares, is a director of Goffs, and has horses in training with Dick Hern, D. K. Weld, L. Brown, B. Hanbury, and David O'Brien, son of Vincent.

Under Sonia, the Airlie studs are continuing 'the Captain's' insistence on the most up-to-date technology. The latest veterinary equipment, such as a blood-gas analyzer, has been installed, and diseases are kept to a minimum by strict hygienic practices on all the studs. The library probably has the most comprehensive set of equine reference books of any stud, which means that pedigrees can be easily validated, not just for Airlie-bred horses but for those from other studs as well. Airlie represents a combination of efficient breeding techniques, good staff relations, and a willingness to help outsiders that is all too rare in the horse-racing world.

ARDENODE AND RAGUSA STUDS, CO KILDARE

Some twenty miles south-west of Dublin, close to The Curragh, is Ardenode Stud, now an extensive estate at the heart of one of the most famous bloodstock areas in the world. In 1963 the estate had acquired extra land to build the public Ragusa stud for four stallions, bringing the total area up to 620 acres, since when it has had a considerable impact on world markets.

The stud stands in beautiful limestone country near the village of Ballymore Eustace and is approached across the salmon waters of the River Liffey, which runs down from the nearby Wicklow Mountains. Like many Irish studs, the centrepiece of Ardenode is an imposing Georgian house shaded by clusters of mature trees. Horses have been bred and raised here for over two centuries. The present owners, Mr and Mrs J. Mullion, purchased the stud in 1956 from Captain Spencer Freeman, who played a major part in establishing the Irish Sweeps Derby. During Captain Spencer's time part of the estate was used as a schooling ground for the famous Punchestown Meeting in late April and the stud was already well known for breeding fine horses for the flat — such as Zucchero, winner of the Coronation Cup, Indian Hemp, a leading American sire, and Royal Mink, dam of Lucky Mel. The Mullions have continued to breed winners, including Floribunda (the leading sprinter of his decade), Ballymore (Irish Two Thousand Guineas winner), and three winners of the Irish One Thousand Guineas — Gazpacho, Wenduyne, and Sarah Siddons. The stud has also produced Princess Pati, who won the Gilltown Stud Irish Guineas Oaks in record time, and the winner of the Poule d'Essai des Pouliches, Ukraine Girl.

The tree-lined drive leading to Ragusa Stud, the stallion complex at Ardenode, one of the most modern in Europe.

In 1958 the stud decided to stand two stallions who had raced successfully in Mr and Mrs Mullion's colours respectively: Court Harwell and the brilliant sprinter Hard Tack. At the same time the lease on the Maddenstown Stud at The Curragh was taken out. Both stallions were successful at stud: Court Harwell sired Meadow Court, who went on to win the Irish Sweeps Derby, whilst Hard Tack sired Right Tack, winner of the 1969 Newmarket Two Thousand Guineas.

In 1963 Ragusa became the leading European Stakes winner, with the Irish Sweeps Derby and the King George VI and Queen Elizabeth Stakes to his credit. It was decided to build a stallion complex at Ardenode itself that would incorporate the latest equipment, including American-type barns. The impressive entrance gates to the yard house the cups won by Ragusa, after whom this new section was named.

Right: Mrs Meg Mullion with the 1984 Irish Oaks winner, Princess Pati, sired by Top Ville.

Below right: View over the extensive Ardenode estate, set in over 600 acres of prime limestone land.

Below: Mrs Meg Mullion with a mare and foal by General Assembly outside the impressive gates of Ragusa Stud.

Mr and Mrs Mullion's son Stuart currently continues this formidable tradition and is one of several young men who now dominate the prestigious bloodstock industry in Ireland. Stuart, who grew up on the stud, has clear long-term policies based on consolidating the great depth of the broodmares and maintaining the well-established family lines. There are three main racehorse families at Ardenode: those of Paddy's Sister, Ela Marita, and Costly Wave. Paddy's Sister, a bay filly by Ballyogan out of Birthday Wood, was bought for the Mullions by the late Paddy Prendergast in 1958, the year Ballyogan's son, Paddy's Point, ran second in the English and Irish Derby. As a two-year-old in 1959, Paddy's Sister won the Queen Mary Stakes at Royal Ascot and the Champagne Stakes at Doncaster. Ela Marita was Ragusa's half sister and produced eight winners, including Mariel (second in the Irish One Thousand Guineas), who in turn produced Sarah Siddons (winner of the Irish One Thousand Guineas and the Yorkshire Oaks). Sarah Siddons was mated with Ballymore, uniting the two principal families and producing Seymour Hicks. Trained by John Dunlop and the winner of five races, Seymour Hicks is now at stud at Airlie. Sarah Siddons was sold, but Seymour Hicks's half-sister Princess Pati was retained and won the Pretty Polly Stakes and the Gilltown Stud Irish Guineas Oaks in record time.

When they are weaned the foals go to Ardenode, while Ragusa concentrates on the stallions and their mares. Besides Ballymore (whose winners include not only Seymour Hicks but also More So and Ex Directory) the stud has Corvaro, son of Vaguely Noble who won the Prix de l'Arc de Triomphe — indeed the only Group-winning son of Vaguely Noble in Ireland or England.

A recent success has been Head for Heights, the son of Shirley Heights and winner of the King Edward VII Stakes at Royal Ascot and the Princess of Wales Stakes, who was sent to Ragusa by Sheikh Mohammed Al Maktoum despite a number of competing offers. Inevitably, Head for Heights has been in enormous demand. In his first season he achieved a fertility rate of over 90 per cent and his future looks assured.

With 6 home-bred Classic winners, 25 Stakes winners, and 15 Group winners, Ardenode's record is an impressive one. The previous policy of selling all the yearlings has been changed, now that it has become difficult to obtain top class fillies. Stuart Mullion plans to build up the filly area and, backed up by the best available facilities for foaling mares, to obtain more high-class stallions. All in all, Ardenode looks set to continue its successes well into the next century.

Head for Heights, by Shirley Heights, owned by Sheikh Mohammed, retired to start his stud career at Ragusa Stud in 1985.

BALLYLINCH STUD, CO KILKENNY

Almost all the prominent Irish breeders and owners of thoroughbred horses live at their studs, among them Major Victor McCalmont and his family, who live at Mount Juliet, the 1,640-acre estate which contains the Ballylinch Stud. This has resulted in a number of important houses in the South of Ireland that have been fully maintained. Mount Juliet is such a house, built in 1672 on a wooded eminence above the main Dublin-Waterford road, on some of the most fertile land in Ireland.

Mares and foals at Ballylinch Stud. Now a commercially-run operation, the stud normally has 49 permanent mares.

At one time it was the seat of the Earl of Carrick, who married a local heiress, so increasing the property to its present size of 1,640 acres. This alliance is commemorated by a charming stone bridge over the River Nore, which to this day joins the two properties, and the house has the tranquillity and peace that only a slow-running river can supply.

The property was bought by the McCalmont family in 1908, and from that date many additions and improvements have been made. The most important addition is the beautiful entrance hall, designed by Sir Edwin Lutyens, from which an elegant stairway leads to the first floor. Lutyens also added a west wing to the house consisting of a small ballroom, which today is used as a picture gallery. Mount Juliet has many examples of the work of the Adam brothers, most notably the dining-room with its original pink setting off the exquisite white plaster medallions and scrollwork. The two drawing-rooms, which lead into each other, have white ceilings enriched with gold, and magnificent carved marble chimney-pieces.

The stud farm, built in 1915, was founded for the benefit of The Tetrarch, the fastest horse of his time. The stallion box, which now houses Scorpio, winner of seven races including the Hardwick Stakes and the Gran Premio del Jockey Club, boasts a mosaic floor with The Tetrarch's name as the central part of the design. Beside this box is a little saddle-room, the walls of which are hung with horseshoes bearing the names of all the winners sired by that mighty horse.

Three of the top stallions standing at Ballylinch Stud in 1975: *(right to left)* Sassafras (FR), by Sheshoon out of Ruta, winner of the 1970 Prix de L'Arc de Triomphe and the Prix du Jockey-Club; English Prince, by Petingo out of English Miss, winner of the 1974 Irish Sweeps Derby and King Edward Stakes; and London Gazette, by Panaslipper out of Court Circular.

The stud, which gets its name from a ruined house called Ballylinch, was built on the site of former farm buildings. In the background is the aqueduct where the farm people used to draw their water. All the buildings, including the horse-boxes and cottages, are of grey stone, with green painted woodwork. Flowers are everywhere. Each cottage has its own small garden. A road connects the stallion boxes and paddocks to the private stud and boxes reserved for the McCalmont broodmares. Beyond the line of cottages there are 60 boxes for visiting mares. A second stallion stands at Ballylinch — Be My Native, winner of three races including the Coronation Cup, and the French Prix de la Force.

Victor McCalmont's son Harry runs Ballylinch Stud. Besides managing the two resident stallions, he looks after the eighteen broodmares belonging to his father. This stud breeds to sell its yearlings, principally at Goffs, or at Newmarket. The rest of the property, employing 45 people, is given over to mixed farming, with 400 acres under tillage. There has always been a tendency to shortage of fodder in Ireland, hay in particular being liable to run short. For this reason Victor McCalmont has made Mount Juliet self-supporting, which in itself is quite an achievement.

Be My Native, by Our Native out of Witchy Woman, winner of three races, including the 1983 Coronation Cup at Epsom, retired to stud at Ballylinch in 1984.

COOLMORE STUD, CO TIPPERARY

In 1970 the Coolmore Stud in Co Tipperary had only two stallions, Gala Performance and King Emperor, American horses with less than inspiring credentials. By 1983 it had become a conglomerate of seven studs, containing sixteen top-class stallions headed by the 1982 Derby winner, Golden Fleece. The Coolmore-Castle Hyde Associates had been formed, one of the most remarkable and successful partnerships in racing history.

The seeds of this partnership had been planted back in 1971 in Kentucky by Jack Mulcahy, who had bluntly said to Vincent O'Brien that he could not understand a man of his calibre remaining 'only a trainer', instead of 'getting part of the action'.

The man dubbed 'only a trainer' by Mulcahy had in fact already won the Grand National three times and the Cheltenham Gold Cup four times. He then turned his attention to the flat. From Ballydoyle, Cashel, O'Brien proceeded to win the Derby (six times), the Oaks (twice), the St Leger (three times), the Two Thousand Guineas (four times), the Irish Derby (five times) and the Sussex Stakes (four times). As if this was not enough, he collected all the French Classics, winning the Prix de l'Arc de Triomphe no fewer than three times.

Aerial view of Coolmore Stud.

When Robert Sangster's The Minstrel won the Derby in 1977, Vincent had been contemplating becoming more involved in the bloodstock industry for several years. He became a key member of the racing syndicate formed by Sangster, which got off to a flying start with The Minstrel's Derby win. The owners of The Minstrel, the Hon. Simon Fraser, Alan Clore, and David Ackroyd, refused a bid of £1 million for the horse a week before the race — a gamble that paid off by bringing in over four times as much when the horse came in first. From then on the Sangster-O'Brien syndicate became a force to be reckoned with.

Vincent O'Brien believes that American horses are raced so hard on their own dirt tracks that they stand up superbly to the kinder grass courses of Europe. He bought the Northern Dancer line before anyone else on either side of the Atlantic had recognized its potential. Sangster says of him: 'When he's looking at yearlings he's visualizing them as three-year-olds. He's got a fantastic feel for a horse, he gives you confidence. I would never have invested a tenth of what I have done, had Vincent not come into partnership with me.'

Unlike O'Brien, who dislikes crowds and shuns parties, Sangster is an excellent salesman and the partnership's front-man. Between them they own millions of pounds' and dollars' worth of racehorses, stallions, broodmares, yearlings, and foals. Both of them are aware that anything bought at the sales must be paid for in cash, whereas there is a long gap between buying a yearling and getting your money back — assuming always that the animal turns out to be a good

Vincent O'Brien, leading trainer in Britain in 1966 and 1977, and whose big wins include the Two Thousand Guineas three times and the Epsom Derby six times, seen here with Baccalauréat.

Mares and foals at Coolmore Stud. At the peak of the season, there are approximately 500 mares at Coolmore and about 200 in the autumn.

racehorse. Vincent O'Brien is ever-mindful of this and admits that he is always learning, developing what is sometimes referred to as his 'magic touch'. He knows very well that he is not infallible, though he takes every precaution to appear so.

With every horse he trains O'Brien decides first on the eventual target (the Derby, for instance). He then plans backwards, working out how many races the horse will need before the big day. He will never run a horse if it is 'only nearly ready'; if the horse shows the slightest signs of stress, O'Brien goes right back to slow exercise and waits patiently until the horse gets his confidence back. He has few interests outside his horses, though he occasionally fishes or plays a round of golf. It is no mere cliché to say that horses are his life.

The 1984 Derby was a magnificent illustration of what racing is all about. The favourite, El Gran Señor, trained by Vincent O'Brien, was beaten by Secreto, trained by his son, David. This coveted prize was snatched from Vincent by Secreto's muzzle being held fractionally higher than El Gran Señor; a mere four inches, the width of a horse's nostril, won the Derby for David O'Brien on a photofinish.

Statue of Be My Guest at Coolmore Stud. Another highly successful horse sired by Northern Dancer, he is the sire of over 111 winners, including Luth Enchantée, currently at the Haras du Mezeray.

Gilltown, one of the best-equipped studs in Europe, is the European headquarters of the Firestone's multinational thoroughbred empire.

GILLTOWN STUD,
CO KILDARE

When Bertram and Diana Firestone decided to move part of their racing empire to Southern Ireland they already had wide experience of breeding thoroughbred racehorses. Their stud farm, Catoctin, 50 miles north-west of Washington DC, is situated in the heart of Virginia. The stone-built house, once inhabited by Quakers and set in a 2,000-acre property, was a Revolutionary stronghold during the American War of Independence. It is now the headquarters of Firestone/McCrann, a property development company of which Bert Firestone is president and chief executive officer. Bert is also Joint-Master of the Kildare, a pack of foxhounds established by the McCalmonts and housed on their Mount Juliet estate.

Whilst Catoctin is curiously Irish in character, Gilltown has the feel of a comfortable American country house. It stands close to the village of Kilcullen, within eight miles of The Curragh, surrounded by 1,200 acres rich in limestone. One of the reasons the Firestones chose to live partly in Ireland was the local pasturage, which Bert believes to be the best in the world for raising thoroughbreds. The house is well stocked with trophies, as well as the portrait by Richard Stone Reeves of the outstanding 'flying filly' Blue Wind, by Lord Gayle out of Azurine. This filly was bred by Miss Laidlaw at Abbey Lodge Stud and bought by the Firestones, who sent her to Dermot Weld for training, with the result that she won both the 1981 Epsom and Irish Oaks, among many other races.

Above: Bertram R. Firestone, who together with his wife, Diana, has established one of the most prolific racing dynasties of the century. With some 4,000 acres divided between Catoctin and Gilltown Studs and over 350 top-class horses, the Firestones aim to provide the best possible facilities for the development of thoroughbreds. Sixty of their horses are currently in training in Ireland.

Right: Broodmares in foal at Gilltown Stud with April Run in foreground.

GILLTOWN STUD

The Stud at Gilltown was created immediately after World War I by Lord Furness. The house, approached along an impressive avenue of trees, is a low two-storey colonial-style building with verandahs and french windows opening on to well-tended lawns. On Lord Furness's death the property was sold to the late Aga Khan and became one of Prince Aly Khan's favourite residences. The Prince had a great affection for Ireland and, like Bert Firestone, was a fine horseman. It was at Gilltown that two of the best Aga Khan-owned horses — Tulyar and Petite Etoile — were bred.

The Firestones acquired the property in 1971 from the present Aga Khan. Bertram Firestone had come into racing via eventing and hunting, having attended the New York Military Academy where he was selected for their showjumping team. While a student at the University of Virginia he became an accomplished competitor in the show ring and appeared regularly at Madison Square Gardens and at the other main venues that make up the American showjumping circuit. Within a remarkably short space of time after buying Gilltown, Mr and Mrs Firestone have achieved tremendous results. Their owner-breeder involvement is a partnership in the fullest

Cure the Blues, one of Gilltown's outstanding stallions and winner of the 1980 Laurel Futurity Stakes, is to stand at Pillar Stud in Kentucky for the 1987 season.

sense, with the fillies running in her name and the colts in his. Their list of winners is a long and impressive one. It includes: King's Company, winner of the Irish Two Thousand Guineas; Blue Wind, winner of the Irish and Epsom Oaks; Half Iced, who flew half around the world to collect the prestigious Japan Cup; and April Run, twice winner of the Aqueduct Turf Classic, New York State, who came within an ace of winning the Prix de l'Arc de Triomphe, the Firestones' greatest ambition. The list continues with Optimistic Gal, winner of the Kentucky Oaks, and Genuine Risk, who won the Kentucky Derby.

While using his own home-bred Gilltown-based stallions, General Assembly and Cure the Blues, to breed with many of his best mares, it is Bert Firestone's policy to buy into other stallions, such as Kris, Blushing Groom, and Ela-Mana-Mou. Though Gilltown is too young an enterprise to have generated foundation families among the forty-two resident mares, General Assembly has already proved himself capable of siring winners: Mrs Meg Mullion sent her Classic-winning mare Sarah Siddons to him, the resulting colt fetching a record-breaking price of £1,400,000 at the 1983 Highflyer Newmarket Sales.

General Assembly, the American-bred stallion who stood at Gilltown since 1980, has also been syndicated to stand at the Pillar Stud. Gilltown has set a pattern by offering European breeders top North American bloodlines.

THE IRISH NATIONAL STUD, TULLY, CO KILDARE

When Tully was handed over to the Irish Government in 1943 it became, as it remains, the Government's responsibility. It has a manager, currently John Clarke, and a Board of Directors, responsible to the Minister of Agriculture and the Minister of Finance.

In May 1966, during Charles Haughey's term of office as Minister of Agriculture, a survey team was set up, comprising Government officials and experts from within the horse-breeding industry. Their brief was to examine all aspects of the industry and make recommendations for its further development. Since then, Irish bloodstock has not only made an impact on the international thoroughbred world, but also has become the country's fourth largest export. At the top of the survey team's list were income-tax concessions, which benefited the small breeder and acted as an incentive to foreigners wishing to set up stud facilities in Ireland.

One of the main functions of the Stud is to make the services of good-class stallions available

The Irish National Stud at Tully comprises 836 acres of prime land.

View through to some of the stables. There are 210 boxes for the accommodation of mares, foals and stallions.

to small breeders. The stud operates a 'no foal, no fee' arrangement, which is particularly valuable to anyone with limited resources. As the team of experts felt that there was a shortage of top-class stallions in the country, it specifically recommended that a sum of between £400,000 and £500,000 should be invested in one prestige stallion to stand at stud. It further suggested that such a stallion should be made available at a commercial fee. The bulk of the capital invested would be recovered in four years, and thereafter the services of the stallion, if he proved successful, could be made available to the small breeder at an attractive price (below its real commercial value).

There has thus always been at least one prestige stallion standing at the Stud. The season of 1986 had nine: Lord Gayle, winner of eight races in England, France, and the USA, including the William Hill Gold Cup; Sallust, winner of seven races including the Prix du Moulin at Longchamps; Tug of War, winner of ten races including the Goodwood Cup; Crash Course, with five races to his credit including the Doncaster Cup and the Ascot Stakes; Ahonoora, a winner of seven races, including the William Hill Sprint Championship and the Stewards Cup at Goodwood; Tap on Wood, who won ten races including the Two Thousand Guineas at Newmarket; Indian King, an eight-times winner; Kafu, a three-times winner; and Krayyan out of Mrs Moss, who won the National Stakes at Sandown Park and the Norfolk Stakes at Royal Ascot.

At the time of the Haughey survey the Tully property was in a state of decline. Now it is a fine example of stud-farm management and, with its nine stallions and twenty-eight brood mares, the stud has been transformed into a viable profit-making organization.

A great deal of the credit for this must go to Michael Osborne, who in 1970 gave up his veterinary practice in Naas to take on the mammoth task of managing Tully. One of his innovations was the introduction of courses on horse-breeding, which take place during the breeding season and are attended by students from all over the world. The courses, offering both practical and theoretical training, cover a wide range of subjects related to animal husbandry and veterinary hygiene, as well as general stud-farm administration. Training is both practical and theoretical.

The Stud also holds open days for stud-farm personnel thrice-weekly during January, February, and March. Breeders attend regularly for advice and discussion on all aspects of bloodstock breeding and have opportunities to see at first hand the most recent innovations and techniques in operation. This has had the added advantage of increasing contact between the general body of breeders and the Stud, a factor of primary importance to the future development of the industry. In addition, training facilities for farriers are provided under the auspices of the Irish Horse Board; and within the environs of the Stud, at Curragh House, the headquarters of

The stallion boxes at the Irish National Stud. The principal role of the Irish National Stud Company is to provide Irish breeders with good-class stallions at a reasonable fee to mate with approved mares. There are nine stallions currently standing, including Tap on Wood, 1979 winner of the Irish Two Thousand Guineas.

the Racing Apprentice Centre of Education was established in 1973.

The Stud has always encouraged general visitors as well as the professionals. In 1977 the Irish Horse Museum was opened close to the main Stud complex. On view here is the illustrated history of the horse in Ireland, from its evolution to the present day. The museum's centrepiece is the skeleton of Arkle, presented to the museum by Anne, Duchess of Westminster, along with a set of her racing colours, including those of Pat Taaffe.

In 1977 a welcome windfall came to the Stud when Garfield Weston, the Canadian millionaire, presented Barretstown Castle Stud and its surrounding 515 acres to the nation. Although the land has not been given permanently to the Stud, it has been made available to them on an indefinite basis, with the result that these excellent pastures – once the stud farm of Elizabeth Arden, whose horses, trained at Newmarket by Captain Cecil Boyd-Rochfort, were highly successful in the years immediately after the war – could be utilized by the Stud. The Stud immediately transferred its band of 15 broodmares and young stock to these additional acres, a move which was to pay handsome dividends: three years later, in 1980, the Irish National Stud sent a draft of yearlings to Goffs Invitation Sales, of which two fetched record prices. The first colt, Americus, by Sallust out of Cat O'Mountaine, sold for Ir.£191,100; the second, Codrington, sold for Ir.£120,750.

Michael Osborne left the Irish National Stud in October 1982 for Kentucky, where he has been building from scratch North Ridge Farm, the property of Mr and Mrs Franklin D. Groves. His place has been taken by John Clarke, who, like his predecessor, attaches great importance to the student training courses, which provide all those who attend with a diploma and a wealth of sound practical experience.

Ahonoora, by Lorezaccio out of Helen Nichols, and winner of seven races, was retired to stud in 1980 and has sired winners of over 33 races to date.

KILDANGAN STUD, CO KILDARE

Kildangan is a beautiful old gabled country mansion, set in 400 acres of prime farm land. Recently acquired by Sheikh Mohammed Al Maktoum, it was begun by its previous owner, Roderic More O'Ferrall, in the late 1930s and considerably expanded immediately after World War II. After the war Roderic took Sir Percy Loraine into partnership, and the influence of well-bred yearlings offered for sale began to make their mark both in England and Ireland.

Sir Percy Loraine, a retired diplomat, was the ideal man both to further the interests of horse-racing, and to promote the bloodstock industry. He was a member of the Jockey Club and the Irish Turf Club, and was the author of the Loraine Report which greatly influenced the future of the British National Stud. Until his death in 1962 Sir Percy was regularly to be seen at major races, a charming elder statesman who, thanks to Roderic and his younger brother Frankie, found an active and fulfilling role after his retirement. On Sir Percy's death Roderic More O'Ferrall went into partnership with Lord Iveagh, a Dublin-based associate who had for many years been chairman of Guinness.

The gabled entrance to the Main Yard at Kildangan Stud.

Katies winning the 1984 Irish One Thousand Guineas. The eleventh Classic winner to have been bred by Kildangan, Katies also beat Pebbles in the 1985 Coronation Stakes at Ascot.

The first of Kildangan's foundation mares was Straight Sequence, bought in 1929 for 130 guineas before the stud had come into existence. She was a three-year-old at the time of purchase, and was the dam of Khosro, grandam of Queenpot, and the great-grandam of Ambergris. Bold Lad, by Bold Ruler, is the present resident syndicated stallion standing at Kildangan. He won five races, including the Middle Park Stakes, the Coventry Stakes, and the Champagne Stakes. Since 1968 he has sired winners of 305 races, among them Waterloo, his Classic-winning daughter who won the One Thousand Guineas at Newmarket.

Over the years Kildangan has bred many Classic winners, taking the Irish Oaks twice with Admirable and Ambergris, the Irish One Thousand Guineas with Katies, the English One Thousand Guineas with Abermaid and Queenpot, the Irish Two Thousand Guineas with Khosro and Linacre, the English Two Thousand Guineas with Darius and Nearula, the Irish St Leger with Parnell, and the Italian One Thousand Guineas with Rosananti.

Roderic More O'Ferrall's horses are trained in England by John Dunlop and in Ireland at Rossmore Lodge, Co Kildare, by Kevin Prendergast who, before becoming a trainer in 1963, was Ireland's leading amateur jockey on several occasions. Kevin's list of owners is as illustrious as John Dunlop's, since he trains for the President of the Irish Republic, and for one of the Al Maktoums, Sheikh Hamadan, as well as for Roderic's sister-in-law, Lady Elizabeth More O'Ferrall, and his partner Lord Iveagh.

Bold Lad, by Bold Ruler, resident syndicated stallion at Kildangan, has sired over 305 winners, including Never So Bold and Waterloo who won the One Thousand Guineas at Newmarket in 1972.

MOUNT COOTE, CO LIMERICK

Mount Coote lies in the south-west of Ireland, in a region known as the Golden Vale, renowned for its bone-building limestone pasturage. On the death of his father, killed in action in 1944, Alan Lillingston inherited the 400-acre Mount Coote estate, including an enormous house in bad repair, and a stud farm without any bloodstock. Six years later, having completed his education, which included a season in France with Edouard Pouret, and a year with his uncle Major Geoffrey Brooke, the Newmarket trainer, he returned home.

After World War II, the stallions Devonian, Cagire and After Midnight had stood at Mount Coote, to be followed by Rustam, who was already in residence when Lillingston took over the management of the stud. There were no brood mares in his inheritance, and the income from standing a single stallion is negligible. His first step was to buy Tudor Melody for £20,000 to stand at Mount Coote. Bred by a neighbour, Jane Moore, the stallion had been sold first to race in England, where he was two-year-old champion, and then sold on to the USA where he failed to live up to his reputation, winning only twice out of ten starts. Back in Ireland, Tudor Melody sired ten individual winners from his first batch of two-year-old runners, his first Classic coming in 1966 when his son Kashmir II won the Two Thousand Guineas at Newmarket. Tudor Melody was now an immensely valuable stallion and the object of enormous American offers to purchase him. Fortunately, the British National Stud stepped in and he was sold for £250,000 to stand at Newmarket.

Alan Lillingston then bought one of the Native Dancer's sons, Native Prince, when he came out of training. Native Prince had been one of the top rated two-year-olds in America and conformed to the high standards Lillingston sought. Like his predecessor Tudor Melody, he stood at Mount Coote for four seasons, though without the same spectacular success. However, he sired a number of good brood mares and many of his daughters produced multiple winners. After selling him to Australia Lillingston decided to revise his breeding policy. He had already sought to improve his cash flow by buying well-bred fillies which had not achieved a great deal as two-year-olds but looked to be likely winners at three years. With this end in view he had several fillies in training with both Vincent O'Brien and Chally Chute, racing them and re-selling them in foal one year later.

Brought up at Mount Coote, Alan Lillingston has grown up with horses and knows all those concerned with them in the South of Ireland. His half-brother, the Earl of Harrington, is an equally astute judge of horses. Alan Lillingston is also a very fine horseman, and when he first returned to live in Ireland he became the foremost Irish amateur jockey, a career culminating in his winning the Champion Hurdle at the Cheltenham Festival meeting in 1963. He also achieved the distinction of winning the Supreme Championship at the Royal Dublin Society's Horse Show with his hunter Josh. His expertise on a horse gained him a place on the Irish team (Three-Day-Eventing) that won a Gold Medal in the European Championships.

When Alan Lillingston decided to concentrate on building up a first-class band of brood mares for re-sale when in foal, with the occasional mare retained for himself, his reputation as a good judge of horses was already well established. From Jeremy Tree came the offer to lodge, on a

permanent basis, ten brood mares belonging to Jock Whitney, the American Ambassador to London and one of the world's great experts on the Turf. Jock Whitney and Alan Lillingston were a natural combination. The Whitney mares remained at Mount Coote until Whitney's death. His widow gave Lillingston a mare called Lacquer in appreciation of all that he had done, while Lillingston describes Whitney as the perfect owner.

Not surprisingly, in view of Mount Coote's record, other clients have sent their valuable bloodstock to be lodged there. Like Jock Whitney, the banker Jocelyn Hambro, whose horses were trained by Alan Lillingston's uncle, Geoffrey Brooke, was a natural client. Jocelyn Hambro has achieved remarkable success as a breeder by going into partnership with Alan Lillingston. Initially they owned six mares in partnership, four being bred in the USA and purchased from the late Charles Engelhard. There are currently nine in this partnership, all proven high achievers. Singe, the dam of One In A Million, winner of the 1979 One Thousand Guineas, has provided the stud with another Classic winner.

The stud comprises a total of eighty boxes including seven large foaling boxes with covered corridor behind leading to the sitting-up room. What was once the covering yard has been turned into an exercise yard for the mares. Visually the old main yard looks much as it always has done, but it is the extensions which give Mount Coote its air of professionalism. The main preoccupation is with feeding, and none of the stock is given river water, as was done in the old days, but water from the well. On a visit to E. P. Taylor in Canada, Alan Lillingston became intrigued by the old man's theories on cube feeding. Naturally that smart old millionaire did not provide him with his actual recipe, but Lillingston prised sufficient information out of him to

Right: View of the entrance to the stable yard at Mount Coote. Renowned for producing winners, Mount Coote's home-bred colt, Armarda by Shirley Heights, made a million guineas at the Newmarket Sales in 1984.

return home and form a foodstuffs line, Pegasus Horse Foods, now a flourishing concern. All the hay at the stud is home-produced.

Right: The main house and estate at Mount Coote.

One of the more onerous tasks that Alan Lillingston has had to tackle is the replacing of Mount Coote's fencing. The vital necessity of providing isolation areas, especially with so many mares arriving from abroad, has resulted in his acquiring an additional 100 acres, in two 50-acre tracts, which have needed post-and-rail fencing backed by neatly trimmed hedges to provide the mares with some shelter.

The mares in foal are wintered out to gain maximum benefit from the rich, bone-building grass for themselves and their future progeny – possible here, because winters in the South of Ireland are mild compared to those in England or Normandy. Foals are weaned at five months, quite early by some standards, which again is part of the toughening-up regime. This has been shown to be a good formula that works well at Mount Coote, since small groups of mares, out in the fresh air, are less likely to succumb to disease or epidemics.

The winners bred at Mount Coote are a formidable list. Apart from two Classic winners, there has been Alia, winner of the Princess Royal Stakes; Armistice Day, who raced with distinction in France, winning the Prix Exbury and the Prix Gontaut-Biron; Ballymacad who won the New Stakes; Blue Yonder, winner of the Jubilee Stakes; Hatta, Sheikh Mohammed Al Maktoum's purchase, who won the Molecomb Stakes; Imprudent Miss, winner of the Leopardstown Silken Glider Stakes; and Intermission, winner of the Cambridgeshire Handicap.

Season by season the list of Mount Coote's racing successes lengthens, and understandably its offerings at the Newmarket Highflyer sales and at Goffs in Ireland are viewed with respect. Partnership bloodstock is sold under the Mount Coote banner; thus new investors profit from the stud's reputation of selling tough, winning animals. William Farish, in partnership with Warner Jones, has mares at Mount Coote to profit from such top nominations as Shareef Dancer and Shirley Heights. Kinderhill Farm, one of the largest American stud farms run as a public company, has sent several of its most valuable mares to Mount Coote for the same reason.

There are a number of factors contributing to the success of Alan Lillingston. He and his wife Vivi are dedicated to the business of thoroughbred breeding, and they are not only in touch with the key Irish owners and trainers, but are equally well connected with the English horse world. The year Alan Lillingston spent in France has also paid dividends in many directions, while much of his successful business has been conducted in Kentucky.

Above all Alan Lillingston is patriotic when it comes to Ireland and its role in the competitive international market. He responded immediately when sponsors for races were called for by making himself financially responsible for the prestigious Mount Coote Stakes at The Curragh. He has modelled himself on no one in particular, though he holds his uncle Geoffrey Brooke in great regard and is pleased to have that great trainer living near him in retirement. Beyond that, he says with youthful gusto, 'bloodstock breeding is something we Irish are really good at, and I'm proud to be a part of this flourishing industry'. He has energy, and has never been afraid to take his coat off. He was brought up to know horses, and by his own initiative has greatly increased his knowledge. Little wonder then that Alan Lillingston and Mount Coote should have had such an impact on the international bloodstock world.

THE THOROUGHBRED
IN FRANCE

THE THOROUGHBRED IN FRANCE

Horse-racing in France stretches back over many centuries, particularly in Brittany and Normandy. In 1066 it was the Normans' superiority in mounted warfare that enabled them to defeat Harold's Anglo-Saxon army; and in the post-Norman period there are records of marathon races lasting several days between knights riding from the south of France as far as Paris. The Limousin horse, from the region of central France round Limoges, was the traditional animal bred by the nobles for hunting. It was originally descended from the North African Barb horses left behind by the Muslims, when they were driven from most of their European empire in the eighth century. The nearness of France to Spain and Italy, where horse-breeding was especially well developed, encouraged a considerable trade in fine horses during the medieval period.

There are several references to organized races in the late seventeenth century. One famous contest took place in the presence of Louis XIV and the court in 1651, when the Prince d'Harcourt rode against the Master of Horse of the Duc de Joyeuse around a lap of the Bois de Boulogne, on the outskirts of Paris. In 1663 the King offered a silver plate worth 1,000 gold *pistoles* for an international race run on the Plaine d'Achères, outside Paris. The start was announced by a flag and the course was fully marked out. In 1700 a grand reunion was organized for the Stuarts in exile in France at the château of St Germain-en-Laye, at which the exiled King James II of England and the French Court were present. This meeting was properly organized and consisted of three races of 2,800 metres, between which the horses were fed and refreshed with Spanish wine. The Marquis de Saillons in the 1720s was notorious for his racing and betting, riding at breakneck speed from the Porte St Denis to Chantilly for a wager of 20,000 *livres*.

Nevertheless, the development of the thoroughbred horse was slow in France, since the French seemed indifferent to the improving strains of Arab blood. The Godolphin Arabian, one of the great influences on British thoroughbred stock, is thought to have been foaled in the Yemen in 1724 and exported to the stud of the Bey of Tunis, who presented him to King Louis XV of France. He was bought by Mr Edward Coke of Longford Hall in Derbyshire and was subsequently owned by Lord Godolphin. It was fortunate for the future of English horse-breeding that the French did not recognize his worth and keep him in France.

Previous two pages: Longchamp in 1886 by Jean Béraud.

Eclipse, with his jockey Jack Oakley, in an engraving by J. Webb after J.N. Sartorius. The reputation of this great horse encouraged the French to import English stallions to improve their own racehorses.

Under Louis XVI (1774–1793) horse-racing in France began in earnest, though the King himself was not particularly enthusiastic, and preferred hunting. It was in part due to the Anglomania that swept France during this period, when it was all the rage to imitate things English. Foremost among those interested in racing were the Comte d'Artois, the Marquis de Conflans and the Duc de Chartres. The exploits of Eclipse, born in 1764, had helped to encourage this enthusiasm, and by 1775 France was importing English thoroughbreds from the lines of the Byerley Turk, the Darley Arabian and the Godolphin Arabian.

The first permanent racecourse was set up by 12 aristocrats on the outskirts of Paris, on flat ground known as the Plaine des Sablons, where the light soil was eminently suitable for testing speed. It was opened in 1776 in the presence of the Court and Louis XVI. The first race was between the horses of the Duc de Chartres and the Comte d'Artois. Many Englishmen came to Sablons, including Horace Walpole, and similarly Frenchmen flocked to English races, so beginning the long-term relationship between racegoers of both countries. In 1776 the first

The New Racecourse at Fontainebleau, a popular venue for French racing since the days of Louis XVI.

Fontainebleau meeting took place when the Court was in residence at the palace there. Marie-Antoinette was a great enthusiast and was all for registering her colours, but the King refused to allow it. Despite his lukewarm approach, the King did take some positive steps. Racing continued annually at Fontainebleau, and also in the park of the royal château at Vincennes, where Louis organized state-backed races called King's Plates and appointed the Marquis de Conflans director of racing, instructing him to draft official regulations which were published in 1780. Until 1790 the King's Plates were all held at Vincennes in the spring, while other meetings, which attracted many English runners, took place there in the autumn. Interest in all these three courses was assisted by regular racing reports in the gazettes of the time, particularly those in the *Journal de Paris*.

During the French Revolution racing was out of the question, stables were destroyed and the horses scattered, and their owners were exiled or guillotined. By 1796, however, races were again being held on the Champ de Mars, together with other sports in imitation of those of the classical republics of Greece and Rome. Under Napoleon, who showed great interest in equine improvement, courses were reorganized in 1806 in various parts of the country, from the Seine to the Pyrenees. All arrangements were organized by the Ministry of the Interior, and the horses raced were aged from five to seven years and ridden only by French jockeys. Grands Prix were established, run over distances of 4,000 metres (2½ miles). This development was short-lived, however, and by 1812 the races were abandoned for lack of good horses, since the importation of British bloodstock into France had been forbidden during the Napoleonic Wars.

The period following the end of the war in 1815 and the restoration of the monarchy gave a boost to racing in France. Many French aristocrats had been exiled in England and had become devoted to the sport. In 1819 Louis XVIII instituted the Prix Royal, which continued under various names until 1869, when it was replaced by the Prix Gladiateur. The races of the Champ de Mars in 1819 were witnessed by all the new Court and the Royal Family, together with a large number of English aristocrats. When the Comte d'Artois, brother of Louis XVIII, came to the throne in 1824 as Charles X, racing in France gained a great supporter. During this period the English thoroughbreds Middlethorpe, Camerton and Coriolanus were imported. The state became firmly involved with bloodstock breeding with the joining of the Pompadour and Le Pin Studs and took a much greater interest when the Royal Stud at Meudon, outside Paris, was established under the Duc de Guiche. The most famous horse from the stud at Meudon was Vittoria, who in 1828 beat the horses of Lord Henry Seymour.

Lord Henry, a younger son of the Marquess of Hertford, was born in Paris and spent his life there. His enthusiasm for the Turf, together with that of the Duc d'Orléans, was instrumental in setting up the Jockey Club in 1833, and Seymour himself was its first President. As France's most exclusive club, it soon became clear that its social functions had to be separated from those of racing and breeding. As a result its founders formed the *Société d'Encouragement pour l'Amélioration des Races de Chevaux en France* (Society to Encourage the Improvement of Horsebreeding in France), which was recognized by the government and took over the Champ de Mars course for meetings. The Société was clear from the start that in order to improve the French thoroughbred, it would have to import from England in order to take advantage of the enormous developments that had taken place there over the past century. It quickly set about its task.

The first great French racecourse was set up at Chantilly, 25 miles north of Paris, and was inaugurated on 15 May 1834. The course measured 2,100 metres (1 mile 2½ furlongs), and more than 30,000 people came from Paris to the opening meeting. Racing had finally arrived. Throughout the reign of Louis-Philippe (1830–1848), the sport's popularity mushroomed. The opening of the Chemin de Fer du Nord (the railway north from Paris) enabled great numbers of

Right: Les courses à Longchamp by Gavarni (pseudonym of Sulpice Guillaume Chevalier, the nineteenth-century French caricaturist). In France as in England, race meetings were social events for the elegant and fashionable.

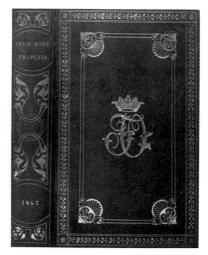

French stud book (1843) from the collection of the Duc d'Orléans.

Parisians to go racing, and Chantilly became part of the Parisian fashionable scene. The Prix du Jockey Club, run over 1½ miles, was founded in 1835 and became the French equivalent of the Derby. The success of Chantilly grew quickly, and soon more than 1,200 horses were in training around the town. The *Journal des Haras* stated in 1841 that Chantilly was decidedly the Newmarket of France. It added that half the population was English and oblivious to anything other than races and horses. Meanwhile the Société d'Encouragement protected the growing French breeding industry by insisting that races promoted by them were to include only French-bred horses. In the 1830s the Derby winners Cadland, Mameluke and Dangerous were all imported into France. Lord Henry Seymour himself imported Ibrahim, who had won the Two Thousand Guineas. He also imported Royal Oak, whose influence on French breeding was to be highly significant. Royal Oak sired Poetess, who won the Prix du Jockey Club in 1841. She was one of France's finest broodmares and was the dam of Hervine and Monarque. Hervine won the Prix du Cadran at Longchamp (2½ miles) and was sent to Goodwood. The first year she was unplaced, but the following year she returned to come second in the Goodwood Cup, becoming the first French-bred winner of an important foreign race. The French had taken great strides after only two decades of serious breeding.

During the 1830s the Champ de Mars course was gradually declining as Chantilly grew in importance. An improvised course was becoming established in the Bois de Boulogne that was to

Chantilly Races, by Eugène-Louis Lami after J.C. Varrall dated about 1840. The Prix du Jockey Club, the French equivalent of the Epsom Derby, has been held here since 1836.

become the famous Auteuil racecourse, while another was beginning close to Versailles. In the provinces, the major courses of the time were developed at Limoges and Aurillac, in central France, Le Pin in Normandy, Bordeaux, Moulins in Burgundy and Tarbes in the Pyrenees. The Second Republic, which lasted from 1848 to 1852, ushered in new enthusiasts including Vicomte Daru and Baron Finot, whose stable was to have an enormous influence for more than 50 years. Prince Louis, later Napoleon III, showed great interest for the whole of his reign. New meetings were established in 1851 at Tours and at Moulins, and by 1851 there were over 50 racecourses operating in France. The Derby of the South was set up at Bordeaux, and that of the West at Saumur. The meetings at Tours during the Second Empire (1852–1870) vied with Chantilly in the calendar of fashionable society. Chantilly retained its monopoly over training, and the Société d'Encouragement extended the training grounds, so that by the end of the nineteenth century these totalled over 550 acres. In its lovely forest setting it could claim to be one of the most beautiful courses in the world.

Monarque, bred by Alexandre Aumont, and half-brother of Hervine, was the best-bred horse of this period. On his third attempt he won the Goodwood Cup in 1857, giving the French further encouragement. In 1856 he had been bought by Comte Frédéric de Lagrange, together with all Alexandre Aumont's bloodstock. Lagrange had made a fortune in the French Industrial Revolution, following the defeat of Napoleon. He maintained stables at both Chantilly and

Mameluke, the 1827 Derby winner under Lord Jersey's colours, by John Frederick Herring. Mameluke was one of several English winners imported to France in the 1830s.

Newmarket and was unusually cosmopolitan for his time; enormously influential, he was a close friend of Napoleon III. He joined with Baron Nivière to form the 'Grande Ecurie' (Great Stable) in 1861-2 and with Joachim Lefèvre in 1874-8. These partnerships were pre-eminent in France. The 'Grande Ecurie' came fifth in the list of winning owners in England in 1861 and top in 1876.

Gladiateur, born in 1862, was the greatest of all Lagrange's horses. He was by Monarque out of Miss Gladiator, and symbolized the new status of the French thoroughbred, making England aware of the new challenge across the Channel. In 1865 he won the English Triple Crown plus the Grand Prix de Paris, and was named the 'avenger of Waterloo' by the French. On his arrival in Paris, the city's shop windows were decked out in tricolours, and speeches were made in the National Assembly in honour of his owner. Yet his significance was only for his lifetime, and he failed to pass on his great qualities. Other horses of the period were also breaking records across the Channel. Fille de l'Air, also owned by Lagrange, won the 1864 Prix de Diane and the Oaks. She was the dam of Reine (sired by Monarque), who won the One Thousand Guineas and the Oaks in 1872. Lagrange had made enormous strides at his stud at Dangu near Compiègne, north-east of Paris. He laid the foundations of the French reputation for toughness and stamina which were to be winning features for generations. At the beginning of the Second Empire the Bois de Boulogne belonged to the state, and Napoleon III gave it and the Bois de Vincennes to the nation. Longchamp was incorporated into the Bois de Boulogne, and in 1856 a lease was given to the Société d'Encouragement to build a racecourse there. It was inaugurated in 1857 by Napoleon III, the Empress and Emperor arriving by yacht to the course on the banks of the Seine, and

Right: A Day at the Races, Longchamp by Lucien Adrion. In the Bois de Boulogne, the Longchamp course was opened in 1857 to meet the demands of Parisians for a local racecourse.

Details of the Chantilly meeting held on Sunday 14 May 1837.

immediately it became part of the established Paris season.

The 1860s were a turning-point for racing in France. The Marseilles course was opened, and the Emperor ordered reforms of the National Studs (Haras Nationaux). Though they had been established in the seventeenth century under Louis XIV, they had little interest in thoroughbred racehorses. Napoleon I had been aware of the need to use thoroughbreds in breeding, but the National Studs had become inflexible, refusing to take note of progress made in England during the eighteenth century and resolutely guarding their position of privilege. After the Revolution and the Napoleonic period, about 1,000 stallions were left in their care, but thoroughbreds were not among them, since Charles X had struck a blow against the National Studs when he set up the Royal Stud at Meudon. Napoleon III instructed Comte Walewski as Minister of State to proceed with reforms long overdue. The rules were modified and altered to ensure that the encouragement of breeding also meant encouragement of the thoroughbred. Moreover, prizes were set up for a variety of equestrian sports that provided a test of quality, amounting to some 600,000 francs.

In 1861 four new big prizes were established, those of the Emperor, the Empress and the Prince Imperial, and the Prix de Longchamp. The last-named became the premier French Classic race and outshone the Prix du Jockey Club in prestige. The Emperor was rumoured to be behind all this, his intention being to raise France's reputation in the racing world. In 1863 the Grand Prix de Paris was inaugurated, financed jointly by the City of Paris and the railway companies, who as in England stood to make large sums from special trains for racegoers. The Grand Prix was

Gladiateur, an outstanding horse owned by Comte Frédéric de Lagrange, winning the Grand Prix de Paris at Longchamp.

intended to promote similar qualities to the Prix du Jockey Club, but it was to be open to horses bred abroad. This was a new departure, marking the maturity of French racing. Runners had to be three-year-old colts and fillies, and the length of the race was 3,000 metres (1 mile 7 furlongs). Run at the end of June, it was a tough test. The opening race attracted more than 100,000 spectators.

Three years later, in 1864, the racecourse at Deauville was opened by its founder, the Duc de Mornay. Designed by the architect of Vincennes racecourse, it was an immediate success, with steamers bringing in the crowds by sea from Le Havre and Honfleur. It remains as it began, one of the most important and elegant events in the European social season. The English were very successful in winning the Grand Prix de Paris, but they were still prevented from running in the other major races, while the French were free to contest all the English ones. Admiral Henry Rous, of the English Jockey Club, brought matters to a head when he wrote to the Société d'Encouragement requesting equal rights, but the only reply he got was that the Société had no authority in the matter, as the rules were set out by those who had given the prizes. French horses were winning considerable prizes in England but the rivalry cooled towards the end of the century. After Gladiateur won the Derby in 1865, no other French horse won it for the rest of the nineteenth century, and by the beginning of the twentieth English breeders were more worried about the American invasion.

Three stallions imported into France from England were of vital importance for the future in founding powerful lines. First among them was The Flying Dutchman, who won the Derby and St Leger in 1849, and went to France in 1858. He sired Dollar, and five generations later in 1910 Brûleur was foaled, who won the Grand Prix and the French St Leger. As a stallion The Flying

The Duke of Westminster's Flying Fox, who won the Triple Crown in 1899 and was sent to stud in France in the same year after his owner's death.

153

Dutchman produced four Prix du Jockey Club winners and three winners of the Prix de l'Arc de Triomphe. Second of the stallions was Rabelais, sired by St Simon, and known for speed and stamina. While not in his sire's class, he won the Goodwood Cup and produced the Derby winner Durbar II, the Prix du Jockey Club winner Ramus and the Grand Prix winner Verdun. In his male line were Rialto, Worden II and Ribot. The third stallion was Flying Fox, exported to France in 1899 after the death of his breeder, the Duke of Westminster. He won the Triple Crown of 1899 and was bought by Edmond Blanc. Flying Fox sired Ajax, who won the Prix du Jockey Club and the Grand Prix, and descended from him in the male line is Tantième, one of the best French sires since World War II.

Fashions in France: *Robe d'après-midi de Jeanne Lanvin*, dated 1921, from the *Gazette du Bon Ton*.

Like England, France saw the opening of many suburban racecourses at the end of the century. Similarly she also experienced a wave of anti-gambling feeling in certain quarters. Crowds as a whole were better organized in France, and the hooliganism the English experienced was noticeably absent, according to contemporary reports. Nevertheless, by the 1890s the French government was showing its concern at the number of courses that had opened. In 1890, 200 meetings were held in the suburbs and only 115 at the racecourses of Auteuil, Longchamp and Vincennes. This meant that 315 days of racing per year were available to Parisians. In 1891 the government decreed that proposals for any new courses must be submitted to the Minister of Agriculture, and only those that would improve the quality of racing were henceforth to be authorized. The Ministry of Agriculture took on more powers: it now had to approve the regulations of the racing authorities, and also exercised control over their accounts. This did not hold back expansion, however. By 1911 France possessed as many as 433 racecourses. The grandstands at Longchamp, built in the Second Empire and rebuilt in the 1870s after the siege of Paris, were quite inadequate for the crowds of 1900 and were completely rebuilt in 1904. The French were successful in maintaining their spectator facilities, whereas in England declining standards in the interwar years contributed to increasing competition from other spectator sports.

Certain horses stand out in the years leading up to World War I. The Grand Prix de Paris of 1914 witnessed the extraordinary excitement of the race between Sardanapale and La Farina, belonging respectively to Edouard and Maurice de Rothschild. Sardanapale was in direct descent from Monarque, the oldest male line in France. The French were overjoyed when Durbar II won the Derby in 1914, the first French winner since Gladiateur in 1865.

By the second week of August 1914, the racetracks had been taken over by the government for military purposes. The 'Belle Epoque' with all its glamour and beauty was over. The courses at Longchamp and Auteuil became cattle pens, and Vincennes was a depot for military equipment. The French bloodstock industry looked doomed. However, after a long gap, the Ministry of Agriculture allowed a few races solely for *épreuves de sélection*, tests of speed and stamina, with no spectators and no betting, which took place at Caen in Normandy, Mont de Marsan in the south-west and Moulins in central France in 1916, and at Chantilly, Maisons-Laffitte and Bordeaux in 1917-18. The only thing an owner could do was to send his horses across the border into Spain, where racing took place at San Sebastian. Teddy, son of Ajax, was sent there, where he won the San Sebastian Grand Prix. His two sons, Bull Dog and Sir Galahad III, eventually went to the USA, while his other sons, Astérus and Aethelstan, remained in France. The latter was the great-grandsire of the influential Tantième, who was to be so important to France after World War II.

After World War I, racecourses were taken in hand, and in 1919 a new society was set up called La Fédération Nationale des Sociétés de Cours de France. Its object was to co-ordinate the activities of breeding and racing, particularly those of the five largest Paris courses. Moreover, it became an important watchdog over the business activities of tracks and breeding. In October 1920, a new international race was founded at Longchamp to celebrate the peace. This was the

Prix de l'Arc de Triomphe, which quickly became as prestigious as the Derby as the test for three-year-olds. The first winner was Comrade, English bred and trained, as were the next two winners. Racing in England had not been reduced in quite the same way as in France, and her advantages were obvious. Nevertheless, France again showed her ability to make up for lost time. By 1921 it was clear that the French-bred Ksar was a star peformer, his sire being Brûleur and his dam Kizil Kourgan. He was bred by M.E. de St Alamy at the Saint-Pair-du-Mont Stud in Normandy and was bought by Edmond Blanc. He won the Prix Lupin and the French St Leger, the Prix de l'Arc de Triomphe and the Prix du Cadran. As a stallion his performance was exceptional. His son Tourbillon was to be an important part of the Boussac empire that was shortly to dominate French racing. The effects of World War I had discouraged many owners, but several important ones survived, and were as ever joined by new ones, who had made fortunes from the war or the new demands of peace. Edmond Blanc and Baron Edouard de Rothschild remained at the fore, and were joined by Jacques Wertheimer and Marcel Boussac. More international colours were to be seen between the wars, as those of Lady Granard, Lord Derby and Martinez de Hoz became familiar sights on French racecourses.

During this period Marcel Boussac was building his racing empire. He had made a fortune from textiles, and after the war he turned to racing. He bought all his own horses, arranged the matings himself and even supervised training from time to time. He began by buying the Jardy

Chevaux de course (devant les tribunes) by Edgar Degas, a prolific artist of racing scenes.

Stud in Saint-Cloud from Edmond Blanc, and took on Charlie Elliott as his stable jockey, when Elliott's gambling debts made it prudent for him to leave England. Boussac acquired what turned out to be four of the best stallions available, Astérus, Djebel, Pharis II and Tourbillon, the foundation of the Boussac empire that came to fruition after World War II. Boussac dominated French racing from the late 1920s to the late '50s, winning the Prix de l'Arc de Triomphe six times, the Prix de Diane five times, the Prix du Jockey Club 12 times and the Prix du Cadran seven times. His success was also phenomenal in England where he won the Derby, the Oaks, four Ascot Gold Cups and two St Legers. His finest year was 1950, when he won no fewer than six Classic races. By 1956 he was the leading French owner for the 19th time.

In spite of the economic depression throughout the world, the interwar years were a period of great progress for French bloodstock breeders. The major studs imported a great deal, their numbers proliferated, and France was beginning to play an international role. Certain long-term figures of the turf were emerging, like Lucien Robert, who became trainer to Edouard de Rothschild at Chantilly in 1932. Perhaps the most publicly admired horse of the period was Brantôme, who appeared in 1933 and in two years won 11 races. In 1935, during the Prix de Diane, he broke away through the forest and the streets of Chantilly. After this he was sent to the Meautry Stud, and during the German Occupation of France he was taken to Germany, where he became hopeless as a stallion. Guy de Rothschild remarked that he had the French Resistance in his soul. After the war, happily back in France at the Meautry Stud, he produced exceptional results. He is deservedly one of the heroes of French racing.

As far as racing was concerned, France was more fortunate than Britain in World War II, as racing continued, albeit with some limitations. There were considerable risks, however. In 1940 the first bombs fell on Chantilly, and by the summer the whole town was evacuated. Vincennes was transformed into a military camp at the end of the war, and Longchamp became a vast anti-aircraft position. Nevertheless, 1941 saw over 200 meetings. In 1943 14 bombs fell on Longchamp in the middle of a meeting, claiming several victims. In 1945 France soon got back to form, despite the havoc caused in Normandy, where over 20 studs had been destroyed in the 1944 campaign. Others, like those of the Rothschilds, had been dispersed by the Germans.

From 1946 the French dominated the racing scene in Britain, as Marcel Boussac's empire reigned supreme, but not alone. Between the end of the war and 1970 one-fifth of English Classic races were won by French-bred horses. The four great stallions Astérus, Djebel, Pharis II and Tourbillon were of supreme importance to Boussac's victories, but they also had to be replaced as time wore on. He bought American stallions, but these proved to be a failure. Pharis II died in 1957 and Djebel in 1958. From the end of the 1950s until 1980 Boussac had only two Classic winners. Other French breeders did extremely well during this period. Baron Guy de Rothschild, having rebuilt his racing empire, put new emphasis on speed, whereas previously, like so many French breeders before him, he had concentrated on staying power. François Dupré took up the 'international outcross' formula and had great success. The British began to ask why the French were doing so well, and the answer was that the Grand Prix de Paris in France had dominated the French breeder's ideal. The French pattern of racing was biased in favour of races with distances of 1,600 metres (1 mile) to 3,000 metres (1 mile 7 furlongs), which offered the most prize money and prestige.

After the war, French racing management was superior to British, and technical innovations on the racecourse were way ahead, although British veterinary science continued to hold its own. The state-owned totalizator, the *pari-mutuel*, conducted all legal betting in France, and its proceeds were shared by the French Government and the Société d'Encouragement. As a result, prize money was much higher in France, and there was money for improved facilities and technical innovations. To this day there are many who feel that Britain should have followed suit when the Betting and Gaming Act was passed in the UK in 1960.

Nevertheless, the attractive prize money had its drawbacks, since foreign competitors were keen to take up the challenge. In 1946 all French races were finally opened to horses bred abroad. French-bred horses held their own brilliantly until 1965, both in France and in England (winning 22 out of 100 Classic races). That the dramatic slump in their fortunes was slowly reversed during the 1970s was largely due to the work of Alec Head and his partner, Comte Roland de Chambure. Alec Head had realized that the best racehorses were going to come from the USA, and by the late 1960s he was a regular attender at the American sales. As a result of these purchases, Riverman and Lyphard became the sire champions of France from 1978 to 1981, the former being syndicated in 1980 for over $100 million. Both sired winners of the Prix de l'Arc de Triomphe, Lyphard, Three Troikas (1979), and Riverman, Detroit (1980).

Throughout all these developments, the French seem to have been able to make the necessary swift responses. The Société d'Encouragement has maximum control over prize money and the organization of French racing. The totalizator funds are a great advantage, and the whole financial side of horse-racing is far less complicated than in the UK, so it was not surprising that the French met the American challenge quickly in the 1970s, when it became clear that the French emphasis on horses with stamina, toughness and middle-distance ability, who reached maturity at three and four years, had to be altered. The changes in the distribution of prize-money in the 1970s made it clear that the emphasis from now on was going to be on speed. While the titles of the races remained the same, the change in distribution of money completely altered their status. The French Derby (Prix du Jockey Club) is now the most important Classic race, with a prize worth more than double that of the Grand Prix.

In the early 1980s rising costs and prices were making the French more pessimistic about their future. Capital gains taxes, a new agricultural income system and the general problem of inflation had all hit the industry hard, and in 1984 some 60 per cent of horses in training belonged to foreigners. This, however, was in part a reflection of the growing internationalization of the thoroughbred world. France has enormous resources to withstand any changes in taxation, which may temporarily upset the industry or suddenly give an advantage to her competitors. Racegoing in France has always been popular and done with great style. The breeding-grounds of Normandy have unique advantages of climate, soil and proximity to the courses. France has an efficient organization and offers attractive prizes, and there is every indication that she will remain in the forefront of the top racehorse-breeding countries.

Spectators watch the parade to the start at Deauville in 1920.

FRENCH STUDS

NORMANDY AND DEAUVILLE

More than 60 per cent of French bloodstock is bred in Normandy where one finds the impressive stud farms for which the region has long been famous. The principal breeding areas are in the north of the region, in the countryside drained by the beautiful valleys of the rivers Touques, Dives, Orne and their tributaries. The area is rich in limestone, providing lush pastures and water rich in calcium, excellent for building strong bones in young horses. For centuries the region has produced superb cattle and is renowned for its fine dairy products, among them world-famous cheeses such as Camembert and Pont l'Evêque. The river valleys are in the centre of the Pays d'Auge, often called 'the heart of Normandy' — a region of half-timbered medieval farmhouses set among orchards (the *clos Normands*') and green meadows full of grazing cattle in top condition, with the occasional château or manor house with an imposing avenue of trees leading from its gates.

This fertile land is perfect for thoroughbred breeding, and the wealth of ancient manors, châteaux and farmhouses are an added attraction to rich French owner-breeders. The French have always looked on the thoroughbred with beauty very much in mind. Their racing and their racegoers have a well-deserved reputation for style and glamour; and it is this approach to the thoroughbred that is epitomized by Deauville, at the mouth of the river Touques.

During the first half of the nineteenth century, Deauville's neighbour Trouville flourished as a fashionable resort. When the Emperor Napoleon III began to visit Trouville in the 1850s, his half-brother, the illegitimate Duc de Morny, cleverly began to invest in land across the river in Deauville. Within two years he had dried out the marshland and created an estate of grand villas. Knowing the Emperor's fondness for racing, he went on to build a racecourse at the back of the town on land bought from the novelist Gustave Flaubert. On 14 August 1864, the La Touques racecourse was opened, named after the river separating Deauville from Trouville. The course was a great success, and although it was some 200 kilometres from Paris, it quickly became part of the Parisian circuit. As with many seaside racecourses, it had excellent turf, brought originally from England, and its facilities and stands were well-maintained and comfortable. The most important race was the Town Prize Race of 6,000 francs, for three-year-olds and over. In 1864 came the Morny Prize of 5,000 francs for two-year-olds, and The Cup, for 20,000 francs, was introduced in 1866.

Deauville soon became the summer resort of Paris racing and an essential part of the social season. Although the Duc de Morny died only a year after the course's inauguration, property development and speculation remained enthusiastic. A casino was built by Léon Vaudoyer, and the scene was set for serious commercial investment in pleasure as well as racing. Success was not without its setbacks, however. During the Franco-Prussian War of 1870-1 several horses were shipped to England to prevent them falling into enemy hands, and the famous Gladiateur and Trocadero were both sold in England at this time. The English prevented the war from reaching the coast, and there were no battles at sea in the Channel itself, but the war was a serious blow to Deauville. France's pride was severely wounded after the defeat, and the 1870s were years of stagnation.

Left: The paddock at Deauville racecourse.

The following decade, however, saw a great revival of fortunes and optimism as the country's economy grew strongly, and unprecedented amounts began to be spent on conspicuous pleasure. In 1887 Deauville's first public sale of yearlings took place. This new event became a great success, involving such names as the Chéri establishment and, by the turn of the century, Tattersalls. The 1890s saw the beginning of the most extravagant period in European racing. American owners, such as W.K. Vanderbilt, Belmont and Duryea, began to arrive, and then came the great showman Tod Sloan and his new American way of riding.

Shortly before World War I the Grand Casino was built and the famous wooden promenade ('Les Planches') constructed; Deauville's two main seafront landmarks, the Normandy and the Royal hotels, were built, grand hotels in an era of the grandest. Deauville became an international centre of fashion, with leading couturiers of the Paris fashion world anxious to have their work paraded as part of the season. It was also a great attraction for the English, and by the time of the Entente Cordiale in 1907 it had few rivals as a resort on either side of the Channel. The sales of yearlings passed all records. In 1912 a 1,600-metre (1 mile) straight track was laid out at La Touques and inaugurated the following year. Gambling in the Edwardian period reached an all-time peak, and the casinos and card clubs operated almost around the clock.

Despite the horrors of the two World Wars and the summer drift south to the Côte d'Azur, the town has managed to retain its position in the French racing world and as a resort of international standing. In 1928 the second racecourse, Clairefontaine, was opened. After World War II, Deauville shared the upsurge of French racing success. A new port with 900 moorings was constructed in 1970 for the international yachting visitors along the River Touques. Deauville's season begins in July and closes with the Grand Prix on the last Sunday in August. Its yearling sales are also held at the end of August.

With its casinos, yachts, film festivals and conference trade, the town has also a great deal to offer outside its short season. Its shops, hotels and restaurants are of a quality normally restricted to the centre of sophisticated cities. With this emphasis on excellence, the town's prosperity and position in the French racing world seems assured for many years to come.

THE THOROUGHBRED EMPIRE OF H.H. THE AGA KHAN

The third Aga Khan photographed at Longchamps racecourse, Paris, in 1948 with the jockey W.R. Johnstone.

The breeding and racing empire of the third Aga Khan (1877-1957) was the first to be considered truly international this century. As such it was on a scale that was to set the style of multi-national operations after World War II.

H.H. the Aga Khan is the hereditary Imam of the Ismaili Muslims. He descends in direct line from the Prophet Mohammed through his daughter Fatima and son-in-law Ali. His followers run into millions and his personal wealth is of equal dimensions. Much of this wealth comes from the first holder of the title Aga Khan, Mohammed Hussaini, who was an immensely rich Persian aristocrat. Internal rivalry with the Shah in the mid-nineteenth century led him to a forced exile in India, where he lived in great state in Bombay. There he was renowned for his feudal style of living and for his stables. His son the second Aga Khan did not long survive him and his grandson the third Aga Khan succeeded to the office of Iman at the age of only eight. Widely respected as an international statesman, he was appointed head of the Indian delegation to the Disarmament Conference at the League of Nations and was made President of the League in 1937.

He began to be interested in racing shortly after King Edward VII came to the throne, when racing was in its heyday in England. He stayed with Colonel William Hall Walker, later Lord Wavertree, at his stud at Tully. This was one of the finest studs in Europe at the time, but despite his friends' encouragement he did not begin to breed and race with any seriousness until after World War I.

His interest in European breeding operations is said to have come from his being placed next to Mrs Asquith at a dinner party in London in 1921. Daughter-in-law of the former Prime Minister, Mrs Asquith was the sister of Cicely Lambton, wife of Lord Derby's trainer. She suggested that he send for George Lambton to buy some horses for him. Together with William Duke, the former trainer of the Vanderbilts, Lambton was instructed to buy yearlings. Dick Dawson was to train for him in England while Duke was to both buy and train for him in France.

At the 1921 Doncaster sales Lambton spent over £25,000 on the Aga Khan's behalf. He was not given carte blanche, however, as the Aga Khan had given instructions to buy a filly, Teresina, and a colt, later named Papyrus. Lambton, who did not agree about the latter, did not bid for him. This was for ever a bone of contention with the Aga Khan, as Papyrus became a Derby winner. Teresina became a successful foundation mare whose influence remains to this day. She won the Goodwood Cup and produced many successful horses, including Turkhan who won the St Leger. Lambton also bought a filly, named Cos, who proved to be a broodmare of note. The Newmarket yearling sales produced equally important purchases including a Tetrarch filly named Paola. Within four weeks Duke had bought a further 15 yearlings at Deauville, the result of which was that by the following year the Aga Khan was already in the top twenty winning owners in France.

1922 was another spectacular year of purchases but in particular that of the filly Mumtaz Mahal, by The Tetrarch out of Lady Josephine. Lambton paid the highest price for a yearling ever known, and she inherited The Tetrarch's renowned quality of speed, becoming popularly known as the Flying Filly. Her victories as a precocious sprinter, together with those of Teresina, made the Aga Khan the leading owner in England in 1924. Mumtaz Mahal's offspring were not really in the same class as she was, but her daughters became mares of enormous influence, in particular Mumtaz Begum and Mah Mahal. Her bloodline produced two Derby winners, an Oaks winner and a winner of the Prix de l'Arc de Triomphe, and remains strong. 1922 also saw the purchase of Friar's Daughter by Dick Dawson. Her influence extended over twenty years. She bred eight English winners and two French, in particular Bahram and Dastur. Bahram won the Triple Crown and Frank Butters believed he was the best horse he had ever trained.

Having made such an impact on the yearling market in the early 1920s, it was inevitable that this approach would stabilize. The first purchase of stud-farm property outside the United Kingdom came in 1923. In France, La Coquenne was followed by Marly la Ville and by St Crespin in 1927, which he purchased on the death of the great French breeder, Edouard Kann. In 1924 the Aga Khan directed his attention to Ireland and bought the Sheshoon Stud at The Curragh from Sir Henry Greer; three years later he added Ballymany Stud, which is alongside the racecourse itself. Two more were added, the Ongar Stud in Co Dublin and the Gilltown Stud in Co Kildare. The present Aga Khan has retained and developed the facilities of Sheshoon and Ballymany, the latter as a public stud where Nishapour and Darshaan, Mouktar and Shernazar now stand.

Darshaan, by Shirley Heights out of Delsy by Abdos, is the winner of five races, including the Prix du Jockey-Club, and £155,403. He was retired to stud in 1985, and now stands at Ballymany Stud in Ireland.

Spectacular purchases were also accompanied by spectacular sales. The Aga Khan always stated publicly that his racing and breeding ought to be self-supporting, but while he emphasized that his motives were always sporting there was no doubt that profit played a large part. By 1936 the Aga Khan had won the Derby three times, had been leading owner in England six times, and had found himself a place alongside the great owner-breeders of the day, such as Lord Derby, Lord Rosebery and the Duke of Westminster, all within only 15 years.

The Aga Khan only just managed to escape from France to Switzerland in 1940. This was the year of the much publicized sale of Bahram and Mahmoud to the United States, which had been preceded by Blenheim. These sales received much criticism and certainly the departure of these top-class stallions had a profound effect on European breeding.

In the dark days of 1940 the Aga Khan bred his most influential horse ever. Nasrullah, by Nearco, had an unspectacular racing career but was his most successful stallion at stud siring, among many others, Never Say Die. He was eventually sold to Bull Hancock and became champion sire five times, dominating American post-war breeding. The Aga Khan's first post-war Derby winner was My Love in 1948, followed four years later by Tulyar.

Attracted by larger prize money, the Aga Khan moved all his horses from England to France in 1952. English racing was at a low ebb and the Aga Khan's departure was a serious blow, even though his son, Prince Aly, retained a few horses, including Petite Etoile, with Noel Murless. Alec Head, his trainer in France, trained many winners for the Aga Khan in the 1950s, sending Palariva (by Palestine out of Rivaz) to England to win two of the top races for fillies and Rose Royale II to win the 1957 One Thousand Guineas.

Lashkari, by Mill Reef out of Larannda, was foaled in 1981. Owned by a syndicate, he stands at Haras de Bonneval in France.

Nasrullah, by Nearco out of Mumtaz Begum by Blenheim, proved to be exceptional at stud despite an inauspicious racing career. He sired such top class horses as Bold Ruler, Never Say Die, Nashua and Grey Sovereign.

The Aga Khan's death in 1957 split the racing empire in three. Two-fifths went to his eldest son Prince Aly, two-fifths to Prince Sadruddin, and one-fifth to his widow. Prince Aly bought the others out and was beginning to expand his racing empire when he was killed in a car crash in Paris in 1960, at the age of 48. In a brief period he had become the leading owner in England, France and Ireland, winning the Prix de l'Arc de Triomphe and four classic races in 1959.

The new Aga Khan, Prince Karim, was only 23 when he inherited from his father. Educated at Harvard, he received two-fifths of the racing empire and bought out the shares of his brother and sister. Death duties made the situation even more difficult and he was obliged to sell many of the best mares, including some of those who traced back to Mumtaz Mahal.

An enormous and unexpected responsibility was thrust on the young man's shoulders and it was clear that careful thought had to go into managing the new racing empire. There were four farms in France and five in Ireland. After the necessary sale of stock there was an over abundance of land to support the remaining horses. The reorganization took some 13 years, leaving two studs in France and two in Ireland. In France he built a new stud at Bonneval which became a public stud in 1973. St Crespin was kept exclusively as a private stud for his own mares. In Ireland, Ballymany became the public stud and Sheshoon was reserved for his own mares.

Alec Head was the foremost trainer in France and trained for both Prince Aly and his father, but the young Aga Khan felt that Alec was too successful in his own right as an owner-breeder to remain part of his new operation. He replaced him in 1964 with François Mathet, a trainer of formidable reputation. On his death, Alain de Royer Dupré succeeded him as principal trainer.

In his first season with Mathet his home-bred colt Silver Shark won him five races. In 1967 Zeddaan won the Prix Robert Papin, the first big two-year-old race in France, and the French Two Thousand Guineas the following year. Zeddaan was by Grey Sovereign out of Vareta and sired Kalamoun, who also won the French Two Thousand Guineas in 1973. Kalamoun went on to sire Bikala, Kalaglow, Shakapour, Kenmare and Persepolis. Zeddaan had an enormous influence on the Aga Khan's stud and was eventually sold to Japan in 1978. Silver Shark, Zeddaan, and Kalamoun were the symbols of the Aga Khan's successful reorganization, winning him some 43 group races between 1960 and 1974.

Broodmares and their foals within the semi-circular foaling unit at Haras de Bonneval, Calvados, France.

By the mid 1970s the Aga Khan had begun to build his magnificent training establishment at Aiglemont, near Chantilly. Many years of research went into it and when it was opened, in 1977, it was one of the finest training operations in the world. Consisting of 102 boxes in six barns, it incorporates electric cars to cut down on heavy labour, so that more time can be devoted to the horses themselves.

In 1974, at the Newmarket December sales, the Aga Khan bought a foal by Red God out of Runaway Bride, already named Blushing Groom who had been foaled at Bonneval. Blushing Groom went on to win the French Two Thousand Guineas and was syndicated in America in 1977 for the sum of $6 million. Part of this money went to purchase the entire bloodstock of Mme François Dupré and, in the following year, that of Marcel Boussac, who had been France's biggest owner-breeders. The Aga Khan calculated that it was necessary to build up his stock of mares, which by the mid 1970s had fallen to about 50. Skilful selection of mares from the Dupré-Boussac acquisitions has enabled him to produce stallions of top rank. Among these Top Ville, Akarad, Vayrann, Darshaan and Mouktar have all shown the wisdom of this policy. Arc-winning filly Akiyda and Prix Vermeille-winning filly Darara were both out of mares acquired from Boussac.

With the stables in France full, in 1978 the Aga Khan decided to train some of his horses in England. He stated that England had made greater progress in racing in the previous five years than any other country, and that his now international reputation would be impaired if he did not race there.

Accordingly, he chose two comparatively young trainers, Richard Fulke Johnson Houghton

From left to right: Petite Etoile with Lester Piggott up, Above Suspicion with D. Smith, and Parthia with W.H. Carr at Epsom in 1960.

and Michael Stoute, who had sufficient experience to give his horses expert training. Shergar was among the yearlings sent over at the end of 1979 and he went to the Newmarket yard of Michael Stoute. He made the name not only of his trainer but of the Aga Khan too. When a horse wins a race by ten lengths it cannot help but capture the imagination. Shergar won the 1981 Derby with incredible ease and the greatest winning margin in the history of the race. The ensuing tragedy, when he was kidnapped at Ballymany, saddened all who had seen him race, but it must be remembered that in his only season at stud Shergar covered 44 mares, resulting in 36 live offspring. Sixty years previously, the third Aga Khan had bought the celebrated Mumtaz Mahal, from which Shergar was descended. Racing empires of the scale of the Aga Khan's can recover with remarkable speed, as his 1986 Derby win with Shahrastani (by Nijinsky out of Shadema) shows.

Shahrastani, by Nijinsky out of Shadema, winner of the 1986 Derby at Epsom, photographed here winning the 1986 Irish Derby.

HARAS D'ETREHAM, NORMANDY

Etreham is just north-west of Bayeux, between the sea and the main highway to Paris. In 1944 it was all too close to the Normandy beaches on which the Allies landed, so that when the Comte Foy revisited his property after the war, accompanied by his friend Comte Hubert de Chambure, they were shattered by what they found. The stud farm, which before the war had been described as one of the best in France, was a wreck. The paddocks were riddled with bomb-craters, petrol and munitions were stored in the farm buildings, and American engineers were quartered in the once-elegant château.

Comte Foy had neither the means nor the energy to repair such devastation. A Parisian who liked his comforts, he sold off the property to Hubert de Chambure. Aided by forty hard-working German prisoners-of-war and his own amazing energy, Hubert de Chambure soon had the stud back in sufficient working order to house his horse Verso II, who sired among many others Lavandin, winner of the 1956 Derby. The stud's foundation mare Nica, a present from Hubert de Chambure's wife, foaled Montenica, winner of the 1947 Prix de Diane, followed by Djebellica, winner of the 1951 Irish Oaks.

The stable yard at the Haras d'Etreham.

In 1953 Hubert de Chambure died, sadly before Lavandin's victory, leaving the property, according to French law, to be divided among his heirs. It was not until 1966 that its present owner, Comte Roland de Chambure, was able to buy the whole stud farm from his family and set about creating what exists today.

The Haras d'Etreham is now without doubt one of the showplaces of the thoroughbred world. The château, built in 1817 and added to at various times, sits squarely in the middle of the well-kept paddocks, an ornamental and well-proportioned reminder of the past.

Combined with his high-powered career in merchant banking, Roland de Chambure chose to breed top-class thoroughbred racehorses. In 1971 he formed the Société Aland in partnership with Alec Head, his trainer and friend of many years' standing. Together they now own around 50 mares, and have 28 horses in training. In addition, Alec Head has his personal bloodstock at his nearby stud farm, Le Quesnay.

In 1981 Christiane (Criquette) Head, Alec Head's daughter, took out a trainer's licence, and was the first woman to train the winner of the Prix de l'Arc de Triomphe (Three Troikas, the 1979 winner). Although on this occasion she was only a private trainer to her mother, it was in fact a team success. The horses owned by the Head-Chambure partnership were leased and ran in the name of Mme Head. Three Troikas had been sent to Etreham in the spring of 1977 to be prepared for the Newmarket Sales. But when Roland de Chambure saw her, he disregarded her somewhat unfashionable breeding, finding her exceptionally well-proportioned. So it came about that Criquette Head offered her breeder, M. Plaff, 41,000 guineas, which luckily for everyone concerned was accepted. It turned out to be a triumph for the family and the partnership, crowned by the fact that Freddie Head, who rides for his sister, rode one of the most brilliant races of his career. Once again a filly had won the biggest race on the French Turf – something which realists like de Chambure view with concern, for in recent years it has been happening all too frequently and points clearly to the lack of top-class male horses in France at present.

The tax system is one of France's greatest handicaps, since the French are required to pay tax on everything. In England a company's losses can be offset against tax, while in Ireland and the USA it is tax-beneficial to go into racing. Roland de Chambure would like to see the French

View across to the Haras d'Etreham which was revived by Comte Roland de Chambure in 1966.

Government returning a little more of the betting turnover to help racehorse owners, which would make little difference to the general tax position but would be of great benefit to the owners. He would also like the Government to encourage more people to go into the breeding business by offering them some form of tax relief or franchise and allowing their losses to be deducted from other income.

Another problem is the disturbing drop in racecourse attendance. This is partly due to the centralization of French racing in the Paris area, and its concentration at Deauville during August. Television in France has not popularized racing as it has in England and Ireland, nor are there huge added cash prizes from various advertising sources.

No European breeder can afford to underestimate the power of the dollar, nor can anyone continually withstand the pressure to sell when the price reaches some staggering sum. However, if any two people are capable of changing the situation, the Head-Chambure association will surely do it. Their mares are sent over to board at Hagyard Farm, Kentucky, and then to all the best stallions. The stallions who stand at Etreham (Fabulous Dancer, Bellman and Sicyos) are all Turf record-holders and are all fully booked each season. Each stallion has his own individual paddock, where he can gallop around at will. Additional boxes have been added, to bring the number up to 160, and cattle — a Friesian milk herd and some Charolais, rotate the paddocks to keep up the quality of the pastures.

Fabulous Dancer, by Northern Dancer out of the American horse Last of Line, is one of the resident Etreham stallions.

France's top internationally-renowned stallion Luthier stood at Etreham until his death of a heart attack in 1981, at the age of 16. He sired 33 winners (22 males and 11 females). For the moment, French breeders are feeling the lack of a top-class stallion; however, it is relatively easy to send a mare to Kentucky, which 85 per cent of French breeders regularly do. It might be argued that they cannot afford *not* to send their best mares to the best American-based stallions; on the other hand, it prevents the establishment of the stallions who stand at Etreham.

All the same, Etreham and Aland partnership-owned racehorses and broodmares seem to go from strength to strength. It is a professional operation, and in order to keep it running horses have to be sold. Both Roland de Chambure and Alec Head are extremely hard-working, and are outstanding judges of bloodstock. Roland de Chambure bought Three Troikas because he liked her looks, and he bought Pistol Packer for the same reason. The day after he had paid $15,000 for her at Saratoga he told Bull Hancock of his purchase and was given a very strange look, for she was by the unfashionable Gun Bow. However, Pistol Packer won the Prix de Diane, Vermeille, St Alary, Chloë, de la Nonette, and Harcourt and ran second to Mill Reef in the 1971 Prix de l'Arc de Triomphe. On that occasion Head and de Chambure were unlucky to come up against one of the best of that year's horses, otherwise Pistol Packer might have been yet another filly to have won this prestigious race.

Three Troikas, by the celebrated Lyphard out of Three Roses, and 1979 winner of the Prix de L'Arc de Triomphe, and the Prix Vermeille, currently stands at the Haras d'Etreham.

HARAS DE FRESNAY-LE-BUFFARD, NORMANDY

The Haras de Fresnay-le-Buffard incorporates a charming manor house, set back from the main stable yard, which looks across a sweep of lawn studded with clumps of beech trees and a small lake. A second small house overlooks the paddocks of this 650-acre stud farm. The whole effect was created by the legendary Marcel Boussac, who dominated French racing from 1928 to 1956. In 1979 Fresnay-le-Buffard was bought by the Greek shipping magnate Stavros Niarchos. For 18 months the paddocks had been resting, after the bloodstock had been bought by the Aga Khan; but the stallion barns, and the stabling in which the broodmares were housed (now generally termed 'American barns'), were there, awaiting resuscitation.

Marcel Boussac was a man ahead of his time, bringing unprecedented scale and originality to the breeding of thoroughbred racehorses. He wanted not just to win races, but to create a breed of racehorse superior to and segregated from the rest of the world's thoroughbreds; and for over half a century his specialized philosophy of inbreeding worked. In less than 60 years he won 1,800 races, of which 140 were races classified as Group 1. He won the French Derby 12 times, the French Oaks five times, the Prix de l'Arc de Triomphe six times, and the Grand Criterium, the most important French two-year-old race, nine times. He headed the list of winning owners in France 19 times and the list of breeders 17 times. In 1950 he was the leading breeder in both France and Britain.

The old half-timbered stables at the Haras de Fresnay-le-Buffard, created by Marcel Boussac. The influence of his powerful racing stable was felt throughout France and Europe in from the 1930s until the 1950s.

He was one of the first owners to make extensive use of air transport, claiming that the shorter the time spent in travelling, the smaller was the disturbance to the horse. This was one of the secrets of his highly successful raids on Newmarket, Epsom and Ascot, where his runners scarcely paused for a meal, and when they did so they brought all their own fodder with them. From the British point of view, the ominous feature of the Boussac horses was not just that they won, but that they did so in such a style that they could only be likened to a whole race of Shergars, giving the appearance of winning a race with casual ease.

The immediate postwar period was tough on the British, who had to accept that nine individually-bred French horses won Classic races between 1947 and 1951, four of them owned and bred by Marcel Boussac. As a breeder, he was very much his own man. He did not want mares sent to his stallions, and seldom used the services of other stallions – a policy that made him great, but finally led to the decline of his Turf supremacy.

At the outbreak of World War II, Boussac's horse Pharis II, having won the 1939 French Derby and Grand Prix in breathtaking style, was retired to stud at Fresnay-le-Buffard; but the following August he was removed by the Germans and installed at the Altenfeld Stud until the end of the war. The high altitude and harsh German climate did not agree with him, and for the five seasons he remained there he was virtually impotent, siring only one top-class filly, Asterblute. But when he came back to Fresnay-le-Buffard after the war his virility returned, and he spent the remaining 12 years of his life siring winners in keeping with his own brilliant racing career. The stallion box in which he lived stands by the entrance to the stud farm, and the legend of Pharis II's reluctance to collaborate with the enemy loses nothing in the telling – although it must be admitted that the temperate climate of that particular corner of Normandy, Orne, is

Pharis II, winner of the 1939 French Derby and Grand Prix, was one of Marcel Boussac's most successful stallions.

regarded as one of the very best areas for breeding racehorses.

Boussac's breeding plan was bold and imaginative. He bought the best outcrosses of both sexes and interbred them, seeking advice from no one except his racing manager, Comte François de Brignac, who once made the marvellous remark about his employer: 'He does everything himself, except cover the mares.' For Marcel Boussac was dedicated, and a demon when it came to detail. He personally designed the broodmares' barns, which are light, airy buildings with two rows of boxes facing one another across a central aisle under a single gabled roof. This economical and efficient design, now used universally, is dubbed 'American-style', whereas in truth it should be called 'Boussac-style'. The concrete fencing, a much-repeated feature on Normandy stud farms, is also Boussac-style and is practical and easy to maintain. The upright posts are set into the ground in such a way as to allow a certain flexibility, as are all the joins in the rails; thus if a yearling gallops into one, which is possible though highly unlikely, there will be sufficient give in

The modern, airy barns used to accommodate the mares and foals.

the fencing to prevent the animal doing itself an injury.

For many years Marcel Boussac was president of the Société d'Encouragement, although nobody who knew him would describe him as social or extrovert, and because of his neat, conservative appearance he was frequently described as a man who lived in the past. In fact, in all his endeavours he had a very progressive attitude. His textile empire, as important in its day as his racing empire, was run on enlightened lines. He instigated housing schemes and pension funds for his employees long before compulsory social services were imposed on employers. Boussac also financed his friend Christian Dior; and in many respects they were not dissimilar in that they were both self-effacing perfectionists.

Now Fresnay-le-Buffard is in the hands of Stavros Niarchos, who receives enthusiastic support from his daughter Maria, one of the new type of women who are becoming seriously involved in the breeding of thoroughbreds. Niarchos gave his son, Philip, and his daughter-in-law, Victoria, the use of the château while he himself moved into the smaller house, preferring to overlook the paddocks filled with his bloodstock.

The stud is now being managed by an experienced Englishman, Tim Richardson. Niarchos has five stallions at stud and 110 broodmares, apart from mares visiting his stallions. Horses are being bred to race, as they were in the days of 'le Patron', as Marcel Boussac is still called by the ageing stable lads who have remained at Le Fresnay. A new Boussac-type of barn has been built to accommodate the increasing number of visiting mares. Le Fresnay has all the activity and hopes of a newly reorganized stud farm, and the list of trainers, on whom so much depends, includes some of the world's best, including Henry Cecil, Jeremy Tree, and the O'Briens, father and son.

View across some of the 650 acres of the Haras de Fresnay-le-Buffard. On the right of the road are the old stables and the entrance to the stud, on the left can be seen the large single-gabled barn which is also used for storage.

HARAS DE MEAUTRY, NORMANDY

The Haras de Meautry is owned by Baron Guy de Rothschild whose family have been involved in racing and breeding for generations.

Three generations of Rothschilds have had a hand in creating the Haras de Meautry in the village of Touques, just outside Deauville. A small château, the ideal size for the Deauville season, lies to one side of this relatively small stud farm with its 500 acres of paddock. Four stallions stand currently at Meautry: the beautiful dapple-grey Kenmare, France's leading sire of 1985; Lightning, the sire of Lypharita, winner of the French Oaks; Blushing Groom's son Crystal Glitters, winner of three important races; and Galant Vert, another young stallion who has won four important French races. Apart from Galant Vert, the stallions are syndicated, with Crystal Glitters commanding 1 million francs a nomination, since he is rightly considered to be the best performer of Blushing Groom's offspring standing at stud in France.

Baron Guy de Rothschild has 36 horses in training in France, divided between two experts. He never sells his yearlings, which means that every animal he breeds is given the opportunity to prove itself. His horses are only sold later in their career — a policy established by his grandfather, who bought first the château and then the surrounding property. The house, in the style of the Belle Epoque, has an air of slightly formal grandeur. The paddocks which adjoin the house are fenced and painted à la Boussac, and the stud farm buildings, including the stallion

boxes and broodmare stalls, are gabled and roofed in deep grey Normandy slate. The rich green of the paddocks, as lush as those in Ireland, remind one that summer on the other side of the Channel is little different to over here. In this part of Normandy each tiny village house, with its timber and plasterwork, seems prettier than the next, Norman churches and castles abound, and the deep grey stone-work makes a stunning contrast to the timber-framed houses. It is easy to understand why the Rothschilds chose to create their stud farm at Touques, and it is equally easy to understand why they continue to maintain it so impeccably.

Unlike the stud farm at Fresnay-le-Buffard, which Marcel Boussac so meticulously created, and where his many famous horses are all buried together in an unnamed grave, the Rothschild bloodstock stars are immortalized. By the main entrance to the farm a large plaque beneath a sculptured horse lists the names of the famous past incumbents: Brantôme, Heaume, Le Roi Soleil, Sans Souci II, La Farina, Bubbles, Vieux Manoir, and Exbury.

The château is opened up each year for the Deauville summer season. From 1900 to the present day the Rothschilds have been among the big names of Deauville; and for three generations their home-bred horses have raced on Deauville's two racecourses, Touques and Clairefontaine.

The stables at the Haras de Meautry.

Le Roi Soleil, one of the famous stallions bred by the Haras de Meautry in 1948.

HARAS DU MEZERAY, NORMANDY

Le Mezeray, near Ticheville, is in the valley of the Touques river, which reaches the sea at Deauville. This famous farming region, known especially for its delicate cheeses, has some of France's best pasture for thoroughbreds. When Paul de Moussac bought the property in 1962 it was a mere 17 acres, with 12 additional rented acres; now a quarter of a century on it consists of 375 acres of fenced paddocks and accommodation for 100 horses.

Paul de Moussac, like every owner, wishes to win as many races as possible; unlike many, he does not rush his two-year-olds. All his horses are trained at Chantilly by John Cunnington Jr, and if a horse needs to be stopped for a few weeks in its training schedule, it is returned to Le Mezeray. The perfect example is Luth Enchantée, who raced only twice as a two-year-old without winning, but reached the peak of her form at Deauville the following year, winning the Prix Jacques Le Marois and the Prix du Moulin at Longchamp, and finishing third in the Prix de l'Arc de Triomphe. De Moussac sold her half-sister by Thatch for 4 million francs. Since he first became involved with breeding and racing, he has always re-invested, and says quite frankly that if one day he owns a champion, he will do everything he can to keep him in France.

The Château du Mezeray, set in magnificent parkland, also houses the public stud farm, which was founded in 1960.

The eighteenth-century Château
du Mezeray.

Luth Enchantée winning the Prix
Jacques Le Marois at Deauville in
1983.

Meanwhile Le Mezeray operates as a public stud farm. There are three stallions standing: Margouillat; Don Roberto, the tough American-bred racehorse sent over by Spendthrift Farm, Kentucky; and the latest arrival, Miller's Mate, bred by Colonel Dick Warden and owned by Sheikh Mohammed Al Maktoum. This unlucky animal was fancied to win the Derby, but broke his near foreleg in the Chester Vase. Thanks to brilliant veterinary bone-pinning by David Ellis of Newmarket, he now has the chance of emulating his famous sire, Mill Reef, at stud.

The building complex at Le Mezeray was designed by the Paris architect Xavier Leplâtre. The stallion barn is large and set apart, and paired with this is a series of barn offices, with all the necessary computer equipment. The foaling units and broodmare barns include a good isolation unit; and the whole is fenced in by posts and rails, unlike the other stud farms of Normandy, where the fencing is Boussac-style (cement railing). The stud farm is roomy, its policy being not to allow more than one horse per acre.

The Haras du Mezeray has 325 acres and includes an all-weather gallop and pre-training centre.

In 1974 Antoine Bozo, a horseman of note, began his collaboration with Paul de Moussac, and now manages Le Mezeray with Pierre Rouxel. Without large cash resources to invest, they work to a very realistic policy, keeping their eyes on the international market. They believe that it is better to breed from strongly-constituted mares that have shown some ability on the racecourse, rather than from top-pedigree mares who may be unable to win or to stand training. Every year they send eight or nine mares to either Spendthrift Farm or to Circle O Farm in Kentucky, and their nominations are among the best in Blushing Groom, Sharpen Up, and Seattle Slew. In Ireland they breed to such horses as Be My Guest and Hello Gorgeous, while in England their mares go to Her Majesty's Shirley Heights, Great Nephew and Known Fact.

Paul de Moussac is a knowledgeable breeder who runs his thoroughbred operation to make money. He takes in a few mares as permanent boarders, including all those belonging to Mme Georges Ohrstom. His own mares, Exclusive Order, Kilmona, and Stresa, are at Mill Ridge Farm, Kentucky, while Right Bank and Trephine are at Circle O. A filly and a colt (Spectacular Voice and Complice) are in training with John Gosden in Los Angeles. He sells horses in training and has developed quite a market for three-year-olds, who go on to win in somebody else's colours. All the yearlings he breeds are broken and taught to walk straight before they leave for John Cunnington. They are schooled under the starting-gate and arrive at Chantilly well-mannered, which helps keep the training costs down. To ensure good management and to keep his staff busy all the year round, de Moussac has developed a maintenance unit with a fully-equipped carpentry shop, so that the fences, which can be a heavy drain on a large property, can be maintained with the minimum outlay. He has also installed a blacksmith with his own forge so that the foals can have their feet attended to at a very early age.

The stable yard at the Haras du Mezeray. The stud has accommodation for 100 horses.

Paul de Moussac has recently built a dirt track with the idea of attracting American owners, who love to race in France but fear that if they subsequently return their horses to the tougher racing conditions of the US dirt track, they risk breaking them down. An all-weather track makes it possible to exercise the horses even when it is freezing. Enclosed by a high fence, its comparative narrowness allows yearlings to be ridden for the first time. Everything at Le Mezeray is similarly well-planned, from the delightful three-storey manor house, which has sufficient room for guests during August when all the racing world converges on Deauville, to the spacious offices. Paul de Moussac is an enthusiast who looks to the future. At a time when so many of the best-bred French horses are being sold to foreign countries, he is doing his best to reverse the trend by standing two top-class stallions from abroad, thus giving French breeders the opportunity to avail themselves of important blood-lines. He would be the first to agree that promotion is the key to standing a successful stallion, for he accepts that he must sell a good brood mare or a good filly if he has several females from the same line.

The recently completed dirt track at Le Mezeray facilitates the training and re-training of horses scheduled to race in the United States.

HARAS DE SAINT-LEONARD-DES-PARCS, NORMANDY

The Haras de Saint-Léonard-des-Parcs, belonging to Jacques Wertheimer, is situated in the beautiful valley of the River Orne. This part of Normandy, with its picturesque half-timbered houses, meandering streams, and gentle surrounding hills covered with the remnants of ancient forests, has some of the best farmland in France. The superb pasture for thoroughbred horses provides opportunities for a stud farm to rotate its paddocks, using its own cattle, or leasing the land for grazing when necessary. All the stud farms back on to farmland proper; and at Saint-Léonard in particular the stud-farm buildings are dispersed among the concrete-fenced paddocks, with regular mixed farming in evidence on either side. Right next to the entrance is a fifteenth-century stone church with a grey-tiled roof, and a handful of cottages in picturesque contrast to the paddocks in which yearlings or mares with their foals are grazing.

Dancing Maid, foaled in France by Lyphard out of Morana, won FF1,398,500 in five races in France. This photograph was taken in 1978, when she was a three-year-old.

HARAS DE SAINT-LEONARD-DES-PARCS

The stud farm was founded by the present owner's father, Pierre Wertheimer, in 1910. The famous horse Epinard, dubbed 'Horse of the Century' in the 1920s, was retired to stud at Saint-Léonard, where he sired two other important Wertheimer horses, La Fayette and Balthazar. It is a working stud farm, well laid out and smartly painted in white and midnight blue; although there is no accompanying stylish manor house as there is at Fresnay or Meautry. However, like Niarchos and Guy de Rothschild, Jacques Wertheimer is a man who breeds to win races, which he has done repeatedly.

Those who succeed in winning that much-coveted French race, the Prix de l'Arc de Triomphe, may justly be proud of their achievement; but when that achievement is turned into a piece of Turf history, there is room for congratulation indeed. Examples are Marcel Boussac, who won the race six times with five different horses; Robert Sangster, who within a four-year span won the race three times with two different horses; and Jacques Wertheimer, whose contribution to the statistics is somewhat unusual, in that he has twice won the race with four-year-old mares. In 1976 he won with Ivanjica (by Sir Ivor), bought at Keeneland, Kentucky, as a yearling for $180,000; and again in 1981 with Gold River. In 1978 Wertheimer was leading owner in France, principally due to two other outstanding fillies, Reine de Saba and Dancing Maid.

Formerly training with Alec Head, he now trains with his daughter, Christiane (Criquette), at Chantilly and has some 60 horses with her. He has approximately the same number of broodmares. His yearlings remain in Normandy, benefiting from those quality pastures until they are ready to leave for Chantilly and the training stables. With little more than 250 acres, he has decided against standing a stallion of his own, preferring to own shares in stallions like Northern Dancer and Nijinsky, and to support some of his former horses like Lyphard, Riverman and Green Dancer in America, all standing in Kentucky. Results prove that Jacques Wertheimer has a flair for sending his top-class mares to the right sires.

Right: Reine de Saba, by Lyphard out of Sirya, was foaled in France in 1975.

Mares and foals in front of the picturesque half-timbered house at the Haras de Saint-Léonard-des-Parcs.

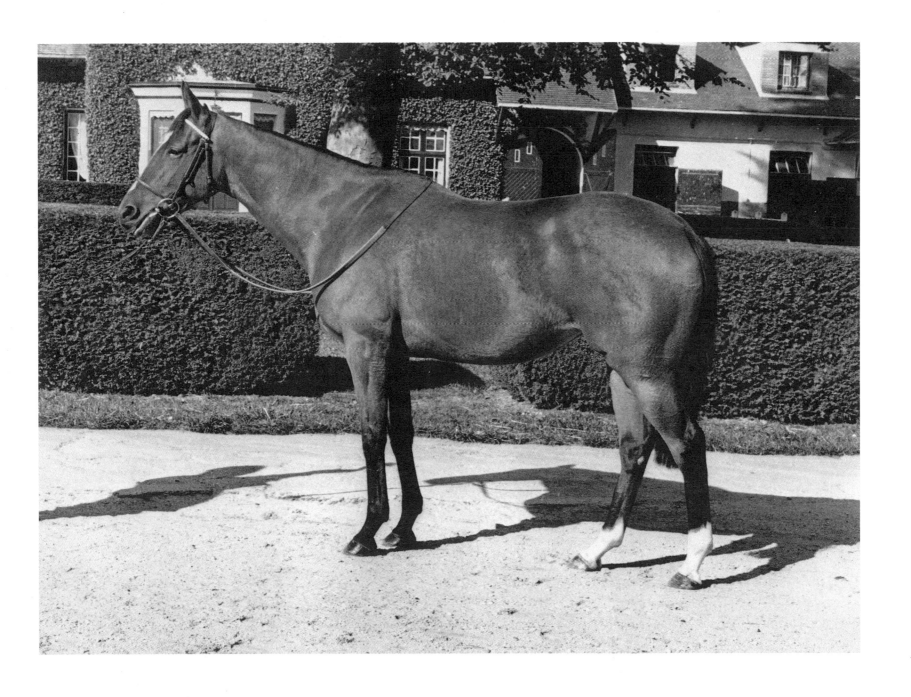

THE THOROUGHBRED
IN THE UNITED STATES

Historians agree that there were no horses in North America when Spanish settlers first landed in the New World in the sixteenth century. The horse's prehistoric ancestors, found throughout the continent, had existed for some 60 million years until the Ice Age destroyed them. In January 1519 Cortes arrived in Mexico with 11 stallions and 5 mares, the first of many imported by the Spanish Conquistadors. These horses would have been Andalusians, the Spanish breed that had been inbred with the Arab horse during the Moorish conquest of Spain. There is some evidence that in South America the horse became extinct much later than the Ice Age, and certainly the horse indigenous to Haiti still poses a mystery as to whether it was derived from an ancient form. In North America the horse was soon adopted by the Indians, who were natural horsemen. In all probability they simply watched the Spaniards with fascination and carefully copied them, acquiring their horses by theft or from illegal horse-traders. Obviously that country suited horses well, as great herds were to be found 150 years later.

Although the English settlers who founded Virginia and settled at Jamestown in 1607 did not import horses in their first ships, throughout the next decades they brought in English saddle horses and expanded contact with the Indian tribes, who by now had bred horses from the Andalusians. Once they had become established by about the mid seventeenth century, Virginian horses bred rapidly, and Virginia began to acquire a name for horse-breeding, so that it was soon selling to other colonies. The horses were tough but so small that stallions under a certain size were forbidden by law to mix with the mares – a common practice in Europe, in England and other countries where the government had tried to improve bloodstock.

As was to be expected from English colonists, racing was soon established in America. As in England, it was confined in general to the upper ranks of the colonists. Several of the mid-seventeenth-century colonists had been Royalists in the English Civil War during the 1640s, and those who were members of the King's Councils would certainly have been well-to-do in England. Often the problem was where to race. The great forests prevented racing on natural heathland, so that the main streets of villages were used as racecourses. As a result, quarter-mile racing was born and the Quarter Horse evolved, the race being a short quarter-mile dash in which collisions and crossings were part of the course. Racing did not appeal to all settlers, and in Puritan settlements it was usually forbidden. Such opposition was to recur frequently in the history of American racing.

New Amsterdam became New York on the surrender of the Dutch in 1664, and in 1665 the English Governor, Sir Richard Nicholls, set up the first full-size racecourse on Long Island. It was situated on an open plain, and so long races on the English model were possible. The Governor's Cup was established in imitation of the Newmarket Town Plate, which had been founded by Charles II to encourage better breeding. Championship races were thus almost simultaneously developed in America and England. Other trophies were offered to stimulate the import of better breeds and encourage horses bred in America.

As the colonies became richer, the courses grew in number. In New York in the early eighteenth century one opened on Manhattan Island, followed by the Greenwich Village course, and by 1725 the Church Farm course was hosting the first New York Subscription Plate.

In Virginia, the tobacco trade had brought considerable wealth and thus greater leisure and investment in horse-racing; but it had also led to the exhaustion of the soil after several tobacco crops, producing waste lands perfect for racecourses. By the end of the seventeenth century the Governor of Virginia was offering prizes. As in most countries at this time, racing was part of the regional fair, where it took place alongside many other amusements. Williamsburg was famous far and wide for its racing, so much so the students at William and Mary College had to be forbidden to keep racehorses. George Washington was a keen supporter of the Turf, keeping a stud at Mount Vernon, in Virginia, and racing his horses as any upper-class English gentleman would.

Previous two pages: Peytona beating Fashion in their historic match for $20,000 over the Union Course, Long Island, in May 1845.

Several owners of the pre-Revolutionary period were of particular importance. John Carter, who was educated in England at Cambridge, raced in Virginia, as did John Tayloe II, whose Mount Airy Stud was extremely important in the second half of the eighteenth century. He imported Childers (by Flying Childers's son Blaze), the origin of much of Virginia's best stock. John Baylor of Newmarket, Caroline County, imported Fearnought, by Regulus, a son of the Godolphin Arabian. Fearnought was 16 hands high and represented a deliberate attempt to increase the size of Virginia's horses which, because they were of Quarter Horse native blood, tended to be small and lacking in staying power.

One exception was Janus who, although only 14 hands high, was the grandson of the Godolphin Arabian. He arrived in Virginia in the late 1750s and lived to be over 30, gaining a notable reputation for producing fast Quarter Horses. Another important horse at this period –

Until the turn of the century, the majority of jockeys competing in heat races in America were black and owned by, or in the employ of, the horse owners.

Copyright, 1890,
BY
FREDERIC REMINGTON

189

again in the Godolphin Arabian line – was Kitty Fisher. Imported in 1759, she produced 13 foals, and her influence was substantial.

Maryland was another important racing state before the Revolution, having some 20 courses, the principal ones being Baltimore (with a three-day meeting) and Annapolis, both of which were well established by the 1740s. Samuel Ogle, who had a stud of considerable importance at Belair in Prince George's County, together with his brother-in-law Colonel Benjamin Tasker, imported many important horses, including Spark and Queen Mab. Tasker imported Selima, who was by the Godolphin Arabian out of a daughter of Flying Childers. After a successful racing career she went to stud at both Belair and Mount Airy. It was the inbreeding of these thoroughbreds with the Quarter Horse that produced the unique quality of the American thoroughbred.

In the first half of the eighteenth century, the Delancey family kept a large stud at Bouwerie Farm, outside New York. They imported Wildair, who was the son of Cade, and sire of Slamerkin, known as the 'Grandmother of the American Turf', since nearly all the best American horses have her in their pedigrees.

Among the Southern states, South Carolina was equally enthusiastic about racing. Charleston had a racecourse founded by its Jockey Club. Edward Fenwick founded his John's Island Stud about the mid eighteenth century and imported several of the Godolphin Arabian's grandsons, including Brutus, whose stock was very important in the colony. Of the mares he imported, Squirt, a granddaughter of Bartlett's Childers, is considered to have been the most influential.

While records are fragmented and obscure, newspapers and advertisements of the period give

Right: Diomed, owned by Sir Charles Bunbury, won the first Derby in 1780. Unsuccessful at stud in Britain, he was exported to Virginia at the age of 21 where he founded one of the great American thoroughbred dynasties. His lineal descendants included such champions as American Eclipse, Boston and Lexington. Painting by Francis Sartorious.

American Quarter Horse by Orren Mixer. Quarter Horses are sprinters and trace their ancestry back directly to the Godolphin Arabian through an English thoroughbred, Janus, which stood in Virginia in the mid eighteenth century.

some indication of the value placed on the thoroughbred at stud, and of the increasing interest taken in improving and importing stock. This was to benefit not only the thoroughbred.

While the War of Independence with Britain was still brewing, Congress was already following a policy anticipating hardship. Extravagance was the first target, and that meant hitting the importation of thoroughbreds, however this might affect the quality of the American horse as a whole. When the war finally broke out in 1776, it caused havoc in the thoroughbred world. Some horses were ridden into battle, others were seized by the British, country meetings were banned, and many records must have been lost. Once peace was signed in 1783, however, normality was restored, and importation began again quite quickly, particularly in the Southern states. In certain other states, however, the war provoked pockets of Puritan opposition. They regarded racing as something that had belonged to the frivolous upper classes and was somehow typically British; now that the latter had been removed, many hoped that the sport would go with them. Happily its roots were too strong in the country at large, particularly in the South. Nevertheless, this attitude, particularly in the North, meant a slow return to racing in some areas.

By the end of the eighteenth century it had been abolished in New York, and was only permitted again in 1821 for a trial period of five years, in Queen's County, New York. The Union Course, built to take advantage of this, was the scene of the famous North-South matches. The first was in May 1823, with Sir Henry for the South against American Eclipse for the North. Sir Henry's sire was Sir Archie, whose success at stud had been phenomenal. He had been bought for stud by General Davie, the founder of the University of North Carolina. Sir Henry's grandsire was Diomed, winner of the first Epsom Derby in 1780. American Eclipse was by Duroc, a son of Diomed, out of a mare by Grey Diomed. He was so named because his breeder, General Nathaniel Coles, considered him worthy of the name of the greatest horse ever known in England. At the time of the race he was already nine years old, some five years older than Sir Henry. The race, witnessed by a crowd estimated at 60,000, was the most celebrated in the States to that date. Sir Henry won the first of the three 4-mile heats and American Eclipse won the second. The final heat was just won by American Eclipse in an incredible show of stamina. One male-line descendant of Diomed and Sir Archie, who was to be of enormous significance to the American racehorse, was Boston, by Sir Archie's son Timoleon. Known as 'Old Whitenose', he won 40 of the 45 races in which he took part. His race against Fashion at the Union course in May 1842 was a celebrated North versus South match. Representing the North, Boston was defeated. He was leading sire from 1851-53, and his most famous sons were Lexington and Lecomte.

Virginia had no such Puritan scruples and was as enthusiastic as ever after the Revolution, boasting four principal racecourses, all with their own jockey clubs. Medley by Gimcrack, foaled in 1776, was imported to Virginia in 1785 by Malcolm Hart. As a sire of broodmares he had a great influence. Calypso was the most significant of these, and several others were outstanding when mated with the legendary Diomed. Diomed, bred in England by Richard Vernon at Newmarket, was by Florizel, a son of Herod. In 1780 he won the first English Derby and all his other three-year-old races. He was sent to stud at six, where he was a failure. By the age of 21 his stud fee had dropped from 5 to 2 guineas. In 1798 John Hoomes, of Bowling Green, Virginia made his historic purchase, buying Diomed from Sir Charles Bunbury for 50 guineas, and reselling him to Colonel Selden, of Free Hill in Virginia, for £1,000. Virginia clearly suited Diomed. Within three years his fertility had returned, and he was champion sire in 1803 at the age of 26. In the next five years of his life his progeny was extraordinary, and he was considered the progenitor of the American racehorse, through his line to Lexington.

Washington became the nation's capital in 1800, and shortly afterwards a new national course was established that became part of a growing social programme. President Jefferson, whose family had long been interested in racing, and Presidents Adams and Van Buren were among

Entrance to the Metairie Racecourse, New Orleans, 1867. It was on the Metairie Course in 1855 that Lexington set the record of 7 mins 19¾ secs over four miles. The importance of the Turf throughout the Southern states in the mid nineteenth century was immense. Few of the wealthy Louisiana planters were without their strings of thoroughbreds, which they raced every other day during the height of the social season.

those who raced at the National Course. However, even sophisticated Washington was not immune to the increasing disapproval of racing, and by the mid nineteenth century the course was dead. Not so in the South, where by 1800 race week at Charleston had become a veritable state carnival. Although the South Carolina Jockey Club went through various difficulties and changes, racing retained its position and respectability and Charleston was one of the few racecourses where women attended without anything being thought amiss. Richard Tattersall, the famous English bloodstock auctioneer, had exported many horses to South Carolina breeders, and in 1837 gave a whip to the South Carolina Jockey Club, as a prize for a race which was run under Newmarket rules. South Carolina owners were unusually military, and this fact, together with the well-ordered races run there, enabled them to stem the tide of Puritanism from the north.

The country was pushing ever westward. Kentucky, which had been carved out of Virginia and North and South Carolina just before the Revolution, developed apace in the years that followed the peace. Part of it was to become famous throughout the world – a large belt of limestone, which was not wooded and in some ways reflected the perfect limestone breeding areas of Europe. Even better, it grew the famous bluegrass, which provided the finest grazing possible for horses. Racing and breeding were quickly established. In 1793 Kentucky became a state, and

by the new century Lexington had established a Jockey Club and eight racecourses. Forty years later Kentucky had more racecourses than any other state, with four more even than Virginia. Its stallions from the stock of Diomed and Sir Archie, and from Blaze, who had been imported from England, contributed to its new-found success. The first Kentucky-bred national champion was considered to be Grey Eagle. He was by Woodpecker, whose grandsire was by Sir Archie. In 1839 Grey Eagle took on Wagner, considered to be the champion of Virginia. Wagner's rider was a slave by the name of Cato, who after two days of heats managed to win for Virginia and was rewarded with freedom.

One immensely influential horse of this time was Lord Jersey's Glencoe, who won the Two Thousand Guineas of 1834 and was the sire of Pocahontas. Bought by James Jackson of Tennessee in 1836, he was champion sire eight times before founding an important male line that included Hanover and Durbar II, both Derby winners. The racing centre of Tennessee was in the west, in an area named Summer County; while Nashville had had a Jockey Club since before the state was founded in 1807. One of Tennessee's most famous inhabitants was Andrew Jackson, a racing enthusiast and a founder member of Nashville racecourse. He raced under a pseudonym while President of the USA in 1828-37.

While expansion of horse-racing had gone westward with the extension of the frontier, the Californian Gold Rush of 1848 brought expansion from the coast. A racecourse was opened at San Francisco in 1851. West Coast enthusiasts took advantage of the developing Australian thoroughbred industry, and began to import horses from across the Pacific. Many courses opened and closed during this foundation period, almost all of which were modelled on those of the East.

In the far South, Louisiana was absorbed into the Union in 1803, but the French upper classes there were simply not interested in racing, and it was left to outsiders to develop it. Yelverton Oliver, from Kentucky, founded the New Orleans Eclipse Course and the Jockey Club, and by 1840 there was sufficient business in the state as a whole to support eight racecourses.

Another outsider in Louisiana, Richard Ten Broeck, came from a distinguished Albany family in New York State. He left West Point under a cloud and became a professional gambler. By 1847 he had bought the Metairie course in New Orleans and made it the best in the Union. In 1852 he bought a bay horse by the name of Darley, who had been bred in Kentucky, and changed his name to Lexington. The first race between Lexington, representing Louisiana, and Lecomte, representing Mississippi, took place on 1 April 1854 on the Metairie racecourse outside New Orleans. This was in the great State Post Stakes, designed to test inter-state rivalry. Lexington won easily, but the following week, in the Jockey Club Purse, Lecomte won both heats. Ten Broeck then issued a challenge of Lexington against any horse over 4 miles or against Lecomte's winning time. Lexington took the prize, beating the best previous time and establishing a record that was not to be broken for 20 years. Two years later Ten Broeck left for England and sold Lexington for the highest price ever paid in America for a horse, some $15,000. His purchaser was Robert Alexander, who owned Woodburn Farm, near Medway, Kentucky. Lexington made Woodburn the biggest stud in the world. He lived to be 25 years old and was champion sire 16 times (1861-74, 1876 and 1878). Of the 600 foals he sired, over 250 were winners.

Lexington's influence was in all good pedigrees of American horses by the end of the century. However, the fact that his pedigree contained some doubtful ancestry was the main reason for the protectionist measures in Britain known as the Jersey Act in 1913. Lexington was not alone in having such an influence. His great-great-grandsire Diomed had been inbred so much that it was clear that new importations were necessary. Eclipse was one very successful import, and his son Alarm was an enormously successful sprinter, as was his grandson Domino. Other descendants include Equipoise, one of the best horses of the 1930s, down to the enormous dollar-earner Dr Fager, and Ack Ack, the 1971 Horse of the Year.

Right: Lexington, by Boston and great-great-grandson of Diomed, was American leading sire 16 times in an almost unbroken line from 1861 to 1878. His influence on the development of the American thoroughbred in the nineteenth century is paramount.

Shortly before the Civil War of 1861-65 an enormous change in the style of American racing began. So far, America had concentrated on long-distance heats which were often cruel tests of endurance. By the mid nineteenth century shorter distances were being introduced, from 5 furlongs to 1½ miles, which were sheer tests of speed. The horses most suitable were two- and three-year-olds, which had the added advantage of bringing a quicker return on the owner's investment. The American thoroughbred, too, was changing as a direct result of importation and breeding policy. The old type of racing between owners to find the best horse was giving way to the public entertainment industry. Speed was a sure winner for public enthusiasm. By the last quarter of the nineteenth century the Americans were placing even more emphasis on speed than the British. The Kentucky Derby, founded in 1875, became the most important of the American Classic races and at 1¼ miles was ¼ mile shorter than the English Derby.

PREAKNESS

"A Classic Race Perpetuates His Name"

Bay Colt, 1867, by Lexington—Bay Leaf, by *Yorkshire

MILTON H. SANFORD, *Owner*   **WOODBURN FARM,** *Breeder*

Preakness, after whom the prestigious Preakness Stakes were named, was the winner of the Dinner Party Stakes which were run in October 1870 to celebrate the inauguration of the Pimlico racecourse in Maryland.

The clubhouse at Belmont Park photographed in 1905, its inaugural year and named after August Belmont, who had helped found the Jerome Park racecourse in 1866 with Leonard Jerome. The prestigious Belmont stakes were also named after him.

The Civil War brought about a sharp shift in the emphasis of racing from South to North. The Southern states were devastated, and many of the studs had been dispersed. Kentucky and Tennessee were neutral and, although they were the scene of fighting, they gained a great deal from the hostilities. Lexington lost only one season in the entire war. Racing was now seen as a popular entertainment that could make considerable sums of money, if properly organized and made attractive and respectable. The developing thoroughbred industries of Kentucky and Tennessee needed new markets now that the South had been impoverished. Two men, Leonard W. Jerome and August Belmont, were instrumental in bringing about a post-Civil War renaissance in racing. Jerome, the son of a rich farmer, was a Wall Street banker. As American Consul in Trieste he had travelled widely in Europe, and had been encouraged by the success of

racing in Paris in the 1850s. Belmont was the Rothschilds' first American agent and was himself a large-scale owner and breeder.

In 1865 Jerome bought an estate at Fordham, Long Island, and there built the Jerome Park racecourse. In 1866 he and Belmont formed the American Jockey Club, based on that of England. Its membership was exclusive, and its aim was to improve the quality of horses and the public's taste in equine sports. It was an immediate success. The Jockey Club leased the Jerome Park racecourse, and the first meeting took place in 1866. Racing became part of the fashionable social calendar, as it had once been in the South, and ladies were once more to be seen on the course. Success was infectious. The Jerome Park course showed that racing could be profitable and enjoyable without attracting Puritan disapproval or gangsterism. In the next ten years the sport began again with some strength – in Maryland with the Bennings and Timonium tracks, in New Jersey with Monmouth Park, and further south at Mobile in Alabama and New Orleans in Louisiana. In Kentucky the first Kentucky Derby was run on Churchill Downs on 17 May 1875. The surprise winner was Aristides, who won by one length.

Aristodes's sire was the famous Leamington, who had been imported by Sir Roderick Cameron for his Staten Island stud in 1865. He was the leading sire four times, and among his best progeny

Left: The Great Metropolitan Stakes at Jerome Park, New York, 1881 by E.P. Sanguinetti.

Iroquois was the double winner of the Epsom Derby and the St Leger in 1881. American leading sire in 1892, he won a total of 145 races.

THE FINISH

CHEERING THE WINNER.

The Suburban Handicap, 1891.
Loantaka, with Marty Bergen up,
captures the rich prize on the
Coney Island Jockey Club Track.
Together with the Metropolitan
Handicap and the Brooklyn
Handicap, the Suburban
Handicap forms the renowned
Belmont's Handicap Triple
Crown, considered one of the
most difficult of all racing
achievements.

were Longfellow, Parole and Iroquois. The last two belonged to Pierre Lorillard, who, with his brother George, had large and influential stables. Their father had emigrated from France and had made a fortune in tobacco. Parole ran a celebrated race at Pimlico, Maryland, in October 1877, beating the Kentucky champion Ten Broeck (named after the famous owner), the favourite, by four lengths. When he was taken to England two years later he won the City and Suburban Stakes and the Great Metropolitan Stakes. Following this success, Lorillard sent Iroquois to be trained at Newmarket. Iroquois was by Leamington out of Maggie B.B., himself out of Madeleine by Boston, and thus combined the strains of the best two horses imported from England at that time. He showed that America could breed the best, for he won the Epsom Derby and the St Leger of 1881. No American-bred horse was to win the Derby again until Never Say Die in 1954.

James Keene, who was English-born, was a Wall Street banker and famous as the owner of Foxhall. The son of Lexington, Foxhall was bred at Woodburn and was sent to Richard Ten Broeck in England. In France he won the 1881 Grand Prix de Paris, and the same year won the English Cesarewitch and the Cambridgeshire, and in 1882 the Ascot Gold Cup.

Throughout the second half of the nineteenth century new racecourses had been opening up in a haphazard fashion in America, and many were suffering from bad management, which in turn led to fraud. To some extent this reflected what was happening in France and England at this time. In short, there had been general over-expansion, but in France and England there had been greater

Foxhall, the only American racehorse in history to win the Grand Prix de Paris in 1881. He was also the winner of five stakes races in England, including the Cesarewitch and the Cambridgeshire in 1881 and the Ascot Gold Cup in 1882.

control. In 1890 Lorillard had managed to get the New York tracks to join together in a Board of Control, which in 1894 became the New York Jockey Club. It gained enormous prestige and, like its English counterpart, licensed trainers, jockeys and racetracks. Nevertheless, within ten years it was clear that it was not strong enough to retain control of racing, since by the turn of the century crime had entered the racing world in a big way. There was much money to be made from gate money, and protection rackets and betting frauds mushroomed. In 1908 betting was made illegal in New York and one state after another followed, so that out of 314 courses in 1897 only 25 remained by 1910. By 1911 there was no racing at all in New York State.

Kentucky racing benefited enormously, but the breeding industry was badly affected. Both England and France, alarmed that they might become flooded with American bloodstock, passed protectionist measures. It was in Kentucky, which had so much to lose, that a breakthrough was finally achieved. In 1906 Colonel Matt Winn had formed the American Turf Association, breaking away from the other Turf Associations that were constantly disagreeing with one another. Such was the importance of the industry in Kentucky that the authorities moved in to form the Kentucky State Racing Commission, which became the most important racing body in the state. Kentucky was quickly followed by all states where racing still existed. A Kentucky legal case in 1908 had a profound effect on American racing finance. When the Mayor of Louisville tried to enforce a law against bookmaking, the Court of Appeal ruled in his favour but allowed pool betting. That same year Colonel Matt Winn found a dozen old *pari-mutuel* (Tote) machines for the Kentucky Derby, which had never become popular. Since then every state has adopted them, making them the only legal form of betting. The *pari-mutuel* machines succeeded because they reduced the crime associated with bookmaking, provided higher winnings and gave the State an enormous new source of revenue. Nevertheless, many of the tracks had gone to the wall. Belmont had absorbed nearly all the customers and important races in New York, and the large similarly absorbed the smaller in most other major cities.

While racing in America was going through hard times at home, the success of Americans abroad was phenomenal. Richard Ten Broeck had arrived with great success in England in the 1850s, followed by Lorillard and James Keane. By the end of the nineteenth century August Belmont and the Whitney family were not only winning many races but were exporting training and racing procedures from America to England. The success of American jockeys in the Derby was astounding. Lester Reiff won on Volodyovski in 1901, J.H. Martin on Ard Patrick in 1902, Danny Maher on Rock Sand in 1903, on Cicero in 1905 and on Spearmint in 1906. Not only did they win the best races, but also a large percentage of races as a whole. Tod Sloan and Lester Reiff at their peak won a quarter of their races. The scale of their success showed how quick the Americans were to take up opportunities abroad when they had contracted at home. American racing had become truly international.

World War I hardly touched American racing and all the major races were run. When August Belmont II sold all his foals in 1917, he included one of the greatest American horses of all time. This was Man O' War, by Fair Play out of Muhubah by Rock Sand, bought by Samuel D. Riddle. He won all but one race, when he was defeated by the Whitney family's Upset, and even beat Sir Barton, the first winner of the American Triple Crown. Man O' War won the Preakness Stakes and the Belmont Stakes, breaking seven American records during his three-year-old season. He exerted an enormous influence on the American racehorse, and is to be found in the pedigrees of Buckpasser and Arts and Letters, as well as those of the Epsom Derby winners Never Say Die, Sir Ivor and Relko.

American racing, which had slumped badly before the war, emerged much slimmer and fitter as a result. With the state governments' new vested interest in a share of betting profits from the *pari-mutuels*, and the resulting increase in prize money, owners and breeders were encouraged to

Right: The first Futurity race at Sheepshead Bay, Long Island, in 1888, painted by Louis Maurer. This six-furlong race commanded prize money of $40,900 and was the richest race ever to have been run at the time. It was won by Proctor Knott out of a field of 14.

invest as never before. Even the Depression of the interwar years did not affect the bloodstock industry as badly as it did others. State budgets were such that the governments were thinking up all kinds of ways of raising revenue. By the mid 1930s another ten states had legalized racing, including California, where the courses at Tanforan and Santa Anita became immensely important.

The achievements of the Hancock family are dealt with elsewhere (see page 218), but their position in American thoroughbred history was extremely important between the wars. Arthur B. Hancock was one of the first owners to buy stallions internationally and was the first to buy as a member of a syndicate, a system which was to have an enormous effect on markets as the twentieth century progressed. He persuaded many leading breeders like William Woodward and Marshal Field to join him and spread the expense of purchase, beginning with the French horse, Sir Gallahad III, bought in 1925. A great success at stud, Sir Gallahad's progeny included Gallant

Whirlaway, sired by Blenheim, was to head the long domination of American racing by Calumet Farm which had been inherited by 1931 by Warren Wright. The 1941 Triple Crown winner, Whirlaway was cured of his tendency to bear out from the rails by the use of blinkers.

Fox, winner of the American Triple Crown. He was champion American stallion four times and was in constant demand for the rest of his life. Hancock imported the Derby winner Blenheim in 1936 from the Aga Khan. Blenheim had been bought for the Aga Khan by George Lambton for 4,100 guineas and was sold to America for £45,000. The English registered their disapproval at this sale, as they were alarmed at the increasing commercialism of racing and at the fact that few could pay such prices. Blenheim proved to be a good buy. His progeny included the Triple Crown Winner Whirlaway, and he was in the top 20 list of stallions for 12 years.

Other of the Aga Khan's stallions followed. In the dark year 1940, Mahmoud and Bahram were exported from England to America; both were Derby winners, and Bahram had won the Triple Crown. The most important horse exported by the Aga Khan to America was Nasrullah, who became leading American sire five times. Nasrullah was highly temperamental, though when his progeny was bred with that of Princequillo, who had been imported early in the war from Ireland, there appeared to be a perfect balance, since Princequillo was notable for staying power and good nature. From these strains came Mill Reef, who won the Derby and the Prix de l'Arc de Triomphe in 1971, and the American Triple Crown winner Secretariat.

The increasing interest in racing of individual states, with their desire to increase tax income, led to their greater involvement as a whole. Racing became the responsibility of the state racing commissions, the local racing associations and the American Jockey Club working together, in sharp contrast to England, where the Jockey Club is still largely the controlling force. The state racing commissions have the power to authorize the meetings of the local associations, and the licensing of jockeys, trainers and owners, and can penalize all those connected if their regulations are thwarted. The commissions pass the regulations of the individual states, and these are automatically ratified and made effective in other states, although each state retains the independent power to grant licences. The local racing associations are the local racecourse authorities, providing facilities for racing, the administration of betting and collection of taxes, in a similiar way to any racecourse operation in the western world.

The Jockey Club's powers are considerably less than those of its counterpart in England. It supervises all aspects of the thoroughbred, from breeding and keeping records to registering owners and supporting research. As regards racing, it provides a representative steward at each meeting and is the body responsible for racing regulations overall. Its members are the most important breeders and owners in the nation, and are elected for life.

The enormous expansion of the thoroughbred industry in postwar America was not without its problems. There was a period in the 1960s when the expansion was felt to be getting slightly out of hand, as more states and racecourse owners fought to squeeze more revenue out of the industry. Annual foal production rose almost three times from 1960 to 1980. Kentucky, the leading producer, sensibly continued to concentrate on quality production and now produces half of the Grade One stakes winners. Nevertheless, in thoroughbred production as a whole Kentucky was overtaken by California in the late 1960s for three years, while Florida came a close third. The rise of California is shown in the number of Grade One stakes held at the Hollywood Park and Santa Anita courses alone. In 1980 these accounted for 23 of the 72 races held throughout America that are considered as Grade One.

By the second half of the twentieth century the top-class American thoroughbred had become synonymous with speed. It was a remarkable achievement of careful selection, which resulted in American-bred horses breaking many all-time records. The American racing programme is such that it makes an extraordinary demand on the racehorse. In terms of investment, it is vital that in its season from late-two-year-old to mid-three-year-old the horse should show its maximum ability over middle distance.

Attention to quality rather than quantity by leading breeders in Kentucky and elsewhere has paid dividends. Their international superiority was increasingly obvious by the 1960s, as American victories in the English and French Classic races became a regular feature. Some buyers in Europe, like Alec Head and Vincent O'Brien, were quick to buy part of this American success. Northern Dancer and his progeny have had extraordinary success in the last 25 years. Bred by E.P. Taylor, he was by Nearctic out of Natalma and won 21 races out of 22 including the Preakness Stakes and the Kentucky Derby in a new record time. When sent to stud he was syndicated for $2,400,000 and when mated with Flaming Page produced Nijinsky who was bought by O'Brien. In 1970 Nijinsky became the first horse since 1935 to win the British Triple Crown. He was never leading sire in Britain, unlike Northern Dancer who achieved this four times. However he has sired many Classic winners including Shadeed, Green Dancer and the 1986 Epsom Derby winner Shahrastani.

Parallel with the stimulation of racing as a means of raising state revenue were the taxation incentives for owners. In America owners can offset losses sustained from owning racehorses against profits made elsewhere. Moreover, to do so the owner has only to make a racing profit in two out of seven years. American owners thus have an enormous advantage compared with their British and French counterparts. It is this concession that has fuelled the extraordinary rise in bloodstock prices of the last ten years, the basis of which is relatively unstable. It is vital that the industry should place as much emphasis on quality as quantity, since that has always guaranteed the success of racing as long-term entertainment. Happily, in America there are enough powerful men steeped in the tradition and love of the thoroughbred over many generations to ensure both quality and entertainment for the future.

Churchill Downs, Louisville, where the Kentucky Derby has been held since its inauguration in 1875.

Mill Reef, by Never Bend out of Milan Mill, was bred in the United States by his owner Paul Mellon in 1968. His brilliant racing record ended when he fractured his near foreleg but his stud career at the National Stud in Newmarket was equally important. Champion sire in 1978, he sired many Classic winners, including Shirley Heights, Acamas and Wassl.

NORTH AMERICAN STUD FARMS

KENTUCKY

Kentucky lies in the heart of America's Middle West. Many of the world's most valuable racehorses are bred there on mile upon mile of rolling pasture, known as the Bluegrass Country. The scale on which these stud farms operate is unprecedented in the history of racehorse breeding. It has always been possible to reap large financial benefits from thoroughbred breeding in Kentucky; it has recently developed into a vast industry, however.

The centre of this industry is Lexington, a small, high-rise town consisting primarily of banks, insurance companies, bloodstock agencies, and specialist advertising and publicity companies. Its lack of character has been severely criticized by John Gaines, whose architectural tastes are well illustrated by Gainesway Farm, though in fairness it should be added that in Lexington entertaining takes place in the home, as it does in Newmarket.

A few miles north of Lexington is what remains of the first of Kentucky's famous thoroughbred farms, Elmendorf. In 1950 this property was divided and 504 acres were sold by P.A.B. Widener III to a Cleveland business consortium, as well as the farm's breeding stock, and two outstanding stallions, Roman and Unbreakable. Two years later these businessmen sold what is today known as Elmendorf to Maxwell Gluck, a New York clothing manufacturer. Since then Elmendorf has added to its reputation by breeding such champions as Protagonist, Shadow Brook and Talking Picture. Sadly, the Wideners pulled down the splendid old colonial house to avoid paying taxes, leaving only the porch with its four magnificent columns topped by a balustrade and reached by a flight of eight steps, with larger-than-life stone lions on either side. Flanking the porch are the remains of a garden, dotted with groups of beech and oak trees. This imposing legacy of bygone days is the focal point of an annual gala fund-raising ball, with the surrounding area tented over for dancing.

Keeneland racecourse, six miles west of Lexington, began back in the 1920s as a private enterprise. Its instigator, Jack Keene, had formerly trained for Czar Nicholas of Russia, and it was his idea to build a race-track, stabling and club house, where friends could meet and race their horses. After spending twenty years and $400,000 of his own money developing this, he sold out in 1935 to the Keeneland Association. From a highly ambitious start Keeneland has developed into a near-perfect park racecourse, landscaped and planned to accommodate the enormous crowds who flock to the 16-day April and October meetings. Race days run from Tuesday through to Saturday, since this is a part of the world where Sunday is regarded as a day of rest.

From April 26 until June 29 racing moves to the more shady course of Churchill Downs, and it is here in early May that the now famous Kentucky Derby is run, with a garland of flowers flung around the victor's neck. There are 70,000 races run annually in the US, of which the majority are 'claiming' races, not always popular with the owner; for when a horse wins, anyone wishing to take over its ownership is entitled to do so for the amount stated on the race-card (i.e. the value of the race), and the only way the owner can avoid losing his horse is to outbid the man who is claiming it. In practice, there is a good deal of the gentleman's agreement in these claiming races.

Left: The Keeneland Race Track.

The Kentucky Training Centre was opened in 1970 by Arnold G. Pennin, a Lexington vet, and Rex Ellsworth, a Californian breeder, on a piece of land on the corner of Paris Pike and Johnston Road. It has stabling for 300 horses, an open mile gallop, and a 3-furlong covered all-seasons track. The Spendthrift Stud Farm also offers trainers facilities to board their horses in training, for unlike Europe there is a migrant pattern to American racing, with Florida making a big effort to attract horses and racegoers south in winter. The Florida racecourses of Gulfstream Park, Hialeah Park and Calder promote themselves vigorously and successfully. Kentucky is under snow in winter; thus all those whose association with racing is not confined to the day-to-day handling of bloodstock take off for the sunshine of Florida, where the events include the month-long Florida Derby Festival at Gulfstream Park every March.

The Keeneland yearling sales are held in mid-July (a three-day sale), followed by further yearling sales for seven days in September. The first of these sales took place in 1943, since when they have gone from strength to strength, due largely to the professional American approach to preparing yearlings for sales. At all the top stud farms where yearlings are sent up for auction there is intensive pre-sale preparation. Nowhere is this more thoroughly understood than at Taylor Made Farm, which takes in yearlings as boarders, breaks them, and teaches them to act and look like grown racehorses, even to the point of learning to parade around an indoor ring, much like the auction ring at Keeneland. There is a waiting list for this specialist treatment of valuable yearlings and there is seldom a vacant stall in the broodmare barns. Here boarders are accepted, who wait to foal before going back to one of the many stallions that are the real life-blood of this community. Everywhere in Kentucky there is an awareness that, however well bred a yearling may be, it will not fetch a top price unless it has the guts and character to become a great racehorse. In Europe yearlings are now being given considerably more attention than previously, and there is growing scope for anyone who is a competent horseman and has stabling facilities to take on this interim period in a horse's education.

Kentucky has become the breeding capital of the racing world for the simple reason that many of the top stallions are at stud there. It therefore influences the transportation business, since many of the world's best broodmares are sent to be covered by these stallions, and the farms which take top care of these horses, like Circle O and Hagyard, which are used by Alec Head and Roland de Chambure, stand to benefit.

BLUEGRASS FARM, KENTUCKY

Nelson Bunker Hunt is the largest private landowner in Kentucky, and one of the leading owner-breeders at an international level. The Bluegrass Farm, the hub of his breeding operation, is on the opposite side of the Versailles Road from Calumet, and right by Keeneland Racecourse and Lexington Airport. Although it is in fact seven farms rolled into one, and comprises 7,500 acres, not all the tracks are adjoining, and the Bluegrass Farm sign can be found swinging by a farm entrance elsewhere in the country. It was natural for Bunker Hunt to base himself as centrally as possible in Lexington, in view of his other farming operations. As well as his stud-farm complex, he owns a herd of 3,000 beef cattle, the largest tobacco base in Kentucky, and 1,000 acres devoted to feed corn and soya beans.

In 1976 Nelson Bunker Hunt won the Epsom Derby with Empery, the French Derby with Youth, and the Hollywood Invitational with Dahlia, all within a one-week period. Dahlia was

Right: Cloud House, the main residence at Bluegrass Farm.

Below: A new-born foal by Youth, the 1976 winner of the French Derby.

bred by Bunker Hunt, and the story as to how he acquired her dam, Pamplona II, is a fascinating one. Nelson was in Lima, Peru, one Sunday, and decided to go to the races. Not knowing a word of Spanish, he looked around for somebody who might speak English and stumbled by chance on Juan Magot, who had been Peru's leading trainer for some fifteen years. Magot and Hunt got into a long conversation, during which Magot told him of a recent disappointment. His best race mare had just bowed a tendon a couple of weeks back and he did not know what he was going to do with her; since he was not a breeder, he supposed he would have to sell her. Hunt asked to see the mare, liked her, and thought that the price Magot was asking seemed reasonable, so there and then he bought Pamplona II.

The success story continued. Pamplona II was the dam of Dahlia, who besides her Hollywood triumph twice won both the King George VI and Queen Elizabeth Stakes at Ascot and the Benson and Hedges Gold Cup at York, with other wins in Ireland and France, before going to stud. By Lyphard she produced Dahar, who remained in training as a four-year-old to win four times out of 12 starts. Dahlia is now featured in the Hall of Fame at Saratoga, New York, as one of two horses by leading sire Vaguely Noble (the other being Exceller) who won more than $1 million. Bunker Hunt bought privately a half-share in Vaguely Noble, having been outbid at the Newmarket December sales by Robert Franklyn of Los Angeles. Vaguely Noble went on to win the 1968 Prix de l'Arc de Triomphe.

When discussing the breeding of horses, this square-shouldered Texan will say that it is an evolving business. Blood-lines that have been good in the 1980s may be no good in the 1990s. He goes on to say that he does not think that anyone has ever quite understood why one horse is good and another is bad. For this reason he feels that nobody is ever likely to gain a stranglehold or dominate racing. Unlike the Sangster-Vincent O'Brien partnership or Sheikh Mohammed Al Maktoum, Nelson Bunker Hunt does not pay phenomenal amounts when he goes to the sales. He also points out that the interest on such sums of money should never be ignored. People who can afford $10-15 million a year *ought* to be buying some good horses.

Nelson Bunker Hunt also owns Waikato Stud in New Zealand, with 40 mares and four good stallions. He says of New Zealand that it is hard to keep up with what is happening down there, and feels that some of his horses sent as foals have not done well in the Southern Hemisphere. The stud farm remains, though he says that it might have worked out better had he been able to spend more time there. Meanwhile he has recently purchased 750 acres in Boyle County, Kentucky, thus increasing his land-holding to over 8,000 acres, and it is on this new track of land that he plans to run his yearlings.

Although he owns a great deal of the Bluegrass Country, he lives and operates out of Dallas. In 1985 he was the winner of the Eclipse Award for the year's outstanding breeder. Both Trillion, who was the dam of the Irish Two Thousand Guineas winner Triptych, and Dahlia are part of the valuable Bunker Hunt brood-mare band, which now numbers 212 mares. Since producing Triptych, Trillion has produced only one foal, a full sister named Barger, who has been placed once in France. Since 1984 she has been barren to covers of Mr Prospector, Nijinsky II and Riverman. Dahlia, however, produced a full sister to Dahar in 1985. She has a three-year-old colt, Delegant, in training in France, and a four-year-old filly, Begonia, who has been taken out of training in California. She is also the dam of Rivlia, on whom great stud hopes currently rest.

Nelson Bunker Hunt takes success and failure in his stride, saying that being in the oil business makes you philosophical. This attitude does, however, waver sightly when it comes to his bloodstock. He also says that nobody should become involved with horses unless they love them.

Right: Some of the top broodmares at Bluegrass Farm, including Dahlia, Gazala II, Goofed and Nobiliary.

CALUMET FARM, KENTUCKY

The Calumet breeding and racing complex lies east of Lexington Airport on 850 acres, impressively fenced by white-painted posts and rails. Every barn and building is smartly painted white, while the doors and windows, and the flooring in the stallion barn, are scarlet. The roofs are high and in green synthetic tiling. From the air the buildings look like a series of sports pavilions set among the trees. The Colonial-style residence is reached from the Versailles Road, through a high black wrought-iron gate. The shutters on the two-storey house are scarlet, as are the two miniature jockeys, wearing the family scarlet and dark blue racing silks, that stand on either side of the front door.

Between 1940 and 1963, Calumet's owner headed the list of winning owners 12 times, was leading breeder 14 times and won the Kentucky Derby eight times. The man who brought all this about was Warren Wright Sr. A businessman from Ohio, he founded this legendary thorough-bred racing stables in 1931, on a farm originally bought in the 1920s by his father, William Monroe Wright, the founder of the Calumet Baking Powder Company, for his Standardbred operation. In 1936 Warren Wright made two important purchases to which the stud farm virtually owes its reputation. His first buy was Bull Lea, bought as a yearling at Saratoga for $14,000; his other buy was a quarter-share in Blenheim II, whom Bull Hancock had bought from the Aga Khan for the then unheard of price of $225,000 to stand at Claiborne.

Bull Lea was to become one of the greatest sires in American Turf history. His runners made him America's leading sire five times from 1947 to 1953. Apart from being the sire of Citation,

who won the Triple Crown for Warren Wright Sr, he sired eight other champions, including three Kentucky Derby winners, and 28 other top-class winners. With his quarter-share in Blenheim II, Warren Wright was rewarded with Calumet's first champion, Whirlaway, the first of Blenheim II's crop of runners as a sire. Thus Calumet shot to prominence, principally due to Bull Lea, to his son Citation and to Whirlaway.

During the whole of this highly successful era the Calumet horses were trained by Ben Jones. Though not a young man – he was 56 when he accepted the job as trainer at Calumet – he won race after race, and his overall management of the racing operation was exemplary. He also established a father-and-son team with his son Jimmy handling all the day-to-day chores. They broke a record with Citation, the first-ever horse to win $1 million.

Secreto, by Northern Dancer out of Betty's Secret, was the 1984 Epsom Derby winner. He returned to the United States after his three-year-old racing career and retired to stud at Calumet in 1985.

On Christmas Day 1950, Warren Wright Sr died. He was succeeded at Calumet by his widow who two years later married Rear-Admiral Gene Markey. Although the Markeys won a number of top-class races, by the mid 1970s they had reduced their band of broodmares. Finally they hired the gifted trainer John Veitch, who inherited what was virtually a group of empty stables. In 1977 he began to pull the stable together. Our Mims was champion filly, and the following year her half-brother, Alydar, began to win a number of good races. Though he never won a Kentucky Derby, this long-striding flashy chestnut was a great favourite with the betting public, and was responsible for reviving Calumet's fortunes. In 1983, Alydar was North America's leading sire of two-year-olds, and he is the sire of 10 stake winners to date.

In August 1982, Mrs Markey died and Calumet was inherited by her grand-daughter, Mrs J.T. Lundy. Lundy comes from the Bluegrass; born and raised in Midway, Kentucky, he worked for his father who is a commercial breeder. Like his predecessor Warren Wright, he is foremost a business-breeder, and openly admits to having little liking for tradition, prestige or public image. John Veitch resigned, and was replaced by another father-son trainer team, Frank and David Whiteley. This new operation has the money, and Lundy knows the breeding business. Four stallions now stand at Calumet Farm: Alydar, who has Native Dancer as his grandsire; Highland Blade; Raise a Cup, sire of 26 stakes winners; and Secreto, who is by the legendary Northern Dancer. There are 50-odd horses in training and a racing stable that races to make money. Under this new and energetic team, Calumet looks set to regain its former Turf glory.

Alydar, by Raise a Native out of Sweet Tooth, was North America's leading sire of two-year-olds in 1983, with record earnings of $1,136,063. Currently standing at Calumet, he has sired 10 stakes winners to date, including Miss Oceana and Althea.

CLAIBORNE FARM, KENTUCKY

Claiborne Farm, near the little town of Paris in Bourbon County, consists of 3,200 rolling acres of pastureland, tree-planted and protected from the winds that sweep across Kentucky. The fencing is all black-creosoted wood. From the road all that can be seen is the front porch of the handsome white two-storey house, reached by a long tree-lined drive. In front of the house is a wide circular sweep of well-tended lawn, a few groups of trees, and beyond a field for yearlings.

Mrs Waddell Hancock created this house during her 42 years of marriage to the famous 'Bull' Hancock, transforming it into the elegant and comfortable six-bedroom house it is today. The flower-filled entrance hall and the three main reception rooms reflect the personality of Waddell Hancock. Pride of place is given to her late husband's gold and silver trophies, set against dark-panelled bookshelves in the drawing-room. For all his success as an owner-breeder, Bull Hancock never won the Kentucky Derby, though both his sons have since done so. When Waddell was asked how he might have felt were he still alive, she replied without a pause: 'He'd have been furious, and then mighty proud of them.'

The main residence, Claiborne House.

Swale, the Claiborne-bred winner of the 1984 Kentucky Derby, was named by Waddell, who has a superstition about names with five letters. She talks with equal enthusiasm about her son Seth, who took over the running of Claiborne on his father's death in 1972. Seth was only 23 at the time, and to find himself the employer of 100 people and responsible for some 500 horses was daunting, even for a boy brought up in the business. Although his mother insists that she is not and never has been involved in the actual operation of the stud farm, she is very much around and about. One of her great pleasures is to escort friends around the property, recalling visits of friends from England and Ireland, describing her late husband's preferences, and above all talking about the enormous success her son Seth has had since he took over the running of the farm.

Only a year after his father's death Seth brought about his first spectacular syndication. Penny Tweedy had just inherited the Meadow Stud racing establishment from her father, Christopher Chenery, and needed money to pay off inheritance taxes. She asked Seth if he could syndicate her two-year-old chestnut colt, Secretariat, who had won the hearts of the racing public and been named Horse of the Year. In four days Seth had sold 28 shares in the horse for the following season, when it would be retired to stud, for what was then a world record of over $6 million. Later in the same year he also put together the syndication of Riva Ridge. Since then, season by season, Seth Hancock has strengthened his position in the racing world. Although it was his father's organization that bred Wajima, the champion three-year-old colt of 1975, and Ivanjica, the filly who won the 1976 Prix de l'Arc de Triomphe, it reflected well on Seth's management. By 1974 Tiller and other horses bred by Seth had begun to make his reputation. Today there are 19 stallions standing at Claiborne Farm and a further ten at Marchmont, an extension of Claiborne.

Kennedy's Creek runs through the extensive acreage of Claiborne Farm.

They include Secretariat, who justified Seth's record syndication fee by going on to win the Kentucky Derby of 1973 in record time, and Sir Ivor, the 1968 Epsom Derby winner belonging to Raymond Guest, then US Ambassador to Ireland.

Bull Hancock and his father Arthur before him were great Anglophiles. After World War II Bull set about drumming up business on an international scale, especially in England. He was an emphatic believer in the outcross and the infusion of different blood into the home-bred lines, and scores of other American breeders followed his example. His syndication of Nasrullah back in 1949 was the beginning of the modern American trend towards buying in Europe, in this instance from the Aga Khan. This great horse was leading sire in England once and five times in America, with a total of 99 stakes winners among his progeny. Nasrullah is to this day remembered at Claiborne for his mean disposition and his many attempts at kicking out at anyone he disliked, including both Bull Hancock and the vet, who on several occasions narrowly missed his flying hooves.

Fortunately Nasrullah seems to have been alone in his dislike of his environment, for great care went into the planning of the stallion barns by Arthur and Bull Hancock, who were believers in tree-shaded paddocks and planted rows of maples, pin oaks and sycamores everywhere on the property. The stallion barns are near each horse's individual paddock, allowing them to see and commune with each other, whether they are out in the field, where they spend most of their day, or back in their stalls. Constantly handled and often being shown to visitors, they all come galloping across the paddock at the call of their name.

The stallion barn at Claiborne Farm. The stud has 300 broodmares and 30 stallions currently standing, including two of America's leading sires: million dollar earner, Secretariat (by home-bred Bold Ruler) and Spectacular Bid, the 1973 American Triple Crown winner by Bold Bidder.

Arthur Hancock, the creator of Claiborne, was principally a vendor of yearlings. He had a flair for salesmanship, and unlike his son and grandson enjoyed this side of the business. When Bull took over the farm, he switched the weight of his breeding operation from selling yearlings to racing them; and now his son Seth is doing the same thing and developing a reputation for his ability to judge, promote and stand stallions. The late Captain Boyd-Rochfort, trainer to King George VI and the present Queen, said of Bull Hancock that he was the finest judge of a horse that he knew. Not surprisingly, the Captain sent his stepson, Henry Cecil, to Claiborne to live on the farm and learn from Bull, one of many young men who came here to learn the ways of breeding and racing horses.

Claiborne's links with Ireland and Newmarket continue from one generation to another. Seth welcomes students from other racing establishments, while his mother continues to play an active role as a hostess. For all Claiborne's outstanding commercial success, it is low-key and run on a very personal basis. Claiborne is for horse people. 'As long as our horses keep winning, people will know what we are doing.' That is Seth speaking, but it might equally well have been his father.

Nijinsky II, bred by E.P. Taylor in Canada, by Northern Dancer out of Flaming Page, raced exclusively in Europe as a two- and three-year-old and was the 1970 winner of the Two Thousand Guineas, the Epsom Derby and the St Leger (the English 'Triple Crown'). Retired to stud in 1971, he has sired many Classic winners, including Shadeed, winner of the 1985 Two Thousand Guineas at Newmarket.

GAINESWAY FARM, KENTUCKY

Gainesway Farm is on the Paris Pike road out of Lexington, on land that once belonged to the Whitneys, with nothing larger than a creosoted post-and-rail fence dividing the two properties. On this recenlty acquired land John Gaines, an East Coast businessman, has created a stud-farm complex that has not only fascinated the whole of the international breeding and racing fraternity, but has won for Gainesway Farm the American Institute of Architect's 1984 Honor Award.

The architect was Theodore M. Ceraldi of New York, who worked in close collaboration with

Aerial view of Gainesway Farm, founded in 1964, showing the neat complex of red-tiled barns. Set in 500 acres, Gainesway currently stands many famous horses of international repute, among them, Lyphard, by Northern Dancer, and Vaguely Noble.

John Gaines and the stud farm's manager, Joe L. Taylor. He created a complex of barns with high-pitched roofs of reddish-brown tiles, linked with pathways of gravel and birch chips, set in the rolling bluegrass countryside. In front of the offices is a stone-sided pool, with jetting fountains.

However, stud farms stand or fall on the results they produce. Apart from the aesthetic standards that have been set by Gainesway, it also stands 41 of the world's most famous racehorses currently at stud in 1986. Within a comparatively short space of time John Gaines has become possibly the world's most important syndicator of stallions. In 1964 he syndicated Crozier, from which point on he has gradually become associated with almost all the top names in racing. Nelson Bunker Hunt of Texas, who owns the Bluegrass Farm at which he boards his many broodmares, always turns to John Gaines to syndicate his stallions. Mrs Jacqueline Getty Phillips sent Bates Motel to stand at Gainesway, and Blushing Groom was sold by the Aga Khan to this farm for syndication. Stavros Niarchos's Femme de Nuit was bred at Gainesway, and is by the Niarchos-owned Cresta Rider. Vaguely Noble and L'Emigrant also stand at Gainesway.

One of Gainesway's stalls. This sophisticated breeding operation boasts some of the most luxurious accommodation for its horses.

Lyphard, who won 14 races in France, Ireland and England for Mme Pierre Wertheimer, is now a constantly visited veteran of Gainesway; his son Lyphard's Wish, who was raced in Europe by Daniel Wildenstein, is also standing there. The list is a formidable one.

John Gaines has concentrated to a large extent on European blood lines. As he points out, it was the imported horse, crossed with the great American stock, that made the American thoroughbred the pride of the world. It becomes clear after only a short time at this stallion farm that it is the horse itself, and the satisfaction derived from breeding a Classic winner, that counts with this man, not just the amount of money any of the horses may represent. His right-hand man, Joe L. Taylor, who has been with him from the beginning, is a third-generation Kentuckian. Like Gaines, he is a stickler for detail. There may be as many as 17 horse-vans arriving together, with brood mares booked to the various stallions, but everything progresses smoothly and efficiently.

The stallions are housed in four-stalled barns, with one man to care for each barn. Each has an independent section where a horse can be hosed down and which supplies the exact amount of food for the four occupants. The ventilation is well thought out; the high roof-pitch is designed to create a soaring interior air space, and the height is sufficient to direct the wind flow through the copper ridge-ventilator that runs along the roof apex. The barns are placed so that prevailing winds hit the broadest side of the ventilator – an important factor, since temperature changes occur regularly in spring, during the day reaching the high 80 degrees F, and at night dropping as low as 45 degrees. Kentucky has snow in winter, and storms and tornadoes at other times, with humidity and temperature rising in high summer. Such stabling tempers all weathers. The covering barn is enormous, with stalls for the visiting mares, and so arranged that two stallions can cover mares simultaneously. All matings are videotaped. The whole farm is as clean and as well-run as an expensive private health clinic.

Joe Taylor, who knows his horses, is fond of saying how much Lexington has changed from his grandfather's day, reminding one that horse-breeding is no longer a cottage industry. The value of the nomination fees is now around $120 million a year, and it is Taylor's job to see that every mare sent to Gainesway leaves the premises in foal. He keeps in touch constantly with all the surrounding stud farms where the mares booked to his stallions are boarded, so that they arrive to be covered only when the moment is correct. Conversely, he does his utmost to conserve the energies of all the stallions under his charge, so they are not overworked or asked to cover a mare unnecessarily. He says that the use of video has helped enormously when, as sometimes happens, an owner says that his mare did not get a good covering.

Walter Hefner, the international industrialist and Swiss-based banker, owns shares in 16 of Gainesway's stallions. He agrees that it has the finest breeding operation in the world, because the horses are meticulously cared for, to a point that seems almost too luxurious for an animal. For John Gaines this luxury is a question of looking ahead to the future. 'I've always been very critical of the buildings put up in downtown Lexington and elsewhere. Since I was going into the breeding business in a big way, I wanted to make an architectural statement as well as a statement in terms of horsemanship.' Indeed, he has done both.

In 1979 John Gaines conceived the idea of a Breeders' Cup, now an important annual event, and set about enlisting others in the thoroughbred breeding business to support him. The idea was triggered off by the disparity between what race mares and fillies were able to win, compared with the stakes earned by the colts. In the USA at the time 30 per cent of the stakes races were for fillies and mares and 70 per cent were for male horses, so the idea of holding a series of races for fillies and mares culminating in a championship was born. After a good deal of groundwork, a ten-man executive committee was formed, consisting of John Gaines, William S. Farish III, Bertram R. Firestone, Charles P. Taylor, Brownell Combs II, Breton C. Jones, Nelson Bunker Hunt, John

A. Nerud, John C. Mabee, and Seth Hancock. The financing was so arranged that each stallion syndicated should contribute the price of its stud fee, and that every owner of a weanling should pay $500 into the corporation, with the result that a $20 million programme has got under way.

One of the four-stalled stallion barns at Gainesway Farm, where possibly the largest number of syndicated stallions currently stand.

GREENTREE STUD, KENTUCKY

The original Greentree Stud Farm, created by Mrs Payne Whitney in 1926, consisted of 750 acres marked out by 30 miles of black fences, on the Paris Pike road. When she died in 1944, the farm was inherited jointly by John (Jock) Hay Whitney and his sister, the first Mrs Charles Payson (who incidentally 'owned' a baseball team, the Mets, in which she took a great interest). Both Jock and his sister were already rich by any standards, having shared an inheritance of some $200 million on the death of their father in 1927. They also shared a love of horses, although for Mrs Payson her baseball team came first. On his wife's death in 1975, Charles Payson inherited her share of the stud. Mr Payson himself died in 1985. This stud farm is still owned by Mrs. John Hay Whitney, widow of the late Ambassador, Jock Hay Whitney, who died in 1982.

Above: Although run on a much smaller scale than when it was founded in 1926, Greentree Stud has 45 permanent mares and seven resident stallions.

Left: Greentree Stud, still privately owned by the Whitney family, is open to the public.

Horses at Greentree are still bred to be privately raced; but the whole operation has been greatly reduced. The old brick Colonial house, with its typical high-columned porch, is the guest-house of the second Mrs Payson, for the present owners tend to fly down just for the day. Greentree is open to the public; it was in fact the first farm to allow tourists to look around, on the grounds that it was pointless for anyone to visit Lexington and not see a stud farm.

From a tourist standpoint the property, which now consists of 616 acres, is both old-world and picturesque, with the residence surrounded by trees, including sugar maples, green cedars and 12 kinds of beech. A road encircles the property, so that anyone can drive past the paddocks on a fine spring day and see the mares with their yearling foals.

Through successive generations the Whitneys have bred to win at the racetrack, and for this reason only the occasional home-bred horse finds its way into the sale ring. Among their most successful horses were two winners of the Kentucky Derby, Twenty Grand in 1931 and Shut Out in 1942. They are both now buried in the Greentree Horse Cemetery. Among the stallions at stud are Arts and Letters, Key to the Mint and Erin's Isle, and there are 45 mares permanently on the farm.

The neatly-kept paddocks at Greentree Stud.

SPENDTHRIFT FARM, KENTUCKY

The man who created Spendthrift, Leslie Combs II, is in his eighties, yet still a remarkable force in the Bluegrass Country. The 2,700-acre breeding and racing establishment which he has built up over 50 years is among the largest in the region. When Spendthrift became a public company in 1983, Leslie Combs II created a stir within the racing community, for it was the first time that a horse-breeding and racing establishment had turned to Wall Street offering the public one-third of the shares in a commodity not easily defined in terms of neat and orderly balance sheets.

Leslie Combs II has retained the white two-storey Colonial house, with its impressive porch, and the 45 acres that immediately surround it. He is still very much the man in charge, with an extraordinary ability to combine a folksy charm with modern business methods. Being both an urban and grass-roots Kentuckian, he has done more for Lexington and North American thoroughbreds than any other person. He now spends his winters in Florida, but returns to Spendthrift before the first day's racing at Keeneland. A legendary host, he welcomes to Spendthrift everyone who is anyone connected with horse-racing, and a great many other notables besides. Leslie Combs II is fond of friendly touches. For instance, when visitors are expected, he has one of the stable lads scatter a little rolled oats close to the fencing, thereby attracting the young foals or yearlings to the section of the paddock where the visitors cannot fail to notice them. Although one realizes that his whole operation has been brilliantly worked out, it is impossible not to respond to this generous outgoing man, who admits quite simply that he likes 'good parties, good horses and pretty gals'.

Combs's first land purchase was the 121-acre Locust Grove Farm, which he rented from a neighbour; later he bought whenever land became available, until he owned 1,000 acres. He boarded broodmares, sold yearlings and bided his time, and by hard work he became the leading vendor at the Keeneland summer sale in 1946. By 1956 he had repeated that success eight more times, and by 1964 he had earned the distinction 16 times in a row. He had no fewer than 30 stallions standing at Spendthrift, including two Kentucky Derby winners and five sons of Nasrullah. In 1967 he was the first man to sell a yearling for $130,000 in North America, Swaps-Obedient. Spendthrift was the first commercial breeding establishment whose runners earned more than $1 million in a single year, and they have never earned less than $1 million since. In 1972 it was the top money-winning stud farm in North America; and so it goes on. Combs has stood eight Kentucky Derby winners and syndicated six stallions for world record prices.

Nashua was one of Leslie Combs's more celebrated purchases, though it came about through sad circumstances, for he was owned by Bill Woodward, who was accidentally shot by his wife. Combs was able to buy Nashua from the executors for slightly more than the horse had won in stakes money, $1,251,200, against winnings of $945,145. This was a group purchase, with Combs owning only one-quarter; however, his other partners were happy to lease him Nashua. The horse went on to win six out of his ten races as a four-year-old in 1956. At stud he stood for 25 seasons, producing 74 stakes-winners, and was ranked No. 6 among North American sires.

Elizabeth Arden was a client of Leslie Combs's for 22 years, and among others were Louis B. Mayer, Harry Warner, Harry Guggenheim, the Phippses and the Whitneys. Although he was the man who pioneered the way for sky-high syndication prices, he now says somewhat wistfully:

Above: Aerial view of the stallion barns at Spendthrift, one of the largest stud farms in Kentucky.

Left: The impressive Colonial-style residence at Spendthrift Farm.

Left: Affirmed, by Exclusive Native out of Won't Tell You, whose victorious dual with Calumet-bred Alydar for the 1978 Triple Crown was one of the most exciting in racing history.

Below: Raise A Native, by Native Dancer, an outstanding sire.

'It's not a gentleman's game any more. For one thing, prices have gotten too high. There are many newcomers in the game that don't understand it. They put up this money – $5 million, $10 million. It means nothing to them.' His son Brownell Combs ran the company for several years, but sold his 33 per cent shareholding in 1986.

There are around 1,000 horses in training, of which only 50-60 actually belong to Spendthrift. Since the facilities arc first-rate, training is a means of providing the organization with a cash flow. Trainers rent the stalls and the facilities, which include an all-year covered gallop, a mile of wood-chip fibre track, a dirt-track, a starting-gate and a time-keeper. Within easy reach there are five other training tracks, River Downs, and the racecourses at Churchill Downs and Keeneland.

Left: The entrance to the 2,700-acre Spendthrift Farm where over 1,000 horses are currently in training.

Spendthrift runs a training programme for grooms and others, mainly from Ireland, wishing to enter the horse-racing industry.

The stallion band consists of 36 top-class horses. Mares are booked to stallions via the booking department at Spendthrift, and the fact that there are so many stallions at this one place means that all the surrounding stud farms do a good business in boarding mares, especially foreign ones. Spendthrift is more like a small town than a farm, and it is so large that it is necessary to tour it in a car. The offices are like those of a large company and include space for sales demonstrations. For all that, the stallions live as they do on any smaller stud farm. They have their stalls with their names in brass beside the door and their individual paddocks where they spend most of their time.

Right: Bronze statue of Nashua, sired by Nasrullah, who stood for 25 seasons and produced 74 stakes winners.

WINDFIELDS FARM, MARYLAND

Windfields Farm was created in 1960 by E. P. Taylor, the Canadian industrialist, affectionately referred to in the horse-racing world as 'Mr Canada'. It is now one of the foremost breeding and training establishments in the world. Built on the site of an old cattle farm, on Maryland's rural upper Eastern Shore, it lies midway between Baltimore and Philadelphia, within a three-hour drive of every racetrack in Maryland, Delaware, New Jersey and New York, with the exception of Saratoga. It consists of 2,562 acres, acquired in 14 separate land transactions, with more than a third leased to local farmers for growing crops, principally corn and soya beans. The prime farmland of the area also produces excellent cantaloupes, watermelons, tomatoes and asparagus.

The breeding establishment is divided into two separate operations, the Main Farm, at which the horses privately owned by the Taylor family are kept, and the Stallion Division, a commercially-run stud farm at which the syndicated horses stand, together with the visiting mares and foals of clients. This Stallion Division is one of the most important in the world, with a syndication value of $100 million represented by the 14 stallions standing here, including The Minstrel and Northern Dancer.

Northern Dancer, born in 1961, sired nine two-year-old winners in a single year, among them

Right: Windfields Farm has established itself as world leader as a breeder of stakes winners. Here (left to right), being led past the main stallion barn are three of the most successful stallions standing at Windfields: Val de l'Orne, The Minstrel and Northern Dancer.

Below: View across the paddocks to the main stallion barn at the Stallion Division at Windfields Farm, Maryland.

Tate Gallery, and season by season the list of his sons now standing successfully at stud grows – Nijinsky II, for example, at Claiborne Farm, and Lyphard, ably managed by Joe Taylor at Gainesway. Shareef Dancer, El Gran Señor, and Devil's Bag are three other famous horses to have been born at Windfields.

The Minstrel, a magnificent chestnut bred in Canada by E. P. Taylor, raced with great tenacity, winning seven top-class races. Bought as a yearling by Robert Sangster for $200,000 and trained in Ireland, he returned to stand at stud in America and was syndicated for $9 million.

The Stallion Division has 12 masonry-walled steel-roofed barns, with stabling for 195 horses. A T-shaped structure combines the breeding area and foaling barn and faces the main stallion barn. There are three stallion barns, and no building is more than 20 years old. There is a reason for this. In 1968 one of the brood-mare barns caught alight and 12 mares, three in foal to Northern Dancer, were trapped and burnt to death. E. P. Taylor resolved only to build barns that were as fire-proof as possible. Indeed the whole complex, with its security fencing (put up in 1983 just three months before Shergar was kidnapped from Ballymany), and its roving personnel on 24-hour alert, is extremely safety- and security-conscious.

At the Main Farm, the privately-owned family horses are housed in four broodmare barns. There are also two training barns and two yearling barns, with assorted other stabling for up to 180 horses. Windfields aims to sell as many as 70 of its 75 yearlings at the summer sales in Kentucky, and there are training and breaking facilities for these. There is also a 5-furlong dirt track, a circular 7-furlong turf strip, a 1-mile turf gallop and a European-style sand gallop, as at Newmarket. Two vets and two farriers look after the general health of all the horses.

The Taylor racing empire includes the 1,250-acre Windfields Farm at Oshawa in Canada, 40 miles east of Toronto. During the first six months of each year around 200 foals are born here, as the mares wait to go back to one of the stud farm's resident 12 stallions, one of whom is Fabuleux Dancer, a French stakes winner by Nijinsky.

At Oshawa they offer the service to their clients of undertaking the preparation of yearlings for sale. This is not unlike Taylor Made Farm, Kentucky (the two Taylors are not related other than in expertise and mutual interests), who also break and train yearlings.

In terms of horse transportation it is a 12-hour van drive from Oshawa to Windfields, Maryland, about the same distance as it is from Kentucky. Since every serious owner holds a portfolio of nominations, brood mares are required to travel, and because of this Northern Dancer, Nijinsky II and The Minstrel were all born at Oshawa.

While E. P. Taylor was creating his dual stud-farm operation, he was also restructuring Canadian racing. He did this by buying up the franchises of 14 chartered racetracks in the Province of Ontario, closing 12 of them, rebuilding Woodbine from scratch and giving it a splendid opening on 12 June 1956. Now all those many years later Woodbine continues as the Ascot of Canadian racing. E. P. Taylor, now in his eighties, is somewhat fragile in health, and has therefore handed over responsibility to his more-than-capable son Charles.

Charles Taylor has played an important part in the thoroughbred industry since 1981. A member and trustee of the Canadian Jockey Club, he is also secretary of the Breeders' Cup. Before this he had worked for many years as a journalist. He worked in Peking as the Bureau Chief for the Toronto *Globe and Mail*, and was the first Western journalist to be accredited to Red China. He reported the Arab-Israeli War of 1967, and the Vietnam War from a helicopter gunship. For many years he was President of the Writers' Union of Canada, and he has written two books on Asia. He writes about Canada's politics as well as its culture, and one feels that he will remain a prime mover in all things that concern Canada, as was his father.

This is not to suggest that either father or son restrict themselves to their Bayview Avenue office in Willowdale, Toronto. Both men have always thought globally; and what began as a

Right: E.P. Taylor with The Minstrel. By Northern Dancer out of Fleur, Nijinsky's half-sister, The Minstrel won all his two-year-old races and beat Hot Grove by a neck in the 1977 Epsom Derby.

pleasurable diversion to get E. P. Taylor out of his office and into the open air has grown into one of the world's largest and most successful thoroughbred breeding establishments. Just as E. P. Taylor turned Leyford Cay, in the Bahamas, into one of the most exclusive golf resorts in the world, so he has consolidated his place in the annals of Turf history by breeding Northern Dancer, winner of the 1964 Kentucky Derby, and by continuing to breed and own racehorses that win, some 300 to date. He has also upgraded Canadian racing, and provided like-minded Canadians with facilities to improve their blood lines by sending their mares to his Canadian or American studs.

The outstanding stallion Northern Dancer, by Neartic out of Natalma, was bred at Oshawa Stud in 1961. Winner of 14 races, he headed the stallion list in the United States in 1971 and 1977 and in Britain in 1970, 1977, 1983 and 1984.

APPENDICES

TRANSPORTING HORSES OVERSEAS

Arrangements for transporting horses overseas are often quite complicated, and veterinary requirements and documentation, which vary from country to country, are stringent. Almost all countries demand blood tests, and no horse can be shipped without a signed veterinary certificate.

The requirements of the countries of destination vary. A European stallion being shipped to stand at stud at an American stud farm, for instance, is required to have Contagious Equine Metritis (CEM) testing and treatment over a five-week period. For a broodmare this extends over six weeks. Horses-in-training travelling to the USA need to be certified by Weatherbys as being of 'in-training' status; the testing then takes three weeks. Geldings and horses under 731 days (two years) of age are exempted from CEM testing.

Having arrived on the tarmac, the horses are led towards the air stable.

Upon arrival in the USA all horses are required to spend three days in Government quarantine at one of the only three airports of approved entry into the United States: New York, Los Angeles and Miami. After this statutory quarantine, the horses-in-training, geldings and horses under 731 days of age are released to go to their final destinations. Stallions are taken in sealed horse vans to a US Government approved farm in an approved State. There they undergo approximately 45 days of testing, including test breeding two mares. Broodmares are also taken to an approved farm in an approved State. If in foal, they have to foal on the approved farm and are then re-tested. If barren, they are kept approximately 30 days for tests then released.

An American racehorse leaving the United States for Europe spends a 30-day period in a Government-approved quarantine facility before being shipped. Having completed their period of isolation, the horses are taken in a sealed van to the airport and go into Government quarantine stables where they are required to have a minimum five hours' rest and are re-inspected before being loaded on to the aircraft.

Horses being shipped between the United Kingdom and France do not need to undergo blood tests, but they do need a veterinary health certificate. Between England and Ireland, however, horses need neither blood tests nor veterinary certificates. Normal customs procedures do apply. Most countries require a Licensed Veterinary Inspector (LVI) to sign the health certificate, and in the case of the United States, it must be countersigned by a Divisional Veterinary Officer (DVO).

Two men, one leading and the other walking behind to make sure the horse goes in smoothly, usually load a horse into the air stables on the ground. These are then high-loaded on to the aircraft.

Every thoroughbred has a passport, which is required if the horse is to be sold, raced or covered in another country. In the United Kingdom, the passport has to be endorsed by and stamped by Weatherbys for export. 'Race Performances' then have to be applied for, which are a complete record of the racehorse's career, listing every race the horse has ever run and detailing its placing, prize-money and location of the race, and origin. A Stud Book Certificate is also mandatory. This certificate is sent directly from Weatherbys to the Jockey Club of the country of destination; without these papers, the foreign Jockey Club cannot register the horse. However, if the horse is only travelling to be covered and returned or sent to race and returned between England, Ireland and France, then only a passport is required.

For entry into the United States, five different views of the horse are photographed when the

Once installed in the air stable, haynets and water are provided to help the horse to settle.

horse lands. An ID certificate showing the horse's markings has to be completed: the passport, race performances, photographs and ID are sent to the US Jockey Club, which registers the horse and issues registration papers allowing the imported horse to race or breed. American horses do not have passports. They have registration papers which are sent in with their markings and Jockey Club photographs to the New York Jockey Club, which then issues an American Jockey Club export certificate directly to Weatherbys in England, for instance, who in turn issue a passport for UK racing purposes.

Horses are transported by specialists in air cargo such as Flying Tigers, which operates the only scheduled all-freighter service carrying horses to and from New York, or on a charter horse flight. Travelling arrangements are handled by specialist companies such as Oakridge International, run from Wantage in Oxfordshire by Margot Wiltshire and Anthony Porter. If travelling by cargo freighter, horses are loaded into an air stable on the ground and then high-loaded on to the aircraft. In the case of charter flights, horses are walked up a ramp and into horse stalls on the aircraft. Specialist flying grooms travel with the horses; they not only know how to handle the horses expertly and look after their well-being during the flight, but are also totally familiar with the horse stalls and their equipment. Loading a charter flight can take a couple of hours, and the load plan is worked out carefully beforehand to ensure, for instance, that stallions are not behind mares. For a load of 50 horses, there will be on average 12 to 14 grooms on board, equipped with medical kits.

The horses' travelling tack takes the form of a head-collar, rope, rug and leg-wraps. Hind shoes are removed so that should the horse lash out during the flight, it will not injure itself, or damage the stall equipment. Normally hay is not provided on the journey to the airport, so that when the horse walks into its stall at the airport, it is ready to start eating. This helps to settle it in its unfamiliar surroundings and to ignore the unusual activities going on around it.

Customs officials check the documents, and when the papers have been cleared the horses are driven out to the airport and loaded. If a horse is required to walk up the ramp, normally one man leads him, while two others walk behind to give a little weight should the horse be reluctant to walk up or enter his stall. Most horses take the whole procedure quite calmly. Hay-nets are filled and hung in the front of their stalls, and water containers are also sent with them on long flights.

In its efficiency, smoothness of operation and modernity, the transport of bloodstock reflects the increasingly sophisticated and international character of the bloodstock industry, and the care taken to safeguard that most valuable of living commodities, the thoroughbred racehorse.

Classic Races

Name of race	Where held	Horses	Distance	Date	1st held
ENGLAND					
Two Thousand Guineas Stakes	Newmarket	3-yr-old colts	1 mile	Sat of Spring Meeting	1809
One Thousand Guineas Stakes	Newmarket	3-yr-old fillies	1 mile	Thurs of Spring Meeting (late April, early May)	1814
Derby Stakes	Epsom	3-yr-old colts and fillies	1½ miles	1st Wed in June	1780
Oaks Stakes	Epsom	3-yr-old fillies	1½ miles	Sat after Derby	1779
St Leger Stakes	Doncaster	3-yr-old colts and fillies	1 mile 6 furlongs 127 yards	1st or 2nd Sat in September	1776
IRELAND					
Irish Two Thousand Guineas	The Curragh	3-yr-old colts	1 mile	Fortnight after Newmarket Sat	1921
Irish One Thousand Guineas	The Curragh	3-yr-old fillies	1 mile	3 weeks after Newmarket Sat	1922
Irish Sweeps Derby	The Curragh	3-yr-old colts and fillies	1½ miles	3½ weeks after Epsom Derby	1866
Irish Guinness Oaks	The Curragh	3-yr-old fillies	1½ miles	6 weeks after Epsom Oaks	1895
Irish St Leger	The Curragh	3-yr-old colts and fillies	1 mile 6 furlongs	4 weeks after Doncaster St Leger	1915
FRANCE					
Poule d'Essai des Poulains (French 2,000 Gns)	Longchamp	3-yr-old colts	1 mile (1,600 metres)	Last Sun in April	1883
Poule d'Essai des Pouliches (French 1,000 Gns)	Longchamp	3-yr-old fillies	1 mile (1,600 metres)	1st Sun in May	1883
Prix du Jockey-Club (French Derby)	Chantilly	3-yr-old colts and fillies	1½ miles (2,400 metres)	1st Sun in June	1836
Prix de Diane (French Oaks)	Chantilly	3-yr-old fillies	1 mile 2½ furlongs (2,100 metres)	3rd Sun in June	1843
** Prix Royal-Oak (French St Leger)	Longchamp	3-yr-old colts and fillies	1 mile 7½ furlongs (3,100 metres)	Last Sun in October	1869

**Not now strictly a Classic race, as it is open to 4-yr-olds as well. Definition of a Classic is for 3-yr-olds.

Name of race	Where held	Horses	Distance	Date	1st held
AMERICAN TRIPLE CROWN					
Kentucky Derby	Churchill Downs, Louisville	3-yr-old colts and fillies	1¼ miles	1st Sat in May	1875
Preakness Stakes	Pimlico, Baltimore	3-yr-old colts and fillies	1³⁄₁₆ miles	2 weeks after Kentucky Derby	1873
Belmont Stakes	Belmont Park, Long Island	3-yr-old colts and fillies	1½ miles	3 weeks after Preakness	1867

Glossary

Age
The birth date of a thoroughbred foal is always assumed to be January 1 – thus even if it is born in December, it becomes a yearling in the New Year. (This applies to horses born in the Northern Hemisphere; in the Southern Hemisphere the crucial date is August 1). A horse is a foal from birth until the age of one, and a yearling from one to two.

Arabian
Horses noted for grace, beauty and speed, originally from Arabia and other countries of the Middle East. Modern thoroughbreds all trace their descent back to three ancestors in the years around 1700, of which two were Arabians (the Darley Arabian and the Goldolphin Arabian).

Barb
Breed of horse originally from Barbary (North Africa). Most famous of such horses was the third of the thoroughbreds' ancestors, the Byerley Turk.

Broodmare
Female horse of any age used for breeding.

Classic Race
The five major flat-races are commonly known as the Classics. In England, they are the Derby, the Oaks, the One Thousand Guineas, the Two Thousand Guineas, and the St Leger. Each of these has its equivalent in Ireland and France.

Colours, Racing
First mentioned in 1762, racing colours distinguish the 'silks' worn by jockeys riding for different owners. They have to be registered each year on payment of a fee.

Colt
An ungelded male horse under five years old.

Cover
Used of stallions, meaning to mate with a mare.

Cup
Any horse-racing prize not given in money.

Dam
The female parent of a horse.

Distance
A point 240 yards from the winning-post on a racecourse. A horse that wins 'by a distance' wins by more than 30 lengths.

Filly
A female horse aged four or less.

Flat-racing Season
Flat races cannot be run before the week that includes 25 March (unless that is the week before Easter Sunday, when races may be run a week earlier), or later than the week that includes 22 November.

Foal
A horse in its first year of life. Used as a verb of mares, to give birth.

Furlong
A distance of 220 yards, ⅛ mile, or about 200 metres.

Gelding
A castrated male horse.

General Stud Book
The pedigrees of racehorses in Great Britain and Ireland are kept in the *Stud Book*, which belongs to the private firm of Weatherbys.

Half-bred
A horse of which one of the parents is not eligible for the *General Stud Book*; in other words, a semi-thoroughbred.

Hand
A horse's height from the ground to the withers is measured in hands, each hand being 4 inches (0.1016 metre).

Handicap
In a handicap race, as defined by the Jockey Club, the horses carry weights that are adjusted by an official known as the handicapper so as to equalize as far as possible their chances of winning.

Heat Race
A race run in different qualifying parts. Early races were often run in three heats.

Inbreeding
The mating of a closely related mare and stallion, opposed to *Outcrossing*.

Jockey
Jockeys have to hold a licence from the *Jockey Club* (or the equivalent body in other countries) to ride for a fee. No one is allowed to ride in a race under the age of 16, and licences may be withdrawn for misconduct.

Jockey Club
The world's premier horse-racing body, founded in England in the mid eighteenth century to promote the interests of the sport and everyone connected with it.

Length
The length of a horse from nose to tail (about 8ft), used as the unit of measurement in recording the results of races.

Mare
A female thoroughbred aged five and over.

Match
A race between two horses belonging to different owners on mutually agreed conditions.

Naming
Once it becomes a yearling, a horse can be officially registered with the name under which it will run. There are various conditions, among them being that the name cannot contain more than 18 characters or spaces. Horses with the same name from different countries are coded with a suffix – e.g. (Ire) or (USA).

Outcrossing
The mating of a mare and stallion that are not closely related, or unrelated, opposed to *Inbreeding*.

Paddock
The part of a racecourse that includes the parade ring, the unsaddling enclosure, and the weighing-room.

APPENDICES

Pattern Races
Races chosen to provide the best conditions for testing top-class horses throughout the season. They are considered annually by the European Pattern Committee, consisting of representatives from the UK, Ireland, France, West Germany and Italy. There are three groups of such races: Group I, championship races, including the Classics; Group II, races just below championship standard; and Group III, races of quality that lead on to Groups I and II. Pattern races are also known as Graded Stakes races.

Quarter Horse
A very fast breed of horse developed in the United States for racing over ¼ mile (440 yards or 400 metres).

Rails
The barriers that define the limits of a racetrack.

Scratch
To take a horse out of a race for which it has been entered.

Selling Race
In this class of race, the winning horse must be offered for sale by auction as soon as the race is over.

Sire
The male parent of a horse. Used as a verb of stallions, means to beget.

Société d'Encouragement pour l'Amélioration des Races de Chevaux en France
The French equivalent of the *Jockey Club*.

Stallion
A male horse kept on a stud farm for breeding.

Starter's Orders
Once the white flag is raised to signal the start of a race, a horse taking part is 'under starter's orders', and if withdrawn at this stage all bets placed on it are lost.

Sweepstakes
Often abbreviated to 'Stakes'. A sweepstake is a race in which entrance fees and other contributions go to the winner or all placed horses.

Syndication
When a stallion is syndicated, it is capitalized into 40 shares (usually 32 shares in the United States), since most stallions cover about 40 mares each season. Purchase of a share entitles a breeder to send one of his mares to the stallion each season, or to dispose of that year's nomination to another breeder.

Thoroughbred
Racehorses of the highest quality whose pedigrees can be traced back to three stallions in the years around 1700 (see *Arabian* and *Barb*).

Triple Crown
In England, to win the Triple Crown a three-year-old must have won the Two Thousand Guineas, Derby and St Leger. In the United States, the American Triple Crown races are the Kentucky Derby, the Preakness Stakes and the Belmont Stakes.

Yearling
A colt, filly or gelding aged between one and two.

Bibliography

Acton, C.R, *Silk and Spur*, Richards, 1935

Aga Khan III (Sultan Mohammed Shah Aga Khan), *The Memoirs of the Aga Khan*, Cassell, 1954

Baerlein, Richard, *Shergar and the Aga Khan's Thoroughbred Empire*, Michael Joseph, 1984

Biracree, Tom and Insinger, Wendy, *The Complete Book of Thoroughbred Horse Racing*, Dolphin Books, New York, 1982

Bird, T.H, *Admiral Rous and The English Turf*, Putnam, 1939

Bland, Ernest, *Flat Racing since 1900*, Andrew Dakers, 1950

Browne, T.H, *A History of The English Turf, 1904-1930*, Virtue & Co, 1931

Cook, Sir Theodore A, *A History of the British Turf*, 3 vols, London, 1904

Curling, B.W.R, *Derby Double: the unique story of racehorse trainer Arthur Budgett*, Luscombe, 1977

De Moubray, Jocelyn, *Horseracing and Racing Society*, Sidgwick and Jackson, 1985

Dossenbach, Monique and Hans, *The Noble Horse*, G.K. Hall, Boston, 1983

FitzGerald, Arthur, *History of the Prix de l'Arc de Triomphe*, Sidgwick and Jackson, 1981

Fletcher, J.J, *The History of the St Leger Stakes*, Hutchinson, 1934

Gaillard, Marc, *Les Hippodromes*, La Palatine, Paris, 1984

Goodhall, Daphne Machin, *A History of Horsebreeding*, Robert Hale, 1977

Guillotel, Gérard, *Les Haras Nationaux*, Lavauzelle, Paris, 1985

Hewitt, Abram S., *The Great Breeders and their Methods*, Thoroughbred Publishers Inc, 1982

Hislop, John, *The Turf*, Collins, 1948

Lambton, The Hon. George, *Men and Horses I Have Known*, J.A. Allen, 1963

Longrigg, Roger, *The History of Horse Racing*, Macmillan, 1972

Lyle, R.C, *The Aga Khan's Horses*, Putnam, 1938

Markham, Gervase, *Cavalrie or the English Horseman*, 1607

McCalmont, Sir Hugh, *Memoirs*, Callwell, 1924

Mortimer, Roger, *The Jockey Club*, Cassell, 1958

Mortimer, Roger, *The History of the Derby Stakes*, Michael Joseph, 1973

Morton, Frederic, *The Rothschilds*, Secker and Warburg, 1963

Neligan, Tim, *The Epsom Derby*, Michael Joseph, 1984

Onslow, R, *Headquarters: A History of Newmarket and its Racing*, Great Ouse Press, 1971

Phillips Browne, Noel, *The Horse in Ireland*, Pelham Books, 1967

Pickering, Martin (Editor), *Directory of the Turf*, Pacemaker Publications Ltd (annual publication)

Robertson, William H.P, *History of Thoroughbred Racing in America*, Prentice-Hall, 1964

Sadler, Julius Trousdale Jr, and Jacquelin, D.J, *American Stables*, New York Graphic Society, Boston, 1981

Siltzer, Frank, *Newmarket: Its Sport and Personalities*, Cassell, 1923

Sloan, J.F, *Tod Sloan. By Himself*, Grant Richards, 1915

Stanley, Louis T, *Newmarket*, W.H. Allen, 1984

Vamplew, Wrag, *The Turf: A Social and Economic History of Horse Racing*, Allen Lane, 1976

Verboom, M.L, *Cent cinquante ans d'élevage du pur-sang en France*, Editions T.E.P.

Welcome, John, *Irish Horseracing, an Illustrated History*, Macmillan, 1982

Willett, Peter, *An Introduction to the Thoroughbred*, Stanley Paul, 1975, *The Classic Racehorse*, Stanley Paul, 1981, *Makers of The Modern Thoroughbred*, Stanley Paul, 1984

Wright, Howard, *The Encyclopedia of Flat Racing*, Robert Hale, 1986

Wynmalen, Henry, *Horse Breeding and Stud Management*, J.A. Allen, 1950

Index

Page references in *italics* indicate illustrations.